"In this fascinating and original book, Michael Oppenheim brings modern Jewish thinkers into conversation with contemporary psychoanalysts. Comparing their profound explorations of love, death, and human relationships, he creates an intriguing conversation between disparate approaches to the human condition."

Susannah Heschel, Eli Black Professor of
Jewish Studies, Dartmouth College

"Oppenheim has a unique ability to create dialogue between thinkers who exist on different planes and registers of meaning. In so doing, the reader is invited to listen to the stories we tell about 'love,' 'relationship,' 'responsibility,' and 'death' in such a way that takes us far beyond their assumed, homogenized, and secularized forms. The dialogues that Oppenheim fosters allow us to speak about love more capaciously and with the dimension it deserves. Oppenheim's sophisticated interdisciplinary scholarship is a model to be emulated."

David M. Goodman, Ph.D., Director,
Psychology and the Other Institute

"Two Languages of Love *deftly weaves together rich insights from Judaism and relational psychoanalysis. Each chapter demonstrates the fresh and original insights that emerge from the confluence of these traditions. When he turns to the subject of death, for instance, Oppenheim relies on both fields to forge a rich conversation about the authentic confrontation of mortality. Clinicians will find these moves innovative and immediately relevant. The author of this book is a teacher; readers of this volume are offered a compelling demonstration of the best in interdisciplinary scholarship."*

Eric Severson, Seattle University

"Building on his previous publications, Oppenheim continues his path-breaking exploration of the interplay between modern Jewish philosophy and psychoanalysis. By generating an original and insightful dialogue between the Jewish philosophers Buber, Rosenzweig, and Levinas and the relational psychoanalysts, Hans Loewald, Stephen Mitchel, and Jessica Benjamin, among others, Oppenheim broadens the cultural significance of modern Jewish philosophy and enriches our understanding of recent developments in psychoanalysis. His interrogation of relationality and inter-subjectivity, of language's role in meaning-making, of meaning and responsibility, and of trust and eternity creatively bridges philosophy, psychology, and religion."

Hava Tirosh-Samuelson, Arizona State University

Contemporary Psychoanalysis and Modern Jewish Philosophy

Relational psychoanalysis and modern Jewish philosophy have much to say about the dynamics of human relationships, but there has been no detailed, thorough, and constructive examination that brings together these two incisive discourses. *Contemporary Psychoanalysis and Modern Jewish Philosophy: Two Languages of Love* explores the critical similarities and differences between the two disciplines, casting new light on both the analytic and philosophical understandings of how relationships develop, flourish, and fail.

For psychoanalysts such as Hans Loewald, Stephen Mitchell, and Jessica Benjamin, love is seen as a fundamental life force, a key to human motivation, and the transformative core of Freud's therapeutic "talking cure." The Jewish philosophers Franz Rosenzweig, Martin Buber, and Emmanuel Levinas envision love as having both a human and divine dimension, expressed through the dual commandments to love God and the neighbor. The two languages are brought to life through chapters that investigate: the relationship between self-love and love of the other, the dynamics of intersubjectivity, the methods and possibilities of human transformation, the "magical" powers of language, the goal of achieving a meaningful life, the significance of responsibility for others, and the challenge that death poses to life's fullness.

This multidisciplinary study, drawing on psychology, philosophy, religion, and feminism, provides an important contribution to contemporary scientific and humanistic interest in the social and relational dimensions of human living. The book will appeal especially to clinicians, theorists, and scholars of psychoanalysis, philosophy of religion, and Jewish studies as well as advanced students studying in these fields.

Michael Oppenheim is Professor Emeritus in the Department of Religion at Concordia University, Montreal. His books include *Speaking/Writing of God* (1997), *Jewish Philosophy and Psychoanalysis* (2006), and *Encounters of Consequence* (2009).

The Relational Perspectives Book Series (RPBS) publishes books that grow out of or contribute to the relational tradition in contemporary psychoanalysis. The term *relational psychoanalysis* was first used by Greenberg and Mitchell[1] to bridge the traditions of interpersonal relations, as developed within interpersonal psychoanalysis and object relations, as developed within contemporary British theory. But, under the seminal work of the late Stephen A. Mitchell, the term *relational psychoanalysis* grew and began to accrue to itself many other influences and developments. Various tributaries—interpersonal psychoanalysis, object relations theory, self psychology, empirical infancy research, and elements of contemporary Freudian and Kleinian thought—flow into this tradition, which understands relational configurations between self and others, both real and fantasied, as the primary subject of psychoanalytic investigation.

We refer to the relational tradition, rather than to a relational school, to highlight that we are identifying a trend, a tendency within contemporary psychoanalysis, not a more formally organized or coherent school or system of beliefs. Our use of the term *relational* signifies a dimension of theory and practice that has become salient across the wide spectrum of contemporary psychoanalysis. Now under the editorial supervision of Lewis Aron and Adrienne Harris, with the assistance of Associate Editors Steven Kuchuck and Eyal Rozmarin, the Relational Perspectives Book Series originated in 1990 under the editorial eye of the late Stephen A. Mitchell. Mitchell was the most prolific and influential of the originators of the relational tradition. Committed to dialogue among psychoanalysts, he abhorred the authoritarianism that dictated adherence to a rigid set of beliefs or technical restrictions. He championed open discussion, comparative and integrative approaches, and promoted new voices across the generations.

Included in the Relational Perspectives Book Series are authors and works that come from within the relational tradition, extend and develop that tradition, as well as works that critique relational approaches or compare and contrast it with alternative points of view. The series includes our most distinguished senior psychoanalysts, along with younger contributors who bring fresh vision. For a full list of all the titles in the series, please visit the Routledge website.

Recent titles in this series:

Vol. 84 *The Neuropsychodynamic Treatment of Self-Deficits: Searching for Complementarity*
Joseph Palombo

Vol. 83 *Trans-generational Trauma and the Other: Dialogues Across History and Difference*
Edited by Sue Grand and Jill Salberg

Vol. 82 *Wounds of History: Repair and Resilience in the Trans-generational Transmission of Trauma*
Edited by Jill Salberg and Sue Grand

Vol. 81 *Body-Mind Dissociation in Psychoanalysis: Development after Bion*
Riccardo Lombardi

Vol. 80 *Psychoanalysis, Trauma and Community: History and Contemporary Reappraisals*
Edited by Judith L. Alpert and Elizabeth R. Goren

Vol. 79 *Contemporary Psychoanalysis and Modern Jewish Philosophy: Two Languages of Love*
Michael Oppenheim

Vol. 78 *Talking About Evil: Psychoanalytic, Social, and Cultural Perspectives*
Edited by Rina Lazar

1 Greenberg, J. & Mitchell, S. (1983). *Object relations in psychoanalytic theory.* Cambridge, MA: Harvard University Press.

Contemporary Psychoanalysis and Modern Jewish Philosophy

Two Languages of Love

Michael Oppenheim

Routledge
Taylor & Francis Group
LONDON AND NEW YORK

First published 2017
by Routledge
2 Park Square, Milton Park, Abingdon, Oxon OX14 4RN

and by Routledge
605 Third Avenue, New York, NY 10017

Routledge is an imprint of the Taylor & Francis Group, an informa business

British Library Cataloguing in Publication Data
A catalogue record for this book is available from the British Library

Library of Congress Cataloging in Publication Data
Names: Oppenheim, Michael D., 1946- author.
Title: Two languages of love: contemporary psychoanalysis and modern Jewish philosophy/Michael Oppenheim.
Description: Abingdon, Oxon; New York, NY: Routledge, 2017. |
Includes bibliographical references and index.
Identifiers: LCCN 2016015993 | ISBN 9781138119420 (hardback: alk. paper) | ISBN 9781138119437 (pbk.: alk. paper) | ISBN 9781315652320 (e-book: alk. paper)
Subjects: LCSH: Jewish philosophy. | Judaism and psychoanalysis. | Psychoanalysis and philosophy. | Love–Philosophy.
Classification: LCC B5802 .P75 O673 2017 | DDC 181/.06–dc23
LC record available at https://lccn.loc.gov/2016015993

ISBN: 978-1-138-11942-0 (hbk)
ISBN: 978-1-138-11943-7 (pbk)
ISBN: 978-1-315-65232-0 (ebk)

Typeset in Times New Roman
by Deanta Global Publishing Services, Chennai, India

To Sarah, Aaron, and David

Contents

Preface

This book emerges out of a passionate interest in the redemptive possibilities of human relationships, which is one way of interpreting what Emmanuel Levinas hints at in writing, "From an ethical perspective, two have a better time than one (*on s'amuse mieux à deux*)!" (1986, 22). This concern was launched many decades ago beginning with the magnetism of Martin Buber's *I and Thou*. It soon widened into the study of Buber's other writings as well as those of his colleague Franz Rosenzweig. The inclusion of Levinas in this trilogy of modern Jewish philosophers of encounter occurred afterward, hampered for a while by the difficulty of his enigmatic inscription. Quite unexpectedly, I later discovered a parallel discourse within some streams of post-Freudian psychoanalysis. The book *Jewish Philosophy and Psychoanalysis: Narrating the Interhuman* (2006) was the first fruit of this additional focus. That work juxtaposed the psychoanalysts Erik Erikson, Melanie Klein, and the Object Relations thinkers, W. R. D. Fairbairn and D. W. Winnicott with Rosenzweig, Buber, and Levinas. Developments in psychoanalysis in more recent times, particularly in terms of the deepened attention to the relation between subjectivity and intersubjectivity, the recognition of the centrality of the human quest for meaning, and the exploration of the intimate dynamics between patient and analyst, sharpen the engagement with the Jewish philosophers. I hope that the philosophers' "dialogue" with Hans Loewald, Stephen Mitchell, Jessica Benjamin, and others pursued in the present work invites and challenges contemporary theorists in all those disciplines who are concerned with the thoughtful convergence of psychology, philosophy, and religion.

Rosenzweig's statement that in the midst of conversation one is "dependent on the other for what is ours" (1999, 87), fittingly expresses the debt that I, as the author of this book, owe to so many others. Discussions over the years with colleagues and students in the Department of Religion at Concordia University have helped, supported, and led me. An appreciative and welcoming environment has been afforded by David Goodman and his collaborators who organize the bi-annual "Psychology and the Other Conference" in Cambridge, Massachusetts. The unwavering support of my colleague and good friend Norma Joseph has been uplifting. Always delightful and positive, Barbara Galli has carefully reviewed most of the manuscript over the years. Lastly, the insightful suggestions of my critic, personal editor, and loving son, David, have enriched the text in innumerable ways.

References

Levinas, Emmanuel. 1986. "Dialogue with Emmanuel Levinas." In *Face to Face with Levinas*, edited by Richard A. Cohen, 13–33. New York: State University of New York Press.

Oppenheim, Michael. 2006. *Jewish Philosophy and Psychoanalysis: Narrating the Interhuman*. Lanham, MD: Lexington Books.

Rosenzweig, Franz. 1999. *Franz Rosenzweig's "The New Thinking."* Edited and translated by Alan Udoff and Barbara E. Galli. Syracuse, NY: Syracuse University Press.

Acknowledgments

Chapter 1 is based upon an article, "Loving the Neighbor: Some Reflections on Narcissism," which was previously published in the journal *Modern Judaism* (2007) 27 (1): 47–71, and is reprinted here with their kind permission. Chapter 4 is based upon an article, "*Langue, Parole et Chanson*: On Language as Song in Psychoanalysis and Jewish Philosophy," which was previously published in the *Journal of Pastoral Psychology* (2013) 62 (4): 403–421, and is reprinted here with their kind permission. Chapter 6 is based upon the chapter "Beyond betrayal: on responsibility in Heidegger, Loewald, and Levinas," in the book *The Ethical Turn: Otherness and subjectivity in contemporary psychoanalysis* (2016), edited by David M. Goodman and Eric R. Severson (London: Routledge/Taylor & Francis publishers), pp. 186–208, and is reprinted here with their kind permission.

Introduction

Love Is...

There are many languages of love. The relational group of contemporary psychoanalysts and the three Jewish philosophers of encounter present two of these. What is meant by a language of love and in what ways do these theorists express two of them? Since the whole book is about love, this Introduction will only touch upon a few features. It offers a brief glance, of love at first sight, *amour coup de foudre*.

Psychoanalysis as a Language of Love

A language of love is a discourse in which the term "love" takes up a central role in the examination of the nature and dynamics of authentic human relationships, as well as what obstacles impede the achievement of these. The meaning of this terse statement is best explored through the two examples detailed below, by particular streams of psychoanalysis and modern Jewish philosophy.

In terms of psychoanalysis, it is appropriate to begin with the discipline's creator, Sigmund Freud (1856–1939). Freud sees love as a fundamental life force and key to human motivation, as well as the core of his talking cure itself. At first he describes the basic human drives or instincts in terms of the sexual instinct or libido and self-preservation. Later, he formulates what is known as the dual instinct theory. This coalesces the two earlier instincts into the term *Eros* (Love), adds a second, *Thanatos* (Death) or "the destructive instinct," and offers them as the elemental forces behind all of life. In his words:

> After long doubts and vacillations we have decided to assume the existence of only two basic instincts, *Eros* and *the destructive instinct*... The aim of the first of these basic instincts is to establish ever greater

> unities and to preserve them thus—in short, to bind together; the aim of the second, on the contrary, is to undo connections and so to destroy things… This interaction of the two basic instincts with and against each other gives rise to the whole variegation of the phenomena of life.
>
> (1949, 20–21)

Freud holds that transference is one of the central, distinguishing concepts within psychoanalysis. It refers to the repetition of patterns of the child's early significant erotic or love relations in later relationships. It is especially germane to the analytic situation. He writes:

> The patient sees in his analyst the return—the reincarnation—of some important figure out of his childhood or past, and consequently transfers on to him feelings and reactions that undoubtedly applied to this model. It soon becomes evident that this fact of transference is a factor of undreamed-of importance—on the one hand an instrument of irreplaceable value and on the other a source of serious dangers.
>
> (1949, 66)

Transference is a danger, because it is part of the patient's unconscious resistance to the analyst's exploration and intervention into fixed past relationships. However, in harnessing the power of the early attachments, it also becomes an absolutely necessary component of therapy. It is in this context that "there emerges the aim of pleasing the analyst, of winning his applause and love. This becomes the true motive-force for the patient's collaboration" (1949, 66). Thus, utilizing the transference means for Freud that psychoanalysis is "actually a cure through love" (cited in Loewald 2000, 255).[1]

The relational psychoanalysts built upon Freud's formulation of this language of love. Although formally a predecessor to the relational stream, the present work includes throughout its discussions the thought of the post-Freudian, Hans Loewald (1906–1993). A partial justification for this arrangement is offered in the seminal book of the leading figure of the movement, Stephen Mitchell (1946–2000). In *Relationality*, Mitchell writes of Loewald that he "was struggling with many of the same issues that now dominate the writings of our most innovative contemporary authors, for whom his work might serve as a rich treasure trove of new ideas and inspiration" (2000, xvi). In this work, I have fully taken up Mitchell's recommendation to delve into the Loewaldian "treasure trove."

The second lecture/chapter, "Transference and Love," of Hans Loewald's elegant but challenging "Freud Lectures" at Yale University, provides a striking example of his creative reworking of the whole array of the master's concepts, in this case especially transference. Transference, as a love event, is no longer primarily situated in the analytic encounter, but is pertinent to the whole history of the individual's life from the mother–infant matrix to mature object relations.[2] In his words, "I shall try to develop the thesis that the concept of transference opened up the historical dimension of man's love life while at the same time disclosing the erotic dimension of his individuation and historicity, of his becoming what may properly be called a self" (1978, 32). In this sense, the history of the individual is the history of love. It includes the genesis of and ongoing relationship between narcissistic love and object love—his terms are "narcissistic libido" and "object libido" (33)—and the development of the mind itself, which he calls individuation. For Loewald, it is through loving the other that one is constituted as a self.

Loewald extends and deepens the term transference to include a number of significant transactions both intrapsychically and intersubjectively. It, first, refers to a wide range of interchanges between the unconscious and conscious. There is also primary or primordial transference that occurs in the earliest postnatal period of life, within the mother–infant psychic unity. Of course, transference still points to the significant exchange between distinct subjects, including the interaction between patient and analyst. Finally, the repetition, re-creation, and reorganization of early love life in later mature interactions are also covered by the term transference in Loewald's lexicon.

The psychic seamlessness or sameness within the mother–infant relation is experienced as a unity where there are no distinctions. This is a level of experiencing without separation between mother and infant, inside and outside, or past and present. The infant functions primarily through identification, enmeshed, as it were, in identificatory love. While the original site of identificatory love is within the matrix, it is a level of psychic life that also lives on beneath the surface in later interactions. With the Oedipal stage, full object love becomes possible, evidencing separation between self and other, along with further distinctions that make experiencing and knowing possible. In object love, both the other and the self come to be as separate, distinct, and thus partners in relation. Paradoxically, Loewald holds that even self-love only emerges at this level, when the self first becomes an entity to itself.

In the posthumous book[3] *Can Love Last?: The Fate of Romance Over Time*, Stephen Mitchell takes up the topic of love, actually narrowing the focus to romantic love and passion, which are the usual associations of the term in the modern West. Over the course of this narrative he addresses underlying aspects of human lives together, as well as revealing both significant features of his own approach to psychoanalysis and wider contemporary developments in the field. In his words:

> The struggle to understand what is involved in the experiencing and sustaining of romance draws us into a thicket of issues and dialectics concerning fantasy and actuality, sameness and otherness, bodies and emotion, love and hate, the controlled and the uncontrollable, pathos and guilt, safety and risk.
>
> (2003, 29)

A recurrent theme in the text is the social nature of human life. While "the view of ourselves as singular, transparent, self-generating, and self-controlling agents" is still pervasive in our culture (Mitchell 2003, 24), it is through relationships with others that we come to be, develop, and strive for lives of richness and meaning. Success in the latter is particularly difficult, because life is not built upon secure foundations or conscious, conclusive choices. Mitchell's psychoanalytic approach, which he labels the "relational-conflict model" (1997, 10), stresses that emotional life is riddled with tensions between competing elements, as noted in the earlier quotation. In these cases, no final resolution or synthesis is possible or even desirable. It is the lived-out tensions that enrich life.

While Mitchell discusses the human need for security and stability, and the difficulty in acknowledging our vulnerability, the book highlights the importance of risk in the nurturing of love over time. He explores:

> the ways in which each of the major dimensions of romantic passion—sexuality, idealization and aggression—undermines our security and sense of self, and the ways in which that very destabilization raises the stakes and makes romantic love dangerous and meaningful.
>
> (2003, 57)

Mitchell departs from the classical Freudian model that regards sexuality and aggression as autonomous drives, which build up over time and seek release. Like many of his contemporary psychoanalysts, he argues that these are actually brought to the fore as responses in relationships, and are shaped by one's particular family and the wider culture.

Love figures prominently in two of the titles of Jessica Benjamin's[4] (b. 1946) major works, *The Bonds of Love: Psychoanalysis, Feminism, and The Problem of Domination* (1988) and *Like Subjects, Love Objects: Essays on Recognition and Sexual Difference* (1995). Together the subtitles reveal some of the many issues that are interwoven with this human affect. At the beginning of *Bonds of Love*, Benjamin writes, "This book is an analysis of the interplay between love and domination... Above all, this book seeks to understand how domination is anchored in the hearts of the dominated" (1988, 5). Benjamin's analysis is based on the view that two desires, for self-assertion and for recognition, punctuate human relationships. It is the latter that is her primary focus, seeing it as the desire "to affirm, validate, acknowledge, know, accept, understand, empathize, take in, tolerate, appreciate, see, identify with, find familiar... love" (15–16). Domination represents a failure of recognition, where the other is merely a fantasized object, not an independent subject of his or her own. In the course of this discussion of love, crucial elements in her overall psychoanalytic theory come to light: The beginning of recognition in the mother–infant relation, the dual pleasure in being recognized by the other and recognizing the other in return, the dynamics of mutual recognition and its inevitable breakdown, and, lastly, the gender polarity that pervades modern society, and its connection to the effacing of the mother's subjectivity.

The complex correlations between two types of love are the platform for Benjamin's *Like Subjects, Love Objects*. She notes that the title "was chosen to highlight the double-sidedness of intersubjectvity and the intrapsychic, as well as the tension between sameness and difference in gender relations" (1995, 7). Identificatory love is both the intrapsychic phenomenon that treats the other as a pawn of inner desire, and what opens the possibility for intersubjective relations with outside loved objects/others to blossom. Continuing and deepening themes in her earlier text, she discusses the fantasy-driven fear of the "omnipotent Mother," the actual fluidity of sexual identities in the development of both boys and girls, and the recurrent rounds of transference and counter-transference in therapy. At the end, she re-visions Freud's dual instinct theory, of *Eros* and *Thanatos*, suggesting that:

> We could consider the distinction between the sexual [where the other is manipulated] and Eros [playful and reciprocal interactions] as coincident with two hypothetical poles of sexuality, the one aligned with omnipotence, death, and fantasy, the other with recognition, life, and reality.
>
> (1995, 208)

The Place of Love in the Discourse of the Jewish Philosophers of Encounter

The topic of love pervades the work of the three Jewish philosophers Franz Rosenzweig, Martin Buber, and Emmanuel Levinas. It is the pivotal axis of Franz Rosenzweig's (1886–1929) signature offering, *The Star of Redemption*, in which he narrates a full philosophical anthropology, esthetics, ethics, and ontology. Rosenzweig describes the section on revelation as "the heart" of the *Star* (1999, 86), and love is its driving force. For he insists that "the allegory of love… goes through the whole [of] Revelation" (2005, 213). The section initially tells of the human transformation from enclosed self to trusting and loving soul that is elicited by God's love. The second act, as it were, concerns the individual's response, which is lived out through the dual love commandments, to love God with all one's heart, soul, and mind, and to love the neighbor as oneself. This choreography is expressed as: "Only the soul loved by God can receive the commandment of neighborly love so far as to fulfill it. God must first have turned toward man before man can be converted to God's will" (231).

Given the transformative power of love, Rosenzweig advances an insight that is repeated in the writings of the two other Jewish philosophers, that love cannot be just a human phenomenon. For him, love as well as its equal companion, language, have their origin and continuing source in the divine:

> For it is not possible for love to be "purely human." When it begins to speak—and this it must do, for there exists no other utterance spoken besides itself than the language of love—so when it speaks, it is already changed into something superhuman; for the sensuous character of the

> word is full to the brim with its divine supra-sensuous meaning; like language itself love is at once sensible and supra-sensuous.
>
> (2005, 216)

Rosenzweig concludes his narrative with the argument that an analysis of the world's most famous love story, the biblical book Song of Songs, repeats and confirms each of the foregoing insights concerning the divine and human, transformation, language, and love.

In Martin Buber's (1878–1965) famous text *I and Thou*, the treatment of love, albeit brief, is a condensed version of the major themes in his entire philosophy of dialogue. He writes:

> Man dwells in his love. This is no metaphor but actuality: love does not cling to an I, as if the Thou[5] were merely its "content" or object; it is between I and Thou… Love is a cosmic force. For those who stand in it and behold in it, men emerge from the entanglement in busy-ness… Exclusiveness comes into being miraculously again and again—and now one can act, help, heal, educate, raise, redeem. Love is responsibility of an I for a Thou.
>
> (1970, 66)

Buber's essential insights about the nature of the human are presented here in a number of ways. He insists that what is significant about a life is not "an attribute of the individual," but emerges only in relation. Thus, one does not have love, but lives in it, as a "cosmic force." It concerns a particular approach to others and to the world. This approach is not about possessing something, treating someone as just a "content or object" of one's own design. Love, as an example of the I–Thou relation, in opposition to the I–It relation of "busy-ness" with things, is built upon a reverence for all life and the acceptance of responsibility for all persons. It is only through such encounters that truly "one can act, help, heal, educate, raise, redeem."

A more concrete examination of love is seen in Buber's discussion of marriage in the essay "The Question to the Single One" (1965, 40–82). He proposes that "marriage is the exemplary bond" between persons. What it essentially teaches is that the "otherness" of one's fellow human beings is not just to be tolerated or even respected, but that it must be confirmed: "This person is other, essentially other than myself, and this otherness of his is what I mean, because I mean him; I confirm it; I wish his otherness to exist, because I wish his particular being to exist" (61). Marriage's lessons concerning authentic human relations extend beyond this welcoming and affirming difference. They include the understanding that one stands before the divine in responsibility not just for oneself, but for one's companions, neighbors, and community. As a consequence, the political arena cannot be excluded from that affirmation of the integrity of the other and its accompanying pursuit of justice.

Just as Buber views love as almost interchangeable with the I–Thou relation, so Emmanuel Levinas (1906–1995) equates love with his paramount concern, one's absolute responsibility for the other. In the following statement he insists that responsibility is the original and enduring meaning of love: "It [responsibility] is all the gravity of the love of the neighbor—of love without lust—on which rests the congenital meaning of this used word and which all the literary forms of its sublimation or its profanation presuppose" (1998, 163).

All the characteristics that congeal in Levinas' philosophy of responsibility apply equally to this view of love. Love is absolute, as is the face-to-face relation with the other, where at the moment of encounter the other is the only one ("the beloved, singular") on the horizon. It is asymmetrical, and not reciprocal: "Love exists without worrying about being loved." There is no hint of reward or any other return for the self. Levinas often cites Pascal in this regard: "And responsibility is actually love, as Blaise Pascal said: 'without concupiscence.'" Love/responsibility is not initiated by the self; one is chosen by the other, a being-designated that cannot be delegated to another. Finally, Levinas sums up an ode to love from one of his many interviews with the comment: "I would say this quite plainly: what is truly human is—and don't be afraid of this word—love" (2001, 143).

Even this first glance at love has produced some dividends. The psychoanalysts and the philosophers share the view that the term covers an extensive range—in ways underlying the totality—of human relationships. Yet, their discourses also reveal distinctive features, which will reappear throughout this book. Starting with Freud, the psychoanalysts describe love in terms of desire, attachment, and connection, a phenomenon of both the intrapsychic and intersubjective registers. The relational psychoanalysts drop Freud's mechanical or hydraulic model of the self, featuring the notion of cathexis, and highlight especially the variegated intersubjective dynamics much more fully. For the Jewish philosophers, love's transformative power can only be unraveled through the dual registers of the human and the divine. For them, love is almost synonymous with responsibility, and coextensive with speech or language. Thus, while the psychoanalysts describe love's "genesis, development, and vicissitudes" as lying behind all human relations (Loewald 1978, 29), the Jewish philosophers' examination of love has a prescriptive dimension; it concerns what constitutes authentic human relations or what is "truly human" (Levinas 2001, 143).

Forays into Love's Terrain

As evidenced above, this book is an effort at what may be metaphorically described as dialogue. It conducts a dialogue between those who foster the two languages of love. Dialogue is not reductionist nor is it synthesizing, as in G. W. F. Hegel's *Aufhebung*. It is about a relation with otherness, where each partner stands in their own integrity. One goal here is to probe that integrity. What are the strengths and weaknesses, the powers and limits of each language? However, integrity is not static; it welcomes challenges and foresees development. Thus, the final question that is continually evoked: How can the dialogue be transformative for each of the partners?[6]

Within a more disciplinary or multidisciplinary context, this approach falls within the parameters of comparative philosophy, and draws upon the insights of a number of philosophic and psychoanalytic theorists. One of its orientations is well reflected in an observation made by the contemporary philosopher Richard Rorty. In the essay "Pragmatism and Philosophy," he describes a shift in how philosophy is seen, aspects of which are also recounted in postmodern and feminist discourses. Some thinkers no longer envision philosophy as a discipline that searches for ultimate truths that transcend cultures, languages, and particular discourses. These adherents of philosophy "compare and contrast cultural traditions" and find that "in the process of playing vocabularies and cultures against each other, we produce new and better ways of talking and acting" (1987, 54). These post-Philosophical philosophers explore "the comparative advantages and disadvantages of the various ways of talking that our race has invented" (58).

Rorty's perspective needs to be augmented by the insights of both the feminist psychotherapist and philosopher Jane Flax and also Jessica

Benjamin. In the process of evaluating the relative strengths and weaknesses of psychoanalytic and postmodern discussions of subjectivity, Flax writes, “Each discourse tries to order the heterogeneous components of subjectivity within one master narrative or category… We will need multiple stories in a variety of styles to appreciate its complexity” (1993, 98). Flax’s thought might be reworked to suggest that philosophy should not just evaluate the relative merits of specific philosophic systems, but that it should recognize that multiple systems, with their diverse perspectives, are required to account for the complexity of existence.

Benjamin’s standpoint often highlights central tensions in human life, such as that between attachment and independence, or between the individual’s need for identifying with what is similar in other persons and being excited by and drawn to what is different. In her view, these tensions are not solved or resolved, but lived with and through (1995, 76). The philosophic lesson here is that sometimes one must withstand the powerful rational urge toward determining a final answer or working toward a synthesis of conflicting ideas. The best accounts often keep in suspense different ideas and approaches reflecting, once again, the complexities of personal and communal life. Bringing together the insights of Flax, Benjamin, and Rorty, this book is an effort to examine “the comparative advantages and disadvantages of the various [disciplinary] ways of talking” (Rorty 1987, 58), while recognizing the need for multiple concurrent perspectives and respecting unresolved conflicts and enduring tensions.

The six chapters and Conclusion that follow are partial[7] forays into the complex terrain that constitutes human relationships. They focus on self-love and love of the other, intersubjectivity, transformation, language, meaning, responsibility, and death. The first three chapters look at the dynamics of what the psychoanalysts describe as intersubjectivity and the philosophers as the interhuman,[8] and the last three chapters and Conclusion examine specific topics in their treatments.

Chapter 1, “Loving the Neighbor: On Self-Love,” introduces some of the major figures in this study, and also provides a reading of Freud and some earlier post-Freudian developments. It is initiated by a paradox, which shadows the reflections of the three Jewish philosophers of encounter. While the biblical commandments to love the neighbor and to love the stranger are central features of their work, in that they see authenticity and meaning as generated solely through the relationship to others, the commandments, read literally, conflict with their position. These conclude that one should love the neighbor *as oneself*, and thus appear to base neighbor-love on self-love. The discussion begins with an examination of the Jewish Rabbis' interpretation of the commandment to love one's neighbor. For them, in contrast to the modern Jewish philosophers, the difficulty in fulfilling the commandment was that it required of persons something the Rabbis saw as inherently impossible: to love others *as much* as they loved themselves.

The conflict concerning the relationship between and relative strength of self-love and love of the other is then shown to have deep resonances within the discourse and development of psychoanalysis. The psychoanalytic side of the examination begins with Freud's insistence that narcissism stands at the origin of instinctual life, and love of the other is derivative. In the work of the post-Freudian Melanie Klein and the object relations theorist W. R. D. Fairbairn, the diametrical opposite understanding is slowly put into play, that love of the other is primary and self-love is derivative. In another important step, Freud's fundamental notion of instincts is subverted by Loewald's attention to the original mother–infant dyad. With Mitchell's most important work, the language of primary narcissism is totally abandoned. The investigation concludes with some wider reflections concerning what is at stake in this argument about the genesis and primacy of love of the self and love of the other.

Jessica Benjamin is the most prominent relational psychoanalyst addressing the topic of intersubjectivity, that is, the relationship between one subject and an independent and outside other. Chapter 2, "Jessica Benjamin and (the Missing) Martin Buber: On Intersubjectivity," advances the argument that despite the lack of references in her work to the writings of Buber, the juxtaposition of their ideas highlights striking similarities and significant disparities that lead to unanticipated insights in understanding each of them. The similarities include their shared understanding of *homo duplex*, and the correspondence between Benjamin's discussion of omnipotence, recognition, the third or in-between, and speech, and Buber's presentation of I and It, I and Thou, the between, and speech or dialogue. One disparity involves Benjamin's view of sharing and the same and Buber's understanding of difference as the foundation for recognizing the other. They also disagree about whether the mother–infant dyad or the divine is pivotal in the genesis of intersubjectivity.

Important challenges for each thinker arise out of the exploration of their differences. Benjamin is asked to consider whether there is something more fundamental than the need for similarity in what she designates as the recognition of the other. Her portrayal of faith in terms of the believer's quest to escape the difficulties of living with freedom and human finitude is also queried. Among other concerns, Buber is asked to remedy the neglect of the crucial early exchanges between mother and infant in his account of individual development. A review of contemporary psychoanalysts who appreciate the affinity between or even influence of Buber's philosophy on their practice and reflections completes the discussion.

Chapter 3, "The Presence of the Other: On Transformation," commences with an examination of psychoanalysis and religion as two systems of transformation, that is, as offering diagnoses of illness, processes of treatment, and promises of health. What is distinctive to the understandings of the post-Freudians and the Jewish philosophers is that the key or catalyst for transformation is the other, the presence of the other. In the case of psychoanalysis this represents a major departure from Freud's view of the role of the analyst, in which the suppression of his or her person-ality is seen as required for the sake of the objectivity of the process. The relational psychoanalysts offer a very different model, of "two-person" psychoanalysis, where the freer and more open exchange between the patient and analyst represents the core of treatment and a model of authentic human relations for the future. The special attention given today to the nature of the analytic interaction and the role and person of the analyst is explored through vignettes focusing on Lewis Aron's discussion of mutuality and asymmetry, Irwin Hoffman's examination of the dynamic between ritual and spontaneity, Thomas Ogden's reflections on reverie, and Steven Cooper's analysis of hope.

For Buber, Rosenzweig, and Levinas the symptoms of illness are feelings of meaninglessness, purposelessness, and the lack of direction/orientation. The cause is an inescapable self-centeredness or egoism, with its accompanying alienation from others. The two "persons" consistently linked together in terms of transformation and genuine relationships with others are the transcendent One and the next one or neighbor. Although there are discrete differences in the understandings of the three Jewish philosophers, they share the view that it is through the encounter with the divine, revelation, that the individual's unique direction in life is illuminated. Following this, authenticity and meaning are expressed through love/responsibility for the neighbor. The chapter continues with focused presentations from the writings of the philosophers that give detail and specificity to their positions. A conversation between the two groups concerning areas of overlap and unique features in the context of diagnosis, treatment, and health concludes the section, highlighted by Buber's own prescient discussion of the dynamics and goals of psychoanalysis.

The point of departure for Chapter 4, "*Langue, Parole, et Chanson:* On Language," is Ferdinand de Saussure's famous discussion of language as *langue* and *parole*, that is, as system and performance. It argues that this viewpoint fails to capture language's sensory, affective, formative, dialogical, ethical, and metaphysical dimensions, which are evoked by the metaphor of "song." Further, it is precisely these linguistic features, which reveal more about the depth and possibilities of human living, that are prominent in the discourses about language in the works of the psychoanalysts and philosophers of this study.

The discussion begins with an examination of the wider "linguistic turn" that has influenced so many of the contemporary human sciences. Mitchell's insight that language is "the very stuff of mind" summarizes the attitude of many psychoanalysts (2000, 5), as does Loewald's analysis of language in terms of early development and unconscious processes. The creative, affective, formative, and performative dimensions of this phenomenon are detailed in the psychoanalytic writings of Thomas Ogden, Roy Schafer, and others. For Rosenzweig, Buber, and Levinas language and the human are synonymous. Their contributions include celebrations of the dynamics of dialogue, the ethical dimension that permeates all linguistic exchanges, and the divine dimension of language. They also share the view that the Holy Scripture is the prototype for understanding the miraculous powers of the word; it constitutes what Levinas terms "language *par excellence*" (1994, xii). The dialogue between the psychoanalysts and philosophers notes the differences in their insights, but also how the two sides provide complementary approaches to appreciating the richness of language.

The title of Chapter 5, "Revisiting an 'Illusion': On Meaning," alludes to Freud's provocative text on religion *The Future of an Illusion* (1964). It inquiries whether a path to the appreciation of religion by contemporary psychoanalysis may be opened as a consequence of the discipline's new emphasis on meaning. Meaning-making is now regarded as a fundamental human activity, as expressed by Anthony Elliott: "The psyche is the launching pad from which people *make meaning*" (1999, 7). Significantly, the methods and goals of psychoanalysis have been correspondingly re-envisioned, as exemplified in Mitchell's words: "In my view, psychoanalysis has become a method for generating a certain kind of meaning, for fostering certain forms of experience and living" (1997, 24).

The brief survey of scholarly examinations of religion, which emphasize its function of providing a meaning schema for individual and social life, leads off the chapter. The psychoanalytic discussion of meaning features the interplay between unconscious and consciousness, rational and irrational, and fantasy and reality. Levinas' "Notes on Meaning" is probed, principally to illuminate what he has in common with Rosenzweig and Buber. In the end, the Jewish philosophers' approach draws attention to the connection between meaning and one's responsibility to the other, and suggests that meaning is carried and even embodied in speech or language. The treatment closes by highlighting the distinctive features of the two discourses on meaning and the nature of a full life, the psychoanalytic appreciation for fantasy and creativity, and the continuing philosophic recognition of the divine dimension of the interhuman.

A historic episode is echoed in the title of Chapter 6, "Beyond 'Betrayal': On Responsibility," which is Martin Heidegger's flirtation with Nazism and what his students felt as his personal betrayal. While many significant thinkers who were Jewish or of Jewish descent, including Hannah Arendt and Karl Löwith, studied under Heidegger, it was particularly Loewald and Levinas who saw their work as direct responses to their teacher. The chapter examines their ambivalent reactions, incorporating both appreciation and rejection, in terms of their understanding of intersubjectivity and responsibility. Responsibility and the relationship to others more widely is first examined in Heidegger's philosophic classic, *Sein und Zeit* (*Being and Time*). In that text the greatest challenge in life, which is death, must be faced by the individual alone, and responsibility essentially concerns the subject's attitude toward his or her own authenticity.

Loewald understands his psychoanalytic work and writings as expanding upon his philosophic training and abiding interests. Responsibility is addressed in his understanding of "owning up" (1978, 19), that is, personally taking up desires, fantasies, and memories embedded in the mind. He also regards his vocation as an analyst as expressing, in the concrete, an abiding love of truth and concern for others. The whole course of Levinas' writings can be seen as a dialectical confrontation with Heidegger. These highlight the ethical call of the other as the only escape from the cycle of violence, meaninglessness, and *ennui* that characterizes the self's original attachment to itself. The last section widens the presentation to examine the emerging importance given by some contemporary psychoanalysts to the idea that a full or meaningful life cannot overlook one's responsibility for others.

The phrase "Strong as Death" again recalls the biblical Song of Songs, with its central assertion that "Love is strong as death" (Song of Sol. 8:6). The meaning of the sentiment about the relation between love and death for the Jewish philosophers is the pivotal issue pursued in the Conclusion. The treatment begins with Irwin Hoffman's sustained discussion of the challenge of death as an example of the approach of many relational psychoanalysts. Hoffman finds that death is the symbol of the meaninglessness and loss that haunt life, as well as providing unique intensity and significance to human existence. The Jewish philosophers share a basic approach to love and death. They acknowledge that death is inescapable, but that it is not stronger than love. They also insist that trust in God provides assurance that nothing significant in life—most assuredly love—is lost. They narrate an alternate story that does not refer to individual survival, but to the endurance of responsibility and love despite death.

Notes

1 Many of the later relational thinkers offer a similar understanding of psychoanalysis as a practice of love. Irwin Hoffman writes of psychoanalysis as a "transformative form of love" (1998, xix), and of the analyst as "a magnet for the universal human appetite to reestablish the earliest conditions for the absorption of love" (12). Reflecting important changes in understanding the nature of the analytic relationship, Lewis Aron highlights the concept of empathy: "Empathy, or analytic love, must be mutually given and mutually accepted" (1996, 136).

2 Freud originally used the term "object" to refer to persons or parts of persons, the object of a particular drive. The phrase "mature object relations" refers to relationships where persons are regarded as separate and having their own integrity.

3 The psychoanalyst Margaret Black, who was Stephen Mitchell's wife, writes a moving tribute to her late husband in the "Foreword" (Mitchell 2003, 11–17).

4 Many of the psychoanalysts in this study were or, if still alive, are Jewish. This includes Freud, Mitchell, Benjamin, and Aron. Loewald's father was also Jewish. This fact is not surprising, since many of the prominent psychoanalysts in the past and in contemporary times were Jewish. Unlike the other figures, there have been many studies of Freud's Judaism; particularly significant is the well-known examination by Yosef Hayim Yerushalmi in *Freud's Moses* (1991).

While this issue is important, it is beyond the parameters of this study. The place and impact of Judaism on the history of the psychoanalytic movement is a major theme in Aron and Starr's *A Psychotherapy for the People* (2013).

5 While in Walter Kaufmann's translation of Buber's *I and Thou* (1970) the German word "*Du*" is rendered "You," I am substituting the more customary word used in Buber studies, "Thou."

6 This question reflects an insight of Rosenzweig's dialogue partner, the Christian philosopher Eugen Rosenstock-Huessy, whose "motto" was "*Respondeo etsi mutabor*," that is, "I respond although I will be changed" (Rosenstock-Huessy 1970, 10).

7 In the article "Epilogue: Prolegomenon to Future Feminist Philosophies of Religion," Marilyn Thie identifies a common understanding among feminist scholars that their "findings, insights, and conclusions are at best partial and limited" (1994, 233). This follows from the recognition that every scholar has a distinct point of departure and presuppositions. It also reflects the view that a whole community of scholars working together is needed to arrive at fuller and deeper understandings of any subject.

8 I will sometimes be using Benjamin's term the "intersubjective" in a generic way to speak of a vision of authentic relationship in reference to what Buber sometimes calls the "interhuman" (Buber 1999, 72–78) and what Levinas describes as the "interpersonal" (1969, 215).

References

Aron, Lewis. 1996. *A Meeting of Minds: Mutuality in Psychoanalysis*. Hillsdale, NJ: Analytic Press.

Aron, Lewis, and Karen Starr. 2013. *A Psychotherapy for the People: Toward a Progressive Psychoanalysis*. New York: Routledge.

Benjamin, Jessica. 1988. *The Bonds of Love: Psychoanalysis, Feminism, and the Problem of Domination*. New York: Pantheon Books.

—. 1995. *Like Subjects, Love Objects: Essays on Recognition and Sexual Difference*. New Haven, CT: Yale University Press.

Buber, Martin. 1965. *Between Man and Man*. Translated by Ronald Gregor Smith. New York: Collier Books.

—. 1970. *I and Thou*. Translated by Walter Kaufmann. New York: Charles Scribner's Sons.

—. 1999. *Martin Buber on Psychology and Psychotherapy: Essays, Letters, and Dialogue*. Edited by Judith Buber Agassi. Syracuse, NY: Syracuse University Press.

Elliott, Anthony, ed. 1999. *Freud 2000*. New York: Routledge.

Flax, Jane. 1993. *Disputed Subjects: Essays on Psychoanalysis, Politics and Philosophy*. New York: Routledge.

Freud, Sigmund. 1949. *An Outline of Psychoanalysis*. Translated by James Strachey. New York: W. W. Norton.

—. 1964. *The Future of an Illusion*. Translated by W. D. Robson-Scott. Garden City, NY: Anchor Books.
Hoffman, Irwin Z. 1998. *Ritual and Spontaneity in the Psychoanalytic Process. A Dialectical-Constructivist View*. Hillsdale, NJ: Analytic Press.
Levinas, Emmanuel. 1969. *Totality and Infinity: An Essay on Exteriority*. Translated by Alphonso Lingis. Pittsburgh, PA: Duquesne University Press.
—. 1994. *Beyond the Verse: Talmudic Readings and Lectures*. Translated by Gary D. Mole. Bloomington, IN: Indiana University Press.
—. 1998. *Of God Who Comes to Mind*. Translated by Bettina Bergo. Stanford, CA: Stanford University Press.
—. 2001. *Is It Righteous To Be?: Interviews with Emmanuel Levinas*. Edited by Jill Robbins. Stanford, CA: Stanford University Press.
Loewald, Hans W. 1978. *Psychoanalysis and the History of the Individual: The Freud Lectures at Yale*. New Haven, CT: Yale University Press.
—. 2000. *The Essential Loewald: Collected Papers and Monographs*. Hagerstown, MD: University Publishing Group.
Mitchell, Stephen A. 1997. *Influence and Autonomy in Psychoanalysis*. Hillsdale, NJ: Analytic Press.
—. 2000. *Relationality: From Attachment to Intersubjectivity*. Hillsdale, NJ: Analytic Press.
—. 2003. *Can Love Last?: The Fate of Romance Over Time*. New York: W. W. Norton and Company.
Rorty, Richard. 1987. "Pragmatism and Philosophy." In *After Philosophy: End or Transformation?* Edited by Kenneth Baynes, James Bohman, and Thomas McCarthy, 26–66. Cambridge, MA: MIT Press.
Rosenstock-Huessy, Eugen. 1970. *I Am an Impure Thinker*. Norwich, VT: Argo Books.
Rosenzweig, Franz. 1999. *Franz Rosenzweig's "The New Thinking"*. Edited and translated by Alan Udoff and Barbara E. Galli. Syracuse, NY: Syracuse University Press.
—. 2005. *The Star of Redemption*. Translated by Barbara E. Galli. Madison, WI: University of Wisconsin Press.
Thie, Marilyn. 1994. "Epilogue: Prolegomenon to Future Feminist Philosophies of Religions," *Hypatia*, 9 (2): 229–39.
Yerushalmi, Yosef Hayim. 1991. *Freud's Moses: Judaism Terminable and Interminable*. New Haven, CT: Yale University Press.

Chapter 1

Loving the Neighbor

On Self-Love

The two biblical commandments in Leviticus to love the neighbor and to love the stranger seem to ground that love of the other in a more original, basic, or given love of the self. This chapter will explore the ways that three modern Jewish philosophers of relation, Franz Rosenzweig, Martin Buber, and Emmanuel Levinas, address these commandments, since for them, love of the other, and not self-love, grounds the self—at least the authentic self—and in this sense is primary, basic, or original. The treatment begins with a discussion of rabbinic glosses on the meaning of these commandments. The focus then shifts to the disagreement concerning narcissism and self-other relations between Freud and some post-Freudian psychoanalytic theorists, which mirrors the opposing standpoints of the Rabbis and the three Jewish philosophers. It concludes with brief suggestions concerning the significance of these two models of love in terms of an array of disciplines and theories.

The book of Leviticus contains the immortal commandments to love the neighbor and the stranger.[1] Leviticus 19:18 states, "You shall not take vengeance or bear any grudge against the sons of your own people, but you shall love your neighbor as yourself: I am the Lord," while Leviticus 19:34 declares, "The stranger who sojourns with you shall be to you as the native among you, and you shall love him as yourself; for you were strangers in the land of Egypt: I am the Lord your God."[2] There is also a formulation of the latter commandment in Deuteronomy 10:19, which does not directly allude to the self: "Love the sojourner therefore; for you were sojourners in the land of Egypt."

These two commandments of love (*ahavah*) are part of the 613 divine commands, the essence of Torah, that the Rabbis—authors of the Mishnah, Talmud, and later commentaries—affirmed were given to Moses at Sinai and that were to punctuate and mold the everyday life of the Jewish people. The task of the Rabbis was to teach and explain the meaning and implications of these biblical injunctions. These traditional biblical commentators seemed to find a dual problematic in fulfilling their tasks in terms of these particular injunctions. They had to translate the commandments to love into specific requirements, that is, to concretize the injunction to elicit and direct that elusive, if also tremendously powerful, passion of love. This effort of concretizing, in this case, loving the other through acts of love, constitutes one of the foremost strengths of the Rabbis.[3] In reference to loving the neighbor (Lev. 19:18), for example, Maimonides (1135–1204) included such social obligations as visiting the sick, comforting the mourners, and giving a dowry to the bride (1967, 221). The love of the stranger entails, according to the Rabbis, providing for such fundamental needs as food and dress, which are alluded to in the verse previous to the Deuteronomy stipulation, where it states that God "loves the sojourner, giving him food and clothing" (Deut. 10:18).

The more interesting problem, in terms of this exposition, refers to rabbinic discussions concerning the relationship between love of the neighbor/stranger and love of the self. The Rabbis felt compelled to attend to this "as oneself" (*kamokhah*). Thus, Nahmanides (1194–1270), in a very influential commentary on the Leviticus neighbor-love, held that the command could not be understood in a literal sense. He wrote:

> This is an expression by way of overstatement, for a human heart is not able to accept a command to love one's neighbor as oneself… However, [because of human nature] he will still not want him to be his equal, for there will always be a desire in his heart that he should have more of these goods than his neighbor.
>
> (translator added words in brackets; 1974, 292–293)[4]

Nahmanides interpreted the verse to mean that an individual should desire the overall well-being of the neighbor, as one desired the good for oneself. In a similar vein, Maimonides wrote:

> By this injunction we are commanded that we are to love one another even as we love ourselves, that a man's love and compassion for his brother in faith shall be like his love and compassion for himself, in respect of his money, his person, and of whatever he possesses and desires. Whatever I wish for myself, I am to wish the like for him.
>
> (1967, 220)

In this quotation, Maimonides ties the two pieces of rabbinic interpretation together—the making concrete and the struggling with a literal loving of the other as one loves the self by channeling the commandment into a "compassion" and desiring the overall good for the other "in respect of his money, his person, and of whatever he possesses and desires." Reaffirming the primacy of love of self as the point of departure for the treatment of the other, Maimonides wrote in his *Mishneh Torah*, "All things that thou desirest that others should do unto thee, thou thyself shouldst do unto him who is thy brother" (1967, 221).

Thus, it is clear that the Rabbis had a particular understanding of the nature of the human. This included the belief that there was something so powerful, primary, and elemental about self-love that they quickly turned from a more straightforward reading of the injunctions, which Nahmanides labeled as an "overstatement." In Nahmanides' words, the literal meaning of loving the neighbor as oneself would be unacceptable to "the heart of man." The love of the other was a divine command, and the Rabbis felt, at least as an ideal, that while one could desire the other person's overall welfare as one's own, it was impossible for there to be a full equation of love of self and love of the other.

Rosenzweig, Buber, and Levinas

The three Jewish philosophers Franz Rosenzweig, Martin Buber, and Emmanuel Levinas also had difficulty in accepting the two injunctions to love the neighbor/stranger as oneself in their literal meaning. However, for them, the obstacle lay in reconciling the meaning of the text with their philosophies that expressed a very different notion of the self, affirming love of the other as the foundation for the authentic life, actually for what it meant to be a person.[5] Thus, their problem was almost exactly opposite of that of the Rabbis. Their question was not how was it conceivable to love the other, possibly all others, as one loved oneself, but how could love of the self, which for these thinkers was problematic, be the basis or model for that highest and divinely sanctioned life-path of love of the other?

The Star of Redemption, Franz Rosenzweig's magnum opus, presents both his interpretation of the commandment to love the neighbor[6] and his view of its centrality for the religious life. Before turning to the specific treatment, it will be helpful to summarize the philosophical anthropology that is narrated in the *Star*. In Rosenzweig's ontogenetic account the individual is not born a self. One is born as just another member of the human species, a creature or "piece of the world" (2005, 80). The full distinctiveness of what one means by a self erupts. At certain points in its maturation, the self wills itself in its particularity, out of the combination of "defiance and character," or alternately, of "*hubris* and *daimon*" (180). With this emergence, the individual is an utterly self-contained entity—one who is a "lonely man in the hardest sense of the word" (80). Rosenzweig looks to the tragic hero of Greek drama to illustrate the basic nature of the human. The hero of tragedy lives a life of isolation and self-containment, which culminates in his or her self-destruction. Living unrelated to others and essentially speechless, the individual is able to trust only in oneself. The central and defining event of that life is the encounter with death. Rosenzweig writes that "death, his own death, has become the event that dominates his life" (85).

The opening of this cage of the self comes through a transcendent call, according to Rosenzweig. He writes, "For it is only in the love of God, pouring into the rock of the Self that the flower of the soul begins to grow; before this, man was turned in on himself, mute and devoid of feeling. Only now is he—beloved soul" (2005, 183). God initiates this relationship with the soul by commanding that the beloved love in return, which introduces the first biblical love commandment of loving God with all one's heart, soul, and mind. In turning to and loving God, the individual is fundamentally transformed. This original love dialogue provides the soul with the basis for an authentic life, including humility, trust, faithfulness, and peace. Most importantly, revelation, which is God's liberating love, elicits in return both speech and love from the individual.

However, Rosenzweig holds that a person who can only love God is at most half a human being.[7] God wishes for complete human beings, those whose speech and love enter the world and extend to others. Further, turning to the other begins again that process—for the neighbor—of hearing of the divine word, feeling the divine presence, and then turning to the next one (*das Nebenmensch*) that is the neighbor. It is at this point that the command to love the neighbor is introduced in the *Star*. Summarizing the dynamic of the commandments to love God and to love the other, Rosenzweig writes, "Only the soul loved by God can receive the commandment of neighborly love so far as to fulfill it. God must first have turned toward man before man can be converted to God's will" (2005, 231).[8]

Rosenzweig's lengthy discussion of the commandment to love the neighbor will be quoted in full:

> For man's act of love is only apparently an act. It is not said to him by God to do unto his neighbor what he would like done to himself. This practical form of the commandment of love of the neighbor, serving as a rule of conduct, really only designates the lower negative limit; the commandment forbids crossing over this limit in action, and already for this reason alone, it will be better to express it, even outwardly, in a negative form. For man must love his neighbor as himself. Like himself, your neighbor is "like you." Man must not deny himself… his Self is finally definitely confirmed in its place… out of the infinite chaos of the world, a neighbor, his neighbor, is placed before his soul, and of him, to begin with exclusively of him, he is told: he is like you. "Like you," hence not "you." You remain You and you will remain You. But he will not remain a He for you and hence only a This for your You; no, he is like you, like your You, a You like you, an I—a soul.
>
> (2005, 257)[9]

Rosenzweig's understanding of the commandment follows from his view of the soul or liberated self's mission in the world. The individual is directed to move from the orbit of revelation, the dialogue of "I" and "Thou" with the divine, to the orbit of redemption, the exchange of "I" and "Thou" between persons. Redemption, for Rosenzweig, is that hidden divine and human process of ensouling (*Beseelung*) the world. The encounter with the other is not fortuitous nor is she or he to be treated as just another piece of the world. The expression to be "like you," in the commandment means that the neighbor is not a mere it or "This," but "like your You, a You like you, an I—a soul." In addition, it is interesting that Rosenzweig refers to an interpretation similar to that of the Rabbis, who translated the injunction into a rule of conduct to do unto the neighbor what one would like done to oneself. He does not reject this view outright, but sees it as "only" the lower limit of its meaning.

The view that "like you" would refer to one's love of self would undermine basic features of Rosenzweig's understanding of the nature of the human and the nature of life. It is only through dialogue that the life of authenticity appears—in speaking, loving, and acting with responsibility. The self is opened up through speech and love and the self opens others to a life of fulfillment through speech and love. Self-love, if having a place at all in Rosenzweig's anthropology, characterizes the shadow of a person wholly turned within, living a solitary life of fear. Actually, the only use for the term "love," which Rosenzweig uses almost as synonymous with speech, is outward-directed. Life is bereft of love until one is called, and then sent to others. However, the lack of reference to self-love does not subvert the importance of the self. For Rosenzweig, it is precisely and exclusively through interactions with others that the self is confirmed in its reality, fullness, and place.

Martin Buber introduces his interpretation of the commandment to love the neighbor in the essay of 1936 "The Question to the Single One." The full force of Buber's exegesis of the command is illuminated by the central argument of the larger essay. It begins with a quotation from his wife, Paula Buber ("Responsibility is the navel-string of creation" [1965, 40]), but its point of departure is a declaration and related essay by the great Danish philosopher, Søren Kierkegaard. The declaration was that he, Søren Kierkegaard, had to give up his *fiancée*, Regina Olson, in order to dedicate himself to God, and the essay, "The Single One," presents Kierkegaard's understanding of the correlation between the relationship to God and the relationship to other persons. Buber is both appreciative and critical of the Kierkegaard missive. He lauds Kierkegaard's understanding that it is as a unique person addressed and answerable to the ultimate that the authentic life is to be lived out, but Buber presents a position that radically departs from what he renders as: "The central event of Kierkegaard's life and the core of the crystallization of his thought was the renunciation of Regina Olsen as representing woman and the world" (40). Buber believes that one cannot find God, or the self, by repudiating the world. In his words, "Creation is not a hurdle on the road to God, it is the road itself. We are created along with one another and directed to a life with one another" (52).

Buber's approach to the commandment to love the neighbor underscores this critique. He continues:

> Both are to be "loved", God and the "neighbour" (i.e. not man in general, but the man who meets me time and again in the context of life), but in different ways. The neighbour is to be loved "as one like myself" (not "as I love myself"; in the last reality one does not love oneself, but one should rather learn to love oneself through love of

> one's neighbour), to whom, then, I should show love as I wish it may be shown to me. But God is to be loved with all my soul and all my might. By connecting the two Jesus brings to light the Old Testament truth that God and man are not rivals.
>
> (1965, 51)

Thus, Buber interprets the *kamokhah* as "one like myself." The German original is "*der mir Gleich*" and not, as Buber puts it, "*wie ich mich liebe*" ("as I love myself" [1962, 229]). The other is to be loved, as a person loves another self or person, and, ultimately, in the same way that one would wish to be loved. He does not see self-love as a reference in the *mitzvah*. Buber insists that "in the last reality one does not love oneself," and, later in the essay, even more insistently: "There is no self-love that is not self-deceit (since he who loves… loves only the other and essentially not himself)" (1965, 43). Further, whatever Buber means here by to "love oneself" (perhaps it would have been more consistent and accurate to write that one learns to respect the self—that elemental sense of dignity or *amour-propre*), one learns to do so by loving others.

Buber's brief discussion of the love of the neighbor underscores important themes in the essay and in his book *I and Thou*. In terms of the former, he maintains that love is other-referential. He also writes that responsibility is other-referential. The panegyric on responsibility affirms that:

> responsibility presupposes one who addresses me primarily, that is, from a realm independent of myself, and to whom I am answerable. He addresses me about something that he has entrusted to me and I am bound to take care of loyally… Where no primary address and claim can touch me… responsibility has become a phantom.
>
> (1965, 45)

Just as there is no meaning to self-love, there is no meaning to being responsible to oneself, although one is to be responsible for oneself. The treatments of love and responsibility elaborate Buber's famous statement in *I and Thou* that "there is no I as such" (1970, 54), but only the I in relation. The most central features of a life of integrity—love and responsibility—are relational through and through.[10] Further, as here Buber states that "one should rather learn to love oneself through love of one's neighbour," the whole structure and message of *I and Thou* places the "I–Thou" relationship with persons as prior even to the "I–Thou" relationship with God. Saying "Thou" to others is the training or discipline to be able to address the divine, which is always and only as "Thou." In addition, the notion of neighbor in the original quotation repeats a primary insight in *I and Thou*, which we also saw in Rosenzweig's *Star*, that the neighbor is not some abstract person, but exactly the one who I meet and who has been placed before me. Responding daily, perhaps hourly, to the commandment to love the neighbor contours a life and aligns it with that mystery which is the divine plan of redemption.

Finally, it is important to note, especially in light of the psychoanalytic treatment that will soon follow, that in *I and Thou* Buber affirms the ontogenetic priority of the I–Thou relationship. He writes, "In the beginning is the relation—as the category of being, as readiness, as a form that reaches out to be filled, as a model of the soul; the *a priori* of relation; *the innate Thou*" (1970, 78). For him, there is a deep interaction between fetus and mother in the womb. Even the prenatal human, the fetus, exhibits the urge toward relation, or "a pure natural association" with its carrier (76). After birth, in the earliest stages, the innate "longing for relation" is clear and dominates the infant's life. Buber writes about the infant's "drive to turn everything into a Thou" (78), that is, a partner in relationship, and sees it as independent of other drives and requirements, such as that of nourishment (77). The natural attitude of the infant, who does not know the distinction between animate and inanimate objects, will even bring her or him to respond to any sound as if to a "conversation" (78).[11] It is on the basis of this desire for relation that all else in the development of the infant unfolds.

Starting in the spring of 1925 and continuing until the death of Rosenzweig in 1929, Rosenzweig and Buber worked on a new German translation of the Bible.[12] The end product was a revolutionary rendering of the text, which is what both thinkers thought was required. This translation was to be the platform for a revival of the Jewish community in Germany, a hope soon crushed by subsequent German history. Rosenzweig and Buber sought to be true to the original text, especially in terms of the Hebrew language and what they saw as the text's oral origin, as well as to have contemporary readers actually feel addressed by the call that animated the biblical words. The two love commandments in Leviticus are rendered in ways consistent with what we have seen above: Leviticus 19:18 as "*halte lieb deinen Genossen, dir gleich*," and Leviticus 19:34 as "*halte lieb ihn, dir gleich*" (Buber and Rosenzweig 1930, 366, 368). The German translation reinforces the directiveness of the commandment to love the neighbor/companion and stranger/sojourner, as well as rendering *kamokhah* as "like you," that is, he is like you.

A meeting with Dutch philosophers at the University of Leiden in 1975 brought Emmanuel Levinas to discuss the commandment to love the neighbor, as well as the Buber–Rosenzweig Bible translation. In a response to a question where *Leviticus* 19:18 was cited, Levinas replied:

> Concerning the biblical text… I am much more perplexed than the translators to whom you refer. What does "as yourself" signify? Buber and Rosenzweig were here very perplexed by the translation. They said to each other, does not "as yourself" mean that one loves oneself most? Instead of translating this in agreement with you, they translated it, "love your neighbor, he is like you." But if one first agrees to separate the last word of the Hebrew verse, *kamokhah*, from the beginning of the verse, one can read the whole thing still otherwise. "Love your neighbor; this work is like yourself"; "love your neighbor; he is yourself"; "it is love of the neighbor which is yourself". Would you say this is an extremely audacious reading? Yet the Old Testament supports several readings and it is when the entirety of the Bible becomes the context of the verse that the verse resounds with all its meaning.
>
> (1998, 90)

This is "an extremely audacious reading," but also one that is consistent with the daring shown by the Rabbis from the beginning of their career as caretakers of the Torah. Levinas, as with Buber and Rosenzweig before, was perplexed by the passage, that is to say, he could not believe that the Bible is suggesting that one "loves oneself most," that self-love is the model or basis for love of the other. Ultimately, Levinas interprets the injunction to mean that one is to love the neighbor for "it is love of the neighbor which is yourself." Loving the neighbor, thus, defines what it means to be a self or person. Levinas justifies this interpretation, in typical rabbinic form, by suggesting that in the face of a "perplexing" statement, one asks its meaning in the context of, or in harmony with, the pervasive spirit of the Torah text.[13] Levinas puts this as: "For the absolute hermeneutic of a verse, the entirety of the book is necessary!" What does Levinas see as the overall message of the Bible? In his response to the original question this is made clear:

> The Bible is the priority of the other in relation to me. It is in another that I always see the widow and the orphan. The other always comes first. This is what I have called, in Greek [philosophic] language, the dissymmetry of the interpersonal relationship. If there is not this dissymmetry, then no line of what I have written can hold. And this is vulnerability. Only a vulnerable I can love his neighbor.
>
> (1998, 91)

For Levinas, the message of the Bible converges on the prophetic call to care for the poor, the widow, the orphan, and the stranger. Levinas also indicates that much was at stake, which is true for both Rosenzweig and Buber, in his "audacious" interpretation of the commandment to love the neighbor. It is nothing less than his whole philosophy: "If there is not this dissymmetry, then no line of what I have written can hold" (1998, 91).

A powerful philosophical anthropology informs the entirety of the Levinas' *oeuvre*. It is a complex portrait of psychic life. Pieced together from his major philosophical works, *Totality and Infinity* (1969) and *Otherwise Than Being or Beyond Essence* (1981), Levinas sees a fundamental tension between one's elemental egoism and that call of the other that resounds in the Torah. He characterizes one polarity of the I as being essentially turned back upon oneself or being self-absorbed. He writes in *Totality and Infinity* that "to be an I is… to have identity as one's content" (1969, 36). This mode of existence is not innocent. Other persons are encountered, but only as objects, subject to my power and freedom. The other is something to be dominated, possessed or discarded, to be incorporated, surmounted, enveloped by my world—the same—or to be wiped out. Here freedom is arbitrary and unjustified, and beneath it lurks a self that is murderous and violent (84). This is the "I" of egoism, which Levinas does not hesitate to characterize from the point of view of ethics as "detestable" (88). It is not too much to identify this self with self-love.

While the self is ruled by its own egoism, enjoyment and happiness, it is also pulled or inspired by a metaphysical desire for what is beyond the self (Levinas 1969, 33). This desire is metaphysical in the sense that it is in a totally different register than drives or needs which emerge from oneself. In *Otherwise Than Being* this dimension is discussed in terms of the way that subjectivity is an openness to the other: "Subjectivity... obligated with regard to the neighbor, is the breaking point where essence is exceeded by the infinite" (1981, 12). The openness to the other, the inability to shut off the other's summons despite one's pretensions to autonomy, is what Levinas in one of the earlier quotations designated as the "vulnerable I."

For Levinas, egoism is not more "original" than love, the unconditioned desire for the other. This love for the other cannot be accounted for in history or biography. It affects the self as "an anachronous birth, prior to its own present, a non-beginning, an anarchy" (1981, 139). Levinas means by this that the seizure by the other is structured into human existence and endures as the basis for subjectivity. The very "corporeality" of the human, the receptiveness of the skin or the breath taken into one's lungs, stand as bodily metaphors for the I's vulnerability (51, 180–181).

The "face-to-face" relationship, particularly as depicted in *Totality and Infinity*, features that "dissymmetry" or asymmetry between the self and other/neighbor that characterizes authentic existence. In the encounter with the other the first impression upon the self is the forcefulness of a command that "Thou shall not kill!" This is correlative with the potential murderousness of one's power and freedom and also the nakedness and vulnerability of the other's face. While a divine voice is not heard here, the command certainly represents a "clandestine dimension of the judgment of God," which has called the self to justify itself (Levinas 1969, 247). The other, or, in biblical language, the neighbor, poor, widow, orphan, and stranger, thus overturns my being-for-myself. He or she is experienced as both commanding and vulnerable, or in Levinas' vocabulary, in both the other's "Height" and "destitution" (200).

Since the egoism of the self is so entrenched, the shattering of the individual's natural attitude must be radical. The language Levinas utilizes is violent; in order to achieve authentic subjectivity, the individual must be hollowed out, inverted, extroverted, denucleated, even persecuted. In his words, "The subjectivity of the subject is persecution and martyrdom." The individual is made nothing less than a "substitute" or "hostage" to the other (1981, 146). Perhaps the most pervasive characteristic of that self given over to the other is responsibility. The self which is turned upon itself and is de-legitimatized in its own eyes becomes subsequently a responsible self. The individual comes to recognize—to be obsessed with—an unrelenting responsibility, where one must answer with a biblical "*here I am*... for everything and for everyone" (114). Importantly, not only is the self made responsible, but it is granted the powers to fulfill that which it is called upon to give (1969, 215).

Thus, for Levinas self-love is in diametrical opposition to love of the neighbor. How could the Bible possibly make this the reference for the commandment? Levinas' philosophical aversion to self-love as the basis for ethics and religion is palatable in "Dialogue with Emmanuel Levinas," an interview first published in 1984. He writes, for example:

> I am trying to show that man's ethical relation to the other is ultimately prior to his ontological relationship to himself (egology).
>
> (1986, 21)

> That is why I prefaced *Otherwise Than Being or Beyond Essence* with Pascal's phrase, "'*That is my place in the sun.' That is how the usurpation of the whole world began.*" Pascal makes the same point when he declares that "*the self is hateful.*" Pascal's ethical sentiments here go against the ontological privileging of "the right to exist." (24)

> The very value of love is the impossibility of reducing the other to myself, of coinciding into sameness. From an ethical perspective, two have a better time than one (*on s'amuse mieux à deux*!) (22)

Psychoanalytic Reverberations

In the discourse of psychoanalysis there are deep resonances of the disagreement between the Rabbis and the three modern Jewish philosophers in terms of the place of self-love in relationships to others. We will find that Sigmund Freud himself mirrors the position of the Rabbis,[14] while one stream of post-Freudian psychoanalysts takes up the standpoint of the modern philosophers. It is fitting to turn to this discourse, because the nature and dynamics of relationships between self and others, whether seen in terms of the "intrapsychic," "object relations," or the "interpersonal," is one of the focal points of those who participate in this discipline.

Sigmund Freud's examination of self-love was presented, of course, through the vocabulary of narcissism, or as he stated it, "*loving oneself*" is "the characteristic feature of narcissism" (1991, 131). His systematic reflections on this topic first appeared in the paper "On Narcissism: An Introduction" of 1914. Freud was firmly committed to the view that the self, actually the ego, was, as it were, the first love object of the infant and that all later love objects derived from and received their energy from this "primary narcissism." In his words, "Thus we form the idea of there being an original libidinal cathexis of the ego, from which some is later given off to objects" (67–68). In a similar way, pleasure is first derived from the self (i.e. auto-eroticism), but when the infant finds that this does not fully meet its needs for pleasure, it turns outside the self. Freud indicates that it is difficult to confirm through the observation of infants the existence of primary narcissism, but, among other reasons, infers this from "the attitude of affectionate parents towards their children," which he finds is "a revival and reproduction of their own narcissism" (84). Narcissism in this sense is thus not a kind of sickness or perversion, but a parallel, expressed through libidinal energy, of another basic instinct, which is that of self-preservation (66). In all, narcissism signals that immensity of self-love, which is actually "the primal state from which instinctual life proceeds" (261). Put in another way, there is an original condition "in which the ego loves itself only and is indifferent to the external world" (133).

There are two paths through which libidinal energy is directed outside of the ego, that is, "object libido." Put in another way, there are two types of adult love according to Freud. The first is "anaclitic" love. The initial attachment or love-object is the mother, or whoever is responsible for care of the infant's needs. Part of the original narcissism has been redirected to her and then may be transferred to others who take up similar functions of nourishment and protection later in life. Freud believed that this type of love, with its overvaluation of the other, was more characteristic of those of the male gender. The second type of love, which is found most frequently in the female, is of a narcissistic type, that is, the original narcissism is intensified rather than displaced. Here one loves the other because the other loves oneself; in Freud's inimical words, "Strictly speaking, it is only themselves that such women love with an intensity comparable to that of the man's love for them" (1991, 82).[15] In this case, if obstacles get in the way of the attachment to the object, it is possible that the cathexis can regress back to the original narcissism (258). Freud closes the circle on, if not closes out, the love of the other as a sui-generis activity. Starting from a primary narcissism that is never extinguished but only partially transferred, one loves the other either because of what the other does for the self or because the other loves the self. Freud's summary typology is only a little more intricate.

A person may love:
(1) According to the narcissistic type:
  (a) what he himself is (i.e. himself);
  (b) what he himself was;

(c) what he himself would like to be;
(d) someone who was once part of himself.

(2) According to the anaclitic (attachment) type:
(a) the woman who feeds him;
(b) the man who protects him.

(1991, 84)

In all, Freud's conception of primary narcissism forcefully embodies his global understanding of the human as turned upon itself and reaching toward others in only derivative ways. As one critical assessment concludes, "Freud's concept of primary narcissism is a stumbling block for any relational/structure model, since it explicitly presupposes that the infant is at first *not* oriented toward others, thereby making object relations secondary and derivative phenomena" (Greenberg and Mitchell 1983, 205). Those psychoanalytic theorists who describe the infant's primary openness to others are thus forced to minimize or outright reject Freud's account of narcissism.

There are a number of psychoanalytic streams that flow out of the extensive Freudian corpus.[16] There were major dissenters from Freud during his lifetime, starting with Alfred Adler and Carl Jung, as well as important changes of emphasis following his death. Freud's own writings are so complex and fecund that almost every innovation in psychoanalytic theory can find its source in the work of the founder. We will trace one of the most important and productive streams, which extends from object relations theory to contemporary relational thinkers. This line of development emphasizes the centrality of relationships to others in the constitution of a self, and echoes many of the positions and themes of the three Jewish philosophers. Still, Freud's emphasis on narcissism has retained its allure for many psychoanalysts.[17] None more so than Jacques Lacan, who sought, according to his motto, a "return to Freud."[18]

This brief narrative of development from Freud to our own day is only suggestive, highlighting a few important steps in a process both complicated and diffuse.[19] Melanie Klein (1882–1960) is often identified with the beginnings of what became the Object Relations school. One of the main features of Klein's work is her insistence that drives and objects (i.e. other persons) are indissolubly linked. For Freud, drives or instincts, particularly the libidinal drive, are not attached to any particular object. The goal of the libidinal drive is either pleasure or the reduction of tension and the object that brings satisfaction is variable. For Klein, instincts are not free-floating. They are always tied to objects and parts of objects. She writes, "From birth onwards, a relation to objects, primarily the mother (her breast) is present" (1997, 51). Additionally, Klein replaces Freud's scheme of early development that describes the progress of psychosexual stages from the oral through anal, phallic, latency, and genital. While Freud defines these stages in terms of the organ that is the central focus of the libidinal drive, Klein's stages are characterized by the type of emotion that dominates the relation to the m/other. For her, two stages govern the infant's first year of life—stages that remain the basis for all later development. The "paranoid–schizoid position" corresponds to Freud's oral and anal phases. The stage is named for the way that the infant deals with its overriding aggression and anxiety, by splitting (schizoid) off the aggression initially targeted within, and for the emotion (paranoid) that dominates, because it experiences that aggression as originating from outside itself. The second stage follows upon the paranoid–schizoid foundation, and embodies the possibility of the infant partially overcoming its powers of destructiveness. The "depressive position" represents the effort to reclaim something good, and comes from the infant's remorseful realization of the aggression and damage wreaked upon the mother, or at least upon her psychic representation. The characteristic feelings are those of love, guilt, loss, and reparation, although Klein has also spoken of this period in terms of gratitude. As she writes:

> When the infant reaches the depressive position, and becomes more able to face his psychic reality, he also feels that the object's badness is largely due to his own aggressiveness and ensuing projection. This insight… gives rise to great mental pain and guilt when the depressive position is at its height… Through mitigation of hatred by love the object improves in the infant's mind.
>
> (1997, 196)

There are important ramifications in Klein's departures for the understanding of narcissism.[20] Since object relations are as original as the instincts, narcissism cannot precede relationships to others. For her, "auto-eroticism and narcissism are in the young infant contemporaneous with the first relation with objects—external and internalized." She also changes the dynamics in understanding narcissism, for she holds that relations to others exhibit narcissism when they are based upon the projection of either good or bad parts of the self onto the other. In this way Klein overturns what she sees as Freud's view of "auto-erotic and narcissistic *stages* which preclude an object-relation" (1997, 51). Finally, since love and gratitude typify Klein's second position, it is accurate to conclude that for her love of the other is an original impulse or emotion, an independent element in the psyche, not derivative from self-love.

Unlike Klein, W. R. D. Fairbairn (1889–1965) was not hesitant to proclaim that his work constituted a fundamental departure from Freud. A familiar refrain in a number of his pivotal essays is: "It would appear as if the point had now been reached at which, in the interests of progress, the classic libido [drive] theory would have to be transformed into a theory of development based essentially upon object-relationships" (1986b, 74).[21] Fairbairn insisted that the central motivation for humans was to relate to other persons, or in his parlance, "The real libidinal aim is the establishment of satisfactory relationships with objects; and it is, accordingly, the object that constitutes the true libidinal goal" (1994, 138). In the wake of making attachment the fundamental motivational precept, Fairbairn jettisoned Freud's notion of the pleasure principle—that humans seek first and foremost their own pleasure (83–84).

Fairbairn is well known for his substitution of a three-stage developmental narrative for the Freudian libidinal model. His stages are not only characterized but labeled in terms of the types of relationships that dominate: infantile dependence, transitional (quasi-independence), and mature dependence.[22] Further, it is noteworthy that Fairbairn's narrative of development goes all the way back to intrauterine life. During this (pre)stage of development the fetus is obviously completely dependent on the mother. Since Fairbairn equates dependence with identification, it can also be said that during this period the fetus exists in the most extreme form of identification (and merger) with the mother. There is no differentiation between self and m/other; the other is "not only his world, but also himself." The developmental stages follow upon or extend this type of relationship. In Fairbairn's words, "identification [and dependence] may thus be regarded as representing the persistence into extra-uterine life of a relationship existing before birth" (1986b, 90).

In the stage of "infantile dependence," which Fairbairn generally equates with Freud's oral stage, the infant's extreme dependence on the mother is both physical and psychological. In terms of the latter, it identifies with her ("primary identification") and relates to her as a part-object, the breast. For Fairbairn, the infant relates orally not because the object/breast brings nourishment and security, but because the infant's access or channel to the world/mother is at this time through the mouth. The basic features of infantile dependence are "an attitude of primary emotional identification" and "a one-sided attitude of incorporation." Between infantile dependence and mature dependence lies a transition, a period of "quasi-independence," which corresponds to Freud's anal and phallic stages. It appears that during this period the child relates to the mother as a whole object and not just to her breast, but the inner attachments, or incorporations of the mother, are not yet cut. At the stage of "mature dependence," which begins at the time of Freud's genital period, the emerging adolescent has more successfully overcome the initial merger with the mother. She or he engages with the mother and other persons as objects outside of the self. There is thus the possibility of cooperation, with the individual being able to both give and receive. Fairbairn defines mature dependence as "a relationship involving evenly matched giving and taking between two differentiated individuals who are mutually dependent, and between whom there is no disparity of dependence" (1994, 145).

Freud's original understanding of narcissism is almost unrecognizable when the term surfaces in Fairbairn's discussions. Fairbairn does retain narcissism as characteristic of the earliest stage, infantile dependence. He writes, "Indeed *primary narcissism* may be simply defined as just such *a state of identification with the object, secondary narcissism being a state of identification with an object which is internalized*" (1994, 48). Fairbairn's change is both subtle and dramatic. Narcissism occurs because one is *first* attached to or loves the other and *then* identifies the self with that other. Primary narcissism develops when the other is outside the self, and secondary narcissism emerges when the other has been internalized as an inner object. This reading is confirmed by another reference that Fairbairn makes to narcissism. In one essay he tries to account for why a subject is depressed following a bodily injury or an illness. Fairbairn insists that it is not the injury to the body that directly causes the depression:

> The true explanation would appear to lie in the fact that the depressive individual still remains to a marked degree in a state of infantile identification with his object. To him, therefore, bodily loss is functionally equivalent to loss of the object; and this equivalence is reinforced by the presence of an internalized object, which, so to speak suffuses the individual's body and imparts to it a narcissistic value.
>
> (1994, 54)

Thus, for Fairbairn, the strong reaction to injury or illness is caused by the subject's identification of her or his body with an internalized other and the subsequent (unconscious) feeling of the loss of that other, rather than by the subject's direct concern about the body itself. It is difficult to imagine a more consistent—or, alternately, labyrinthine—object-relations approach to mental life.

Hans Loewald was a brilliant and original psychoanalytic theorist whose work is yet to be fully appreciated. His reflections on the role of the m/other in terms of the instincts and primary process mentation, that is, on unconscious mental life, lead to further re-envisioning of the concept of narcissism. A unifying feature of Loewald's work is a heliotropism, not in the direction of Freud's son–father Oedipal crisis, but the mother–infant dyad, that original "cosmos"[23] that provides the enduring foundation for mental life and behavior (2000, 566–69). Loewald invariably cites Freud and William James in introducing this phenomenon. He finds an imprimatur in a famous letter Freud wrote to Romain Rolland,[24] where Rolland's questioning of Freud's understanding of religion brought the latter to ruminate about an original psychic state of merger between ego and world that takes place at the very beginning of individual life, and which leaves traces in some persons as an "oceanic feeling."[25] James' statement about the first events in the infant's life being experienced as "one buzzing blooming confusion" provides Loewald with a helpful description of the environment out of which development takes place (185). Loewald takes the notion of the unity or merger of mother and infant with absolute seriousness.[26] There is no differentiation between ego and world, self and other, mine and yours, or more poignantly, between "a mother's contentment and an infant's quietude," in this state (554). Mind is collective, the mental integration of the two physical presences in "being" (553).[27] Overturning the presupposition that separation rather than unity constitutes the originary state, he portrays the "global experience within the mother–child field" (185). Turning to the nursing experience, Loewald formulates powerfully suggestive alternatives to the typical descriptions of the mother offering and the infant finding the breast. He writes:

> Perhaps we can come closer to an adequate understanding by introducing the concept of *invention* here. Mother and infant may be said to invent each other in the mouth–breast encounter: they come upon

> something and, out of need or desire, invent—jointly—its utilization… [The] infant/mother invents the mouth–breast "combination," which comes into existence in the manner of a newly invented instrumentality.
> (2000, 513)

Just as in the analytic situation the patient and therapist are the artist and medium for each other, "one may say that the maternal breast is the medium of the infant's creative tension even as the infant in its creative tension is the medium of the mother's creative breast" (2000, 511). It is as if the tension in the infant and the mother bring them to find/create each other. Through these joint experiences of satisfaction and others of dissatisfaction, the mother and infant slowly differentiate, which from the infant's side is the formation of the correlate ego and world.

The mother's impact upon the developing infant is difficult to overestimate.[28] The mother not only sustains the infant physically, she shapes, forms, actually structures its mental life. Through her attention and care, responses and interactions, the infant's "buzzing confusion" is organized into self and other, including the self's psychic contents. The mother's, and later parents', image of the infant is internalized as part of the infant's self, and their "vision" of where development should lead helps to direct the child's growth. This imparting and giving direction through sounds and activity is well summarized by Loewald:

> The bodily handling of and concern with the child, the manner in which the child is fed, touched, cleaned, the way it is looked at, talked to, called by name, recognized and re-recognized—all these and many other ways of communicating with the child, and communicating to him his identity, sameness, unity, and individuality, shape and mold him so that he can begin to identify himself, to feel and recognize himself as one and as separate from others yet with others. The child begins to experience himself as a centered unit by being centered upon.
> (2000, 229–30)

As with psychoanalytic narratives of development offered by other theorists, Loewald holds that these earliest of experiences constitute the base of mental activity and are in various ways repeated in later, especially intense, relationships with others. Again borrowing and adapting terms from

Freud, Loewald labels the infantile and foundational psychic operations as "primary process" activity. The primary process is unconscious and primitive, "unitary, non-differentiating, non-discriminating between various elements or components of a global event or experience." Unconscious identification with the other is a dominant operation here. What have been described as higher mental operations constitute Loewald's "secondary process" mentation. Here "*duality* and multiplicity are dominant, i.e. differentiation, division, a splitting of what was unitary, global, unstructured oneness" (2000, 196). These mental operations and behavior are ascribed by Loewald to the preconscious, that is, as ways of operation susceptible to conscious direction. Engagements with others and the environment that presume some differentiation, that is, separation and distance, between selves or between the self and the world are secondary process. This is the realm of rationality, the abstract, of those positions that we normally label as "objective." Both processes play roles in our everyday activities, although one or the other may be dominant, in shifting constellations. In therapy, for example, there may be unanalyzed emotions, moods, words, and identifications which sweep over patient and analyst, and resonate with the layer of primary process experiences. Examining these through language in either analytic or synthetic ways would constitute secondary process mentation. For Loewald, health and meaning arise from the creative interweaving of the two processes, of these two ways of addressing worlds (562).

These views about merger and development subvert the Freudian notion of instincts. Since there is no original self, the infant cannot have or be ruled by instincts. Relationality takes the upper hand over pre-existing biological drives. "Motivational psychic forces" inhere in the original mother–infant matrix (2000, 292), and are patterned, or even created, through interaction. Dispositions take shape, but they always correspond or correlate to the taking shape of objects. Loewald writes, "Organism and environment in their differentiation from one another and in their interactions produce the individual's death instinct and life instinct, and their origins and vicissitudes are not primarily independent of the caring persons" (322). He eventually discusses aggressive/destructive and libidinal drives in terms of *Thanatos* and *Eros*, which further transforms their character. *Thanatos* is the drive toward dissolution of structure and ultimately an undifferentiated state; *Eros* is the drive toward more inclusive and complex relationship (320).

What then becomes of primary narcissism, that self's earliest love of itself? As we have seen, a language of earliest self is impossible to use in conjunction with the mother–infant field. The identification of infant with mother, and conversely of mother with infant, may be said to inhere in love. The possibilities of love of the other and love of the self develop together, when the other can be differentiated from the self and one can be "an object to itself," through responding and caring (Loewald 2000, 556). Loewald speaks of primary narcissism always in reference to this relational situation. In the following passages, primary narcissism is even equated with the mother–infant dyad: "Narcissistic and object libido, identification and object cathexis, are products of differentiation *within primary narcissism, that is, within the mother–infant matrix of psychic life*" (461; my emphasis); "*Primary narcissism* then is a title for the instinctual life of the mother–infant matrix" (471). Paradoxically, Loewald describes love of the self as secondary narcissism. In his words, "It is secondary insofar as it arises only on the basis of that primary, identificatory form of love which leads to the *formation* of an ego" (556). One learns of love, and learns to love others and the self—as well as to be a self—out of that original "love-matrix" of mother and infant (555).

Stephen Mitchell's work can be seen to crystallize the post-Freudian line of development narrated here. He was one of the leaders of what has become known as Relational Psychoanalysis, a "tradition" that has emerged starting in the 1990s.[29] Unlike some post-Freudians, who have written essays about particular issues but have not put together their ideas in a systematic fashion, Mitchell has written a number of books to integrate his overall standpoint. His comprehensive perspective, especially as seen in one of his last works, *Relationality*, highlights the impact of the other on the self in terms of the dialectic between the interpersonal and the intrapsychic. The interpersonal represents interactions with external persons in the world, and the intrapsychic is understood as the internalization by the psyche of such interactions. In the context of evaluating Loewald's contributions, Mitchell expresses this understanding of the interrelation of self and other: "Our minds are open systems embedded in an interactive matrix with other minds, and our sense of self is a function of the internalization and continual reproduction and memorialization of those relationships" (Mitchell 2000, 48). The sense of self and other are thus produced through relational processes, or, in words that vibrate with Mitchell's distinctive tone, "An individual human mind is an oxymoron; subjectivity always develops in the context of intersubjectivity" (57). Mitchell's discussion of the dimensions or modes of human relationality and his brief note on narcissism will conclude this treatment of the post-Freudians.

Mitchell reads object relations theorists, such as Fairbairn or D. W. Winnicott, to be saying something more revolutionary than that persons seek other persons, replacing Freud's view that persons seek pleasure or release. He posits a Copernican revolution,[30] another attack upon the human-centered, here individual-centered, universe, illustrated through quaint allusions to bees and leaves. Mitchell queries, "In what sense does a bee *seek* other bees? (2000, 105), or does the leaf ask, "Why am I hanging around with these other leaves?" (xii). There is no need for accounts of why individuals are motivated to be with others, as presented in theories about drives. Humans are embedded in a social matrix from the start, the types of relations crossing and re-crossing those permeable boundaries between past and present, inner and outer, fantasy and reality. Persons are designed, as it were, for social living:

> Human beings, starting as small babies, seek other human minds to interact with, not for the satisfaction of some discrete need, but because we are wired to respond visually to the human face, olfactorially to human smells, auditorially to the human voice, and semiotically to human signs.
>
> (2000, 106)

In Chapter 3 of *Relationality*, Mitchell elaborates four axes of the individual's life with others, "both our relational embeddedness with others (in the interpersonal field) and the embeddedness of others within our own minds (in the internal world)" (2000, 69). This represents one attempt to bring together insights from a number of post-Freudian relational streams—among these are self psychology, object relations theory, interpersonal psychoanalysis, and relational psychoanalysis—along with recent discoveries in the study of infant development. Mitchell's four-stage "interactional hierarchy" includes dimensions of affect, behavior, and language in dynamic configurations. The four developmentally emerge sequentially, show increasing sophistication, and in adult life are always operative, though at any one time a particular axis will be more dominant than the others. Together they offer an excellent charting of various intrapsychic and interpersonal dimensions.

The earliest form of interaction is between infant and mother, which takes place below conscious awareness. This dimension of "nonreflective behavior" (2000, 59) is constituted by the intricate choreography of mutual actions through which the two partners impact each other in cycles of exchange. Discrete exchanges of eye movements and facial expressions, as well as the infant's instinctual actions of sucking and clinging, wind into cycles of give and response. In adult life these patterns are seen in, and help constitute, intimate relationships between partners.

The second form, "affective permeability," points to the transpersonal and contagious features of human emotions. Vital emotions such as terror, rage, love, anxiety, and fear can seem to capture those in intense relationships. The question of who has what emotion evaporates when, as one of Mitchell's patients expressed it, "love is in the air" (2000, 67). A good example of this affective phenomenon is illustrated in recent work on analytic interactions, in which the analyst sometimes reflects on her or his own litany of emotions as guides to both what the patient feels and to what is taking place between them.

"Self–other configurations" are patterns of interaction which are put in symbolic forms of "me" and "you," as in father–son, mother–daughter, older to younger sibling, and so on. In terms of the former, Mitchell writes, "In each of these relationships, I have both shaped myself in relation to my parents and internalized a sense of my parents in relation to me" (2000, 62). These multiple symbolic patterns are carried both unconsciously and consciously, and powerfully illustrate the great number and discontinuous features of what we wish to see as a single, harmonious self.

The last mode of relationality is "intersubjectivity," defined by Mitchell in terms of the relations between persons "with self-reflective intentionality (thinking about and trying to do things) and dependency (upon other agents for completing)" (2000, 64). This primarily concerns the dynamic of being recognized as a subject by another person. Mitchell notes that particularly in the West, such recognition is regarded as both elemental and essential to human life. This understanding has had significant impact on theorizing about the analytic situation, which recently has moved from Freud's basically subject–object model (the analyst as observer and interpreter) to a subject–subject model, or "two-person" therapy, where the dynamic respects the intentionality and dependency of the two partners in dialogue.

In *Relationality*, Mitchell abandons the language of primary narcissism;[31] the single reference to narcissism sounds almost a note of relief that the early object relations thinkers were able to provide an "antidote" to this misleading Freudian concept (2000, 111). While love certainly retains its force in this vocabulary, there is no way to even voice a notion of a primary love of the self for itself. What is primary is the mother–infant dyad where no distinction or differentiation between self and other exists (mode one). Love often evaporates or overwhelms such differentiation; intense love is infectious (mode two). There is no isolated self to love itself, in the sense that the self is made up of identifications with and internalizations of various others (mode three), as well as the recognition of our subjectivity by others (mode four).

Two Models

The juxtaposition of the examination of the meaning of the biblical commandments to love the neighbor/stranger as the self with the chronicle exploring the viability of the notion of primary narcissism has illuminated two models of love—actually, of the nature of the human. One view, which seems to have the agreement of the Rabbis and Freud, holds that love of self is the baseline of human motivation. Part of the power of self-love can be extended to others through divine command or because some basic needs cannot be met by the self alone, but in both cases self-love is the original force behind human behavior, which can at best be mitigated or deflected. The other position, offered by the three Jewish philosophers and some post-Freudian psychoanalysts, suggests that persons are always in relationship with other persons and that humans are motivated, first and foremost, to seek out and interact with others. Our orientation to the world, and to ourselves, comes through experiences of attachment, relationship, and love of the other.

Of course, there are significant differences in the discourses of the Jewish philosophers and the psychoanalysts. The Jewish philosophers accentuate the ways that others bring the mature self to fruition. Most importantly, they find that the fullness of the person requires connections both with other humans and with God. Mere existence is possible bereft of the divine, although that way of living is equally missing significant relationships with other persons. The inauthentic life is portrayed by Rosenzweig as the fear of death, by Buber in terms of the I–It, and by Levinas as the *ennui* of the life of egoism. Through a transformative contact with God, the relation to other persons is opened—Rosenzweig's love of the neighbor, Buber's mutuality and reciprocity of the I–Thou, and Levinas' responsibility. The relationship with God leads to a life of meaning, purpose, and orientation. Both the fruit and the proof, the sole proof, of the authenticity of that connection is the change in relations with others. For all three philosophers there is a subtle systole and diastole between the relation to the divine and the relation to other persons. This fluctuation is often so discrete that its elements cannot be distinguished. There is an additional role that the term "God" plays. It provides a way to acknowledge astonishment at the transcendent possibilities of the human. Human life is more than a product of the past. Its possibilities for transformation cannot be foreseen; they are incalculable.

The post-Freudian psychoanalytic discourse is usually framed in terms of a narrative of development, of stages over time. The narrative focuses on the mother–infant cosmos, although some, as with Fairbairn, begin with the intrauterine. In this telling, the mother–infant relationship is the basis for psychic organization, psychosocial development, and future patterns of relationship. Loewald, following Fairbairn, has the mother organizing the infant's very psyche through her loving initiatives and responses. As Mitchell indicates, not only do later relationships mirror the first experiences with others, but self–other interactions, both unconscious and conscious, are the foundation for even the most mature understandings of the self and experiences in the world. The psychoanalysts also highlight the complexity that all relationships exhibit, those tensions between past and present, unconscious and conscious, inner objects and outside others, *Eros* and *Thanatos*, fantasy and reality, attraction and autonomy, integration and disintegration.

Despite these differences there are overlaps in the discourses of the Jewish philosophers and the psychoanalysts, in Buber's "There is no I as such" (1970, 54), and in Mitchell's "Subjectivity always develops in the context of intersubjectivity" (2000, 57). Especially in the work of later theorists such as Loewald and Mitchell, the original psychoanalytic concern with the earliest years and on working health as the therapeutic goal has been broadened to include an interest in mature relationships and the centrality of meaning in human life. For both sets of thinkers, the highest achievements of the human, including trust, integrity, responsibility, and meaning emerge out of and are reconfirmed through relationships to the other.

The ramifications of the disagreements about the meaning of "as thyself" (*kamokhah*) and the viability of the concept of primary narcissism go beyond our interlocutors, the Rabbis and the three Jewish philosophers, Freud, and some of the post-Freudians. The arguments bring to light fundamental notions of what it means to be a person, notions that have had a great impact upon extensive disciplines and fields of activity such as philosophy, psychology, religion, ethics, politics, economics, and social theory more widely. One model, most explicitly in Freud, sometimes surreptitiously and at other times quite manifestly grounds the ideology of individualism, or the individualistic mode, so prevalent in the modern West.[32] We have examined two fundamental constituents of this model: that the individual is the basic unit for understanding the human, and that humans are first and foremost motivated by self-love or self-interest.

Individualism comes in a number of varieties and its development is complex. As a substitute for a long argument about its dominance, which for many readers is probably not necessary, a few allusions will be offered. The individual's autonomy, especially in terms of self-consciousness and the pursuit of truth, are installed at the beginning of modern philosophy through René Descartes' *cogito* and radical doubt. Baruch Spinoza maintains in the *Ethics* that the essence of finite being is expressed in seeking its own preservation, *conatus essendi*. Thomas Hobbes is particularly important, for both philosophy and social theory, in terms of his view that persons are independent entities, monads, and that their exclusive pursuit of their own interest makes conflict inevitable and some kind of social contract necessary.[33] Martin Hollis encapsulates Hobbes' understanding as: "The unit of analysis here was man, conceived as a self-interested, rational, essentially presocial animal. Rationality lay in the shrewd calculation of individual advantage, with conflicts of interest reconciled in principle through a notional social contract" (Hollis 1985, 225). In economics the single, self-interested individual is usually an unexamined presupposition, which is summed up well in F. Y. Edgeworth's statement that "the first principle of economics is that every agent is actuated by self-interest" (cited in Hollis 1985, 226).[34] In psychology, drive theory, with its emphasis on the single individual and on primary narcissism, deeply influences not only Freudians but also many schools of psychology as well as what is often labeled as "pop-psychology." In all, this model of the person is so interwoven into Western life that it is usually not even identified as a model or construction, but as something natural, self-evident, given.

Levinas argues in many places that the autonomy and self-interest expressed in the first model are endemic in both philosophy and political theory. The beginning of *Otherwise Than Being* critiques the notion of peace offered in philosophy and in politics. He finds that this is a peace that presupposes the war of individuals, a peace that brings at most moments of relief to the underlying, constant state of war. Referring to the *conatus essendi*, he writes, "*Esse* is *interesse*; essence is interest… Being's interest takes dramatic form in egoisms struggling with one another, each against all, in the multiplicity of allergic egoisms which are at war with one another and are thus together" (1981, 4). In the essay "The Bible and the Greeks," Levinas refers again to the *conatus essendi*, with its "original perseverance of realities in their being," and its "war among 'owning and interested men'" (1994, 133).

The second model of the nature of the human offers a view that persons cannot be understood or extracted from their social matrix, and that love or attachment to the other both grounds and motivates the self. In this connection, Levinas speaks of the Bible's opposition to "Greek" thought, expressed through its teachings of "answering for the other" and its "Thou shalt love thy neighbor" (1984, 133). In psychoanalytic language, this second view is expressed most concisely in Loewald's notion of an original "love matrix" that is both foundation and enduring presence in the human (2000, 555). Social theory is not bereft of some aspects of this model. For example, Isaiah Berlin in *Two Concepts of Liberty* (1958) demonstrates that Hobbes is not the sole option for an understanding of the social contract. Another view of human nature with roots in Jean-Jacques Rousseau, G. W. F. Hegel, and additional Continental thinkers holds that humans are intrinsically social. For this stream of theorists, a supportive social order is required not to prevent a war of "all against all," but because the highest human experiences and expressions take place in the social realm. For example, while Rousseau still holds that private interest is intrinsic to the individual, he also appreciates the genuine significance of society, that "larger whole, from which he [the individual] in a sense draws life and being'" (cited in Greenberg and Mitchell 1983, 402). Commenting on this, Greenberg and Mitchell write, "Through the social contract, the individual transcends his private, isolated existence to become part of something broader and more meaningful" (402).

The significance of these arguments over the love-commandments and narcissism is that they provide the opportunity to examine our presuppositions about the nature of the human and about social life. They put philosophical, psychological, religious, ethical, political, and economic views of the natural, the possible, the "realistic," into relief, that is, into question.

Notes

1 There is also a third love commandment, to love God: "And you shall love the Lord your God with all your heart, with all your soul, and with all your might" (Deut. 6:5). See Maimonides' treatment of "Love of God" (1967, 3–5), and Rosenzweig's *Star* (2005, 169–220).

2 Bible translations are from *The Oxford Annotated Bible with the Apocrypha, RSV*.

3 This formalization of love into its acts, and of those acts in terms of requirements for the other's physical needs, is often referred to by Levinas as: "The other's material needs are my spiritual needs" (1986, 24).

4 This reference is noted in Steven Harvey's "Love." Harvey explains that Nahmanides' interpretation reflected the opinion of earlier commentators such as Ibn Ezra, who wrote that "a person should love the good for his fellow as he does for himself" (Harvey 1988, 558). It is interesting that Harvey's fine essay takes for granted a model of the self that sees self-love as basic, and finds the literal meaning of *kamokhah* as problematic. Harvey also reflects on the other issues that the Rabbis felt were raised by the two commandments, including who constitutes the neighbor and stranger, and how love could be commanded.

5 The issue was of particular importance for them, not only because of their philosophic objections. Especially for Rosenzweig and Buber, in the wake of Jewish Emancipation and the Jewish Question, the latter being the widespread opposition throughout Europe to granting Jews citizenship, there were numerous discussions about the referents of the dual commandments to love the neighbor and the stranger. See David Novak's *The Election of Israel* (1995, 96–97).

6 As we will see, love of the neighbor for him includes love of the stranger, for the neighbor (*der Nebenmensch*) is anyone who stands near.

7 Rosenzweig characterizes the mystic as one who loves God but turns away from the world, and is thus "scarcely half a man" (2005, 224).

8 In the *Star* it appears that only within the two communities of Judaism and Christianity does this fullness of love and speech take place. While, ultimately, all persons will be included in these communities, the question of what type of love and speech takes place outside of these is not fully clear.

9 At another place in the *Star*, Rosenzweig reiterates this understanding of the commandment: "Love your other, for he is not an other, not a he, but an I like you, 'he is like you'" (2005, 292).

10 In *I and Thou* Buber ties the two together in the statement, "Love is responsibility of an I for a Thou." His discussion of love itself in this text

argues for its relational character in a somewhat different way: "Love does not cling to an I, as if the Thou were merely its 'content' or object; it is between I and Thou. Whoever does not know this, know this with his being does not know love" (1970, 66). Buber's statement comes in the context of arguing that love is not a feeling one possesses, but a "cosmic force," in the between, which one enters.

11 Buber's explicit portrayal of what object relations thinkers might describe as the drive for an object is dramatic. *I and Thou* was written between 1918 and 1922, just as psychoanalysis was turning to studying children and the British Psycho-Analytical Society was being founded (1919).

12 Essays by Buber and Rosenzweig on their understanding of the Bible and the principles behind the translation can be found in their work *Scripture and Translation*.

13 Levinas appears to be referring to the famous first-century rabbi Hillel's seventh principle of biblical interpretation, "*Davar halamed me-inyano*," deriving an interpretation of a verse from the wider context of the text.

14 However, there is no direct influence of the Rabbis on Freud's position. Freud was not trained in Jewish law and literature, and his relationship to Judaism was both complex and ambiguous. The literature on this topic is substantial; a good start might be with Yosef Yerushalmi's *Freud's Moses* (1991).

15 Luce Irigaray provides a powerful critique of Freud's wider understanding of "woman" and "the little girl" in *Speculum of the Other Woman* (1985, 13–129). The colonial and anti-Semitic contexts of Freud's misogyny are presented in Aron and Starr's *A Psychotherapy for the People* (2013, 293–303, 316–17).

16 See, for example, Mitchell and Black's *Freud and Beyond*.

17 See the collection of important essays in *Essential Papers on Narcissism* (1986), edited by Andrew Morrison. None of the post-Freudians discussed in this article are included in the collection, indicating that they did not have an important role in advancing the concept of narcissism.

18 While there might be a little hyperbole in Jane Flax's treatment of Lacan in *Thinking Fragments* (1990), I do not dispute her basic judgment, which comes through quite vividly in the subtitles of her chapters on him, such as "Jacques Lacan: Narcissism and the Fetishism of Language and the Phallus," and "Not a Ladies' Man: Gender, Knowledge, Language, and Castration."

19 As we will see in Chapter 2, Jessica Benjamin's work highlights a fundamental conflict within the self between omnipotence, which is somewhat reminiscent of Freud's primary narcissism, and recognition of the other. She also objects to "pejorative notions about narcissism implicit in some psychoanalytic thinking" (1995, 71).

20 Klein characterizes Freud's view of auto-eroticism and narcissism as being "not unequivocal" (1997, 51) and inconsistent (52), but her position is complicated by keeping Freud's terminology while departing from many of his views.

21 Fairbairn's break with Freud's libidinal theory is again announced in an important later essay (1986a, 102–103, 115).

22 There are some minor differences in terminology and characterization in Fairbairn's treatment of the stages over the years. One overall treatment is summarized in an article of 1941 (1986b, 81–84).
23 See Jonathan Lear's "Introduction" in *The Essential Loewald* (Loewald 2000, xxviii). Also see Loewald's essay "The Waning of the Oedipal Complex" (384–404).
24 An account is given in Freud's *Civilization and Its Discontents* (1961, 11–12).
25 Loewald's use of this remark about the "oceanic feeling" serves as a good example of his reticence to reject the Freudian vocabulary, which he finds resonates more deeply than any particular interpretation can fathom (2000, 193–94).
26 Loewald does not overlook the influence of the father, even as being absent (2000, 7–8).
27 Of course, even during this period the mother has engagements with others much different from this preoccupation and attunement with the infant. Loewald is one of the few theorists, in my experience, who begins to ponder the ramifications for the mother both at that time and later on of this at-one-ment. In terms of her earliest interaction with the infant, he has written: "She speaks with or to the infant, not with the expectation that he will grasp the words, but as if speaking to herself with the infant included" (2000, 185; see also 215). An important exception to this neglect of the mother's psychological transformations is Daniel Stern and Nadia Bruschweiler-Stern's *The Birth of a Mother* (1998).
28 While Levinas does not present anything comparable to Loewald's portrait of the mother–infant matrix, it should be noted that in *Otherwise Than Being or Beyond Essence*, Levinas sees maternity as the highest example of being for the other (1981, 74–75).
29 Some of the most important essays in the evolution of this stream of psychoanalysis are collected in the work *Relational Psychoanalysis: The Emergence of a Tradition* (1999), edited by Mitchell and Aron.
30 This is a term Freud liked to use for his own work, often comparing it to the impact of Darwin's writings. See *A General Introduction to Psychoanalysis* (Freud 1969, 252).
31 Mitchell did write an important chapter on narcissism, "The Wings of Icarus" (1988, 175–203). However, it did not focus on Freud's notion of the original state of self-love, but on the role of those narcissist illusions of self-grandiosity and idealization of the other in development and human relationships.
32 The parameters of this examination have been limited to so-called Western cultures, to that intellectual inheritance of the Greeks and the religious endowment of the three biblical religions, that has been developed particularly in Europe and North America. It cannot be presumed that these issues and models have a universal applicability to other cultures and periods. See, for example, the collection *The Category of the Person*, edited by Carrithers, Collins, and Lukes, which takes as its point of departure Marcel Mauss' famous essay "A Category of the Human Mind: The Notion of Person, The Notion of Self."

33 Hobbes provides a dramatic illustration of the way that the emphasis on the autonomy of subjectivity can lead to the erasure of the actual origin of the subject. Although only in terms of a thought-experiment, he suggests to consider that "men spring up from the ground like mushrooms" (cited in Katz 2003, 78).

34 In terms of the history of individualism, see the essays in *The Category of the Person*, especially those by Michael Carrithers, "An Alternative Social History of the Self" (Carrithers 1985, 234–56), and Charles Taylor, "The Person" (257–81).

References

Aron, Lewis, and Karen Starr. 2013. *A Psychotherapy for the People: Toward a Progressive Psychoanalysis*. New York: Routledge.

Benjamin, Jessica. 1995. *Like Subjects, Love Objects: Essays on Recognition and Sexual Difference*. New Haven, CT: Yale University Press.

Berlin, Isaiah. 1958. *Two Concepts of Liberty: An Inaugural Address Delivered Before the University of Oxford*. Oxford: Clarendon Press.

Buber, Martin. 1962. "Die Frage An Den Einzelnen." In *Werke*, Erster Band, 215–65. München: Kösel-Verlag.

—. 1965. *Between Man and Man*. Translated by Ronald Gregor Smith. New York: Collier Books.

—. 1970. *I and Thou*. Translated by Walter Kaufmann. New York: Charles Scribner's Sons.

Buber, Martin, and Franz Rosenzweig. 1930. *Die Fünf Bücher Der Weisung*. Berlin: Lambert Schneider.

—. 1994. *Scripture and Translation: Martin Buber and Franz Rosenzweig*. Translated by Lawrence Rosenwald and Everett Fox. Bloomington, IN: Indiana University Press.

Carrithers, Michael, Steven Collins, and Steven Lukes, eds. 1985. *The Category of the Person: Anthropology, Philosophy, History*. Cambridge: Cambridge University Press.

Fairbairn, W. R. D. 1986a. "The Repression and the Return of Bad Objects (with Special Reference to the 'War Neuroses')." In *Essential Papers on Object Relations*, edited by Peter Buckley, 102–26. New York: New York University Press.

—. 1986b. "A Revised Psychopathology of the Psychoses and Psychoneuroses." In *Essential Papers on Object Relations*, edited by Peter Buckley, 71–101. New York: New York University Press.

—. 1994. *Psychoanalytic Studies of the Personality*. London: Routledge.

Flax, Jane. 1990. *Thinking Fragments: Psychoanalysis, Feminism, and Postmodernism in the Contemporary West*. Berkeley: University of California Press.

Freud, Sigmund. 1961. *Civilization and Its Discontents*. Translated and edited by James Strachey. New York: W. W. Norton and Company.

—. 1969. *A General Introduction to Psychoanalysis*. Translated by Joan Riviere. New York: Clarion Books.
—. 1991. *On Metapsychology: The Theory of Psychoanalysis*. Translated by James Strachey. London: Penguin Books.
Greenberg, Jay R., and Stephen A. Mitchell. 1983. *Object Relations in Psychoanalytic Theory*. Cambridge, MA: Harvard University Press.
Harvey, Steven. 1988. "Love." In *Contemporary Jewish Religious Thought: Original Essays on Critical Concepts, Movements, and Beliefs*, edited by Arthur A. Cohen and Paul Mendes-Flohr, 557–63. New York: The Free Press.
Hollis, Martin. 1985. "Of Masks and Men." In *The Category of the Person: Anthropology, Philosophy, History*, edited by Michael Carrithers, Steven Collins, and Steven Lukes, 217–33. Cambridge: Cambridge University Press.
Irigaray, Luce. 1985. *Speculum of the Other Woman*. Translated by Gillian C. Gill. Ithaca, NY: Cornell University Press.
Katz, Claire Elise. 2003. *Levinas, Judaism and the Feminine: The Silent Footsteps of Rebecca*. Bloomington, IN: Indiana University Press.
Klein, Melanie. 1997. *Envy and Gratitude: And Other Works 1946–1963*. London: Vintage.
Levinas, Emmanuel. 1969. *Totality and Infinity: An Essay on Exteriority*. Translated by Alphonso Lingis. Pittsburgh, PA: Duquesne University Press.
—. 1981. *Otherwise Than Being or Beyond Essence*. Translated by Alphonso Lingis. The Hague: Martin Nijoff Publishers.
—. 1986. "Dialogue with Emmanuel Levinas." In *Face to Face with Levinas*, edited by Richard A. Cohen, 13–33. New York: State University of New York Press.
—. 1994. *In the Time of the Nations*. Translated by Michael R. Smith. Bloomington, IN: Indiana University Press.
—. 1998. *Of God Who Comes to Mind*. Translated by Bettina Bergo. Stanford, CA: Stanford University Press.
Loewald, Hans W. 2000. *The Essential Loewald: Collected Papers and Monographs*. Hagerstown, MD: University Publishing Group.
Maimonides, Moses. 1967. *The Commandments: Sefer Ha-Mitzvoth of Maimonides: The Positive Commandments*. Translated by Charles Ber Chavel. New York: Soncino Press.
Mitchell, Stephen A. 1988. *Relational Concepts in Psychoanalysis: An Integration*. Cambridge, MA: Harvard University Press.
—. 2000. *Relationality: From Attachment to Intersubjectivity*. Hillsdale, NJ: Analytic Press.
Mitchell, Stephen A., and Lewis Aron, eds. 1999. *Relational Psychoanalysis: The Emergence of a Tradition*. Hillsdale, NJ: The Analytic Press.
Mitchell, Stephen A., and Margaret J. Black. 1995. *Freud and Beyond: A History of Modern Psychoanalytic Thought*. New York: Basic Books.
Morrison, Andrew P., ed. 1986. *Essential Papers on Narcissism*. New York: New York University Press.

Novak, David. 1995. *The Election of Israel: The Idea of the Chosen People*. Cambridge: Cambridge University Press.
Rosenzweig, Franz. 2005. *The Star of Redemption*. Translated by Barbara E. Galli. Madison, WI: University of Wisconsin Press.
Stern, Daniel N., Nadia Bruschweiler-Stern, and Alison Freeland. 1998. *The Birth of a Mother: How the Motherhood Experience Changes You Forever*. New York: Basic Books.
Yerushalmi, Yosef Hayim. 1991. *Freud's Moses: Judaism Terminable and Interminable*. New Haven, CT: Yale University Press.

Chapter 2

Jessica Benjamin and (the Missing) Martin Buber

On Intersubjectivity

Missing: Not present; not found; absent; gone.[1] The term "missing" refers to a prior condition of anticipation and expectation. For various reasons, one anticipates the presence of something, but the expectation is left unrealized. The object is not found; it is absent, gone. In this case, what is missing is any reference in the work of the contemporary relational psychoanalyst Jessica Benjamin to the insights of the twentieth-century Jewish philosopher Martin Buber.

Two main sections constitute the following presentation. After a brief introduction to the two thinkers, it commences with a comparison of the basic similarities and differences in the thought of Benjamin and Buber. The first phase of the comparison starts with their shared understandings of *homo duplex* and then juxtaposes Benjamin's views of omnipotence, recognition, the third or in-between, and speech, with Buber's presentation of I and It, I and Thou, the between, and speech or dialogue. The second phase contrasts Benjamin's view of sharing and the same and Buber's understanding of difference as the foundation for recognizing the other. They also disagree about whether the mother–infant dyad or the divine is decisive in the genesis of intersubjectivity. However, the claim that significant reference to Martin Buber's work is more than not present, but missing from the writings of Jessica Benjamin requires something further than this comparison. The second part argues both that there is a justified expectation by those familiar with Benjamin's work that references to Buber would be present, and that the remedial juxtaposition and analysis of the central insights of these theorists leads to fertile insights and new directions in understanding each of them.

Jessica Benjamin (b. 1946) and Martin Buber (1878–1965) are two of the most well-known, often-cited, and productive thinkers in their respective disciplines in terms of the view that persons develop and mature through substantial relationships with other persons. In their first edited volume on the emerging tradition of Relational Psychoanalysis, Stephen Mitchell and Lewis Aron preface one of Benjamin's essays with the accolade that she is "one of the most profound psychoanalytic theoreticians of this generation" (1999, 181). Benjamin frequently describes her work in terms of the overriding concern with intersubjectivity, that is, with the relationship between one subject and an independent and outside other. In her words, "The problem of how we relate to the fact of the other's independent consciousness, a mind that is fundamentally like our own but unfathomably different and outside our control, has been a through line in my work" (1998, xii). Her three principal books, *The Bonds of Love: Psychoanalysis, Feminism, and the Problem of Domination* (1988), *Like Subjects, Love Objects: Essays on Recognition and Sexual Difference* (1995), and *Shadow of the Other: Intersubjectivity and Gender in Psychoanalysis* (1998), are multifaceted forays into the overlapping areas of Freudian and post-Freudian psychoanalysis, developmental psychology, feminism, modern philosophy, and social theory.

Martin Buber, whose name is frequently associated with the term "dialogue," was already regarded as a significant European thinker at the beginning of the twentieth century. His book of 1923 *I and Thou* is a philosophical and religious classic, as well as the cornerstone of all the multidisciplinary presentations that he later authored. The beginning of his essay "The History of the Dialogical Principle" features a statement emblematic of his presentation of the interhuman sphere: "Through the fact that he enters into essential reciprocity, man becomes revealed as man… the saying of Thou by the I stands in the origin of all individual human becoming" (1965, 209).

Similarities

From the beginning of psychoanalysis with Sigmund Freud and continuing through to contemporary analysts, the view that psychic conflict is endemic and inescapable in human life has been ubiquitous. Benjamin offers her own distinctive portrayal of *homo duplex*, of the two-sidedness of human desire or what she terms "the inherently problematic and conflictual makeup of the psyche." In her words, "Our psychic makeup is such that we are torn between omnipotence, illusion of control, on the one hand, and the wish for contact with the different, the external, the not-me, on the other" (1999, 202). She uses multiple terms to describe one side of this tension, such as omnipotence, narcissism, aggression, and destruction, while the singular term recognition stands for the other side. Ultimately the first psychic force is the drive to fashion the other into the same or to destroy difference. The second is the desire to make contact with what is outside and different—with another mind.

Buber's work also features the portrayal of human engagement with the world in terms of *homo duplex*. The first sentence of *I and Thou* introduces the idea that persons have a "twofold attitude," expressive of the two different aspects of the self: "For the I of the basic word I–Thou is different from that in the basic word I–It" (1970, 53). The I–It attitude, the relation of experience and use, is "goal-directed," that is, it treats the other, whether person, piece of nature or of art, as an object. The second approach of I and Thou is not dominated by any concrete goal, but by the willingness or openness to be "drawn into relation" (58). In a later essay, "Distance and Relation," Buber offers a slightly different perspective, describing "the two-fold principle of human life" (1999, 8) as the "primal setting at a distance" and the "entering into relation" (4).

The concept of omnipotence plays an essential role in the work of Benjamin. It is the desire, in the realm of fantasy and the intrapsychic, to be the only one. She concretizes this absoluteness of the self as "the insistence on being one (everyone is identical to me) and all alone (there is nothing outside of me that I do not control)" (1995, 36). Otherness is then known and mastered, the individual treated as an ideal figure or denigrated as alien. Many of us have experience of this in contact with a young child, and not so young others, who unabashedly insist that things be done their way, or in our own desire to have another not just "understand" but agree with what we say or do.

Benjamin relates omnipotence to Freudian theory in two ways. It is her expression for Freud's primary narcissism (1995, 36, 89), that libidinal drive turned toward the self, and thus self-love. At times she also sees omnipotence as corresponding to Freud's death instinct. The wish to obliterate otherness ultimately translates into the desire to end all distinctions, that is, for nothingness or that ultimate stasis of death. In her words, "It corresponds to the zero point of tension between self and other" (1988, 67).

Buber's I–It relation objectifies the other, since the other is just a means to one's own end, whether this might be the self's pleasure, power, or profit. It is fundamentally about appropriation, although this action can be pursued with courtesy or affability. Since the individual's prior desire or design defines the relation, Buber holds that the relationship has no presence, that is, does not breathe in the present. He writes, "Insofar as a human being makes do with the things that he experiences and uses, he lives in the past, and his moment has no presence. He has nothing but objects; but objects consist in having been" (1970, 63–64). Still, the I–It relation is not inherently bad, as it is necessary for navigating the basic necessities of life.

The concept of recognition is the key to Benjamin's deep concern with intersubjectivity, as she writes, "Intersubjective theory postulates that the other must be recognized as another subject in order for the self to fully experience his or her subjectivity in the other's presence" (1995, 30). Mutuality and reciprocity are the defining features of this relationship between subjects (1988, 23–31). Benjamin's understanding of recognition can be seen to include four important insights: There is a basic human need to be recognized; persons have the capacity to recognize others; there is a corresponding pleasure or pleasures in the fulfillment of this need and capacity; and lastly, recognition rests upon prior experiences of having things in common, and sharing emotions and experiences.

The first major claim about recognition is that "we have a need for recognition" (Benjamin 1995, 30). This obviously constitutes a break with the Freudian model of the human, which explained behavior in terms of a rather closed system of drives or instincts. She draws her evidence from revolutionary observations about early mother–infant interactions, especially the phenomena of play and attunement, by the developmental psychologist Daniel Stern.[2]

Second, Benjamin speaks of a capacity to recognize others. Of course, human life would be even more tragic than we usually find it if there was only the need for recognition without the corresponding capacity or possibility of recognizing others. Thus, the full sentence cited above is: "We have a need for recognition and… we have a capacity to recognize others in return, thus making mutual recognition possible" (1995, 30).

Third, there are specific pleasures linked to this need and capacity. Earlier the infant, and later mature persons, are driven to and find pleasure in connecting with another mind, with being known and acknowledged, and knowing and acknowledging in return. As the interactions are mutual, so the pleasures are experienced by both sides.[3] The significance of this for her is seen in the flow of synonyms that Benjamin employs—pleasure, joy, enjoyment. Her references cover both those early foundational interactions and later experiences:

> The joy of intersubjective attunement [between mother and infant]. (1995, 35)
>
> The parent is in fact taking pleasure in *contacting the child's mind.* (35)
>
> The *pleasure* of the evolving relationship with a partner from whom one knows how to elicit a response but whose responses are not entirely predictable and assimilable to internal fantasy. (31–32)
>
> By our very enjoyment of the other's confirming response, we recognize her in return. (33)

This pleasure in recognition makes up for that privation of the drive of omnipotence, of mastering the other: "The subject is compensated for his loss of sovereignty by the pleasure of sharing, the communion with another subject" (1988, 53).

Finally, a fourth insight relates to the understanding that two minds can "share common states, feelings, or experiences" (1995, 183). Benjamin's terminology of "share common" is vital. The infant discovers that while the mother is separate from itself, she or he does share some things with that outside person, does have things in common. For Benjamin, the common and sharing are what make possible mutual and reciprocal recognition between two persons. They overcome the different and alien (other). She writes:

> The recognition by separate beings of commonality is the central phenomenon referred to in the intersubjective dimension. (182) [...] Recognition means that the other is mentally placed in the position of a different, outside entity but shares a similar feeling or state of mind. (184)

For Buber "free giving between I and Thou" is the essential feature of the interhuman sphere (1999, 79). This relationship is characterized by mutuality and reciprocity (1970, 67). Since it is not defined in terms of goals and objects, it is of a different order than that demarcated by the human-projected space–time grid. To be in an I–Thou relation is to live in the present, that is, to allow the flow of the relationship itself to determine what is to happen. In Buber's words, "Only as the Thou becomes present does presence come into being" (63). The exclusiveness and openness of the encounter is also detailed by him in terms of "sacrifice" and "risk" (60).

To enter into an I–Thou relation requires what Buber terms "will and grace" (1970, 58). The first of these words stands for the aforementioned openness—something that borders on passivity—and the second, "grace," points to the notion that the relation is not just in one's hands. Here, the other is not reduced to any particular feature, but taken in his or her entirety, as a full person, and the I is not limited to an aspect but allowed to address the other in one's wholeness. He writes of this transformative feature, "I require a Thou to become; becoming I, I say Thou" (62).

Buber highlights three important dynamics in the correlation between I–Thou and I–It. First, phylogenetically, the I–It relationship has increased in human culture throughout time, in terms of knowledge of the world, technology, and social organization, and has become especially dominant with modernity (1970, 88). Second, in terms of the history of the individual, ontogenetically, the I–Thou at least in nascent form is prior. Buber describes the "prenatal life of the child" in terms of "a pure natural association" (76), and finds that in the earliest stages in the life of the infant one can detect a "longing for relation" and a "drive to turn everything into a Thou." There is a reaching out for the other even when that other is a physical object. From this Buber concludes, "In the beginning is the relation—as the category of being, as readiness, as a form that reaches out to be filled, as a model of the soul; the *a priori* of relation; *the innate Thou*" (78). Third, while the I–Thou encounter is elusive and ephemeral, its influence can be lasting. A life that recognizes and realizes its moments has the ability to transfigure, to introduce "the spirit" to the more normal and mundane events in the world (99).[4] Buber encapsulates this interhuman dimension of the life of persons:

> For the inmost growth of the self is not accomplished, as people like to suppose today, in man's relation to himself, but in the relation between the one and the other, between men, that is, preeminently in the mutuality of the making present—in the making present of another self and in the knowledge that one is made present in his own self by the other—together with the mutuality of acceptance, of affirmation and confirmation.
>
> (1999, 15–16)

In the last decade-and-a-half, with articles starting around 1999, Benjamin's published writings and presentations show some important developments.

She builds up a large vocabulary around the term thirdness, including the "shared, intersubjective third," the "primordial third," the "symbolic third," and the "moral third." Overall thirdness refers to a type of interaction where a transpersonal dimension is created that cannot be said to be the product of either partner. Benjamin relates:

> To construct the idea of the shared, intersubjective third, I have brought together two experiences of thirdness: the differentiating aspect that needs to inform even the oneness of accommodation, empathy, and resonance; and the rhythmic aspect that informs shared reflection, negotiating, and repair of ruptures.
>
> (2012, 106)

In this interactive space, which she sometimes makes reference to as "the in-between" (2007, 3, 5), there is both respect for difference and a shared experiencing of recognition. The primordial third describes the relation in terms of the maternal dyad, where both sides establish or give in to a rhythm of interaction that precedes any conceptual/symbolic exchange. The symbolic third "makes use of more developed narrative elements and involves procedural rules based on consensus, negotiation, and recognition, especially recognition of the other's separate subjectivity" (2009, 441). Lastly, the moral third involves the idea that in thirdness there is a moral dimension, a respect for some lawfulness or for the value of human life overall that guides the relationship (2009, 447; 2012, 98).[5]

Rhythmicity is a term Benjamin uses to give a sense of the cadence and symmetric dimensions of some human relations. It is a major feature of thirdness, and her obvious references are to music and dance. In musical improvisation the artists give in to a developing work that has its own integrity and demands. In this process the individuals mirror and match each other. Benjamin comments that "I am trying to capture, at least metaphorically, the harmonic or musical dimension of the third in its transpersonal or energetic aspect" (2012, 101). Following Louis Sander, she sees this feature as pervasive in human interactions, and actually in relationships exhibited by all life-forms (2007, 7).

A short but electric treatment of "the between" constitutes the climax of Buber's essay "What is Man?" He describes "the between" as a "primal category of human reality," which goes beyond seeing humans in terms of individuals or aggregates. In essence, it designates a relationship rooted in the uniqueness of the participants, but has a transcendent dimension in the sense that it is "a third," which "reaches out beyond the special sphere of each" (1965, 203). This sphere or dimension, not determined by the past, is a spontaneous happening that is also fleeting: "a narrow ridge" (204). While Buber ties it to the place where "I and Thou meet," and describes it as a "dialogical situation," he is insistent that it also pertains to communities (204–205). Communal life is an element in all authentic existence, and in this context, "the between" is the ground for true community.

One of the most important insights which Benjamin and Buber share concerns what she calls speech and he designates as language, speech, or dialogue. Her idea that genuine speech or what she calls "communicative speech" is a dimension arising between persons rather than a "property" or ability of an individual is revolutionary. In her words, "Because communicative speech establishes a space of dialogue potentially outside the mental control of either or both participants, it is a site of mediation, the 'third term'" (1998, 28). Through speech both subjects are set free to bring about something new. Put in another way, the transcendence of each subject's past limits or control is best exemplified in dialogue.

The topic of language or speech, which for him are often interchangeable terms, traverses Buber's work.[6] Language—as *langue* (grammar) and *parole* (spoken)—is both crucial to understanding human relationships and is actually synonymous with them. The first paragraph in *I and Thou* establishes that the two basic word-pairs "I–Thou" and "I–It" are nothing less than the fundamental ways that humans address or approach the world. The life of thoroughly attentive and respectful relations to others, whether in the realm of nature, humanity, or art, is the "life of dialogue" (1965, 19). Buber also uses the metaphors of speech and address to describe God's contact with and direction to individuals and communities. He writes, "God's address to man penetrates the events in all our lives and all the events in the world around us, everything biographical and everything historical, and turns it into instruction, into demands for you and me" (1970, 182).

The theme of language is also central to Buber's discussion of human relationships in "Distance and Relation." He insists that language or speech is "the great characteristic of men's life with one another" (1999, 12). Through it the most significant features of true relationship are realized, which are the recognition and confirmation of the other in his or her distinctiveness. He writes, "Genuine conversation, and therefore every actual fulfillment of relation between men, means acceptance of otherness." The opposite of true relation also has its linguistic counterpart. Buber sees "propaganda" as the use and manipulation of the other, which treats her or him as an object, robbing persons of "their distance and independence" (13).

Differences

The second section of this comparison will feature two diagnostic differences in the works of Benjamin and Buber: the conflict between Benjamin's view of sharing as the foundation for recognition and Buber's insistence on separation and difference as the presupposition for authentic encounters, and the role of the mother as the initial agent of transformation as against the role of the divine. These two discussions will include reflections about gender, trust, and religion.

The notion that similarity and sharing are the ground for recognition is a crucial aspect of Benjamin's work.[7] In *Bonds of Love* she states that "the sharing of affective states is the baseline of intersubjectivity" (1988, 255). In *Like Subjects, Love Objects* Benjamin argues that inner identification with the other is the presupposition for love of the outside object. In *Shadow of the Other* (1998) she writes that "for the sense of difference to be exciting and pleasurable rather than merely threatening, the self must be able to bear an attunement with the other that revives earlier feelings of identification" (1998, 70), and that "identification must be tolerated in order that the other's qualities not evoke intolerable envy or fear" (64). Finally, the themes of similarity and sharing continue to hold a central position in her later discussion of the topics of thirdness and rhythmicity.

Buber sees difference or "separation" as the underpinning for true relation. Separation refers to the initial independence and distinctiveness of both partners. With Buber this is clearest in "Distance and Relation," where he writes, "That the first movement [distance] is the presupposition of the other is plain from the fact that one can enter into relation only with a being which has been set at a distance, more precisely, has become an independent opposite" (1999, 4). Buber also holds that the quintessential expression of authentic relation—speech—requires this independence, separation, and difference.

The starkness of the two overall positions—whether similarity or difference grounds genuine relationship—is mitigated somewhat by some secondary considerations on the part of both sides. Benjamin sees difference as ultimately a crucial element in intersubjectivity, writing: "One of the most important insights of intersubjective theory is that sameness and difference exist simultaneously in mutual recognition" (1988, 47). She defines recognition's opposite, omnipotence, as the eradication of difference, and posits true relation as the confirmation of the other as separate and different from oneself. Her insistence on the ultimate unknowability of the other reinforces this point (1995, 22). On the other hand, Buber can speak of similarity. For example, he interprets the command to love the neighbor as oneself not as a reference to egoism, but to what can be seen as the commonality of being a person or "Thou." He writes, "The neighbor is to be loved 'as one like myself'" (1965, 51).

Even if at times there appears some agreement between Benjamin and Buber, an enduring contrast in their treatments still remains. What may account for this? A number of factors influence Benjamin's view concerning sameness and difference. Obviously, it is important to remember her overall disciplinary commitment to psychology.[8] The earlier quotation from *Bonds of Love* about emotional sharing as the "baseline for intersubjectivity" (1988, 255), begins with a reference to Stern, whose findings about infant development, as well as other theorists in the area, are extremely important to her. Benjamin's dedication to feminist psychoanalysis, emphasizing the mother–infant relation of attunement and sharing, as well as the overall role of gender in development, are also part of the background.

Buber is, among other things, making a philosophical or even logical point, that a relationship requires two separate sides; A = A is not a pattern for human relationship. He also recognizes that his overall position does not directly coincide with psychology.[9] However, the main point of contention remains: Benjamin's view that the recognition of the other requires a sense of the similar and experiences of sharing, and Buber's insistence that an authentic relationship rests upon the acceptance of otherness.

At this point, it can be asked of Buber what allows such a relationship if the other is just totally different. Or perhaps the question is whether there is something that allays the other as alien. There is an answer and this points to the religious dimension that permeates his work. I would suggest that the relationship to God provides the individual with a sense of the meaningfulness of life, a feeling of being given a direction or mission, and ultimately a trust in oneself and in life that underlies the turning to and trusting of the other.

Buber's understanding of trust is first fully enunciated in *I and Thou*. In the pivotal section of the book, on revelation, he gives expression to this in terms of the concept of meaning. Revelation, that is, the experience of and relation to God, furnishes:

> the inexpressible confirmation of meaning. It is guaranteed. Nothing, nothing can henceforth be meaningless. The question about the meaning of life has vanished... The guarantee does not wish to remain shut up within me, it wants to be born into the world by me... The meaning we receive can be put to the proof in action only by each person in the uniqueness of his being and in the uniqueness of his life.
>
> (1970, 158–159)

Buber holds that the relationship to God provides a guarantee, or a trust, in the meaningfulness of life, and this guarantee must be lived out by each person in her or his uniqueness. It should be added that *I and Thou* sees this living-out primarily in the life with others. In the "Afterword" he writes, "The central significance of the close association of the relation to God with the relation to one's fellow-men... is my most essential concern" (172).

For Buber, the Hebrew term *emunah*, which is customarily translated into English as "faith," ought to be translated as "trust" (2003, 28). This is the main message of his late book *Two Types of Faith*. In the work, he describes *emunah* as a fundamental trust in God that permeates all of one's life. He writes:

> The realization of one's faith... [takes place] in the man's whole life, that is in the actual totality of his relationships, not only towards God, but also to his appointed sphere in the world and to himself... By its very nature trust is substantiation of trust in the fullness of life in spite of the course of the world which is experienced. (40)

These features of trust—that a trust in God translates into a trust in one's "appointed sphere in the world," a trust in oneself, and a "trust in the fullness of life"—are carried as a pervasive expectation in spite of whatever is experienced. Said again, the relationship to God results in a trust.

This trust in life is not a conclusion drawn from a variety of experiences in the world, but a presupposition carried as an expectation or confidence. It is an outlook that affects "the totality of his [the believing/trusting individual's] relationships."

At this stage new questions can be raised concerning Benjamin's position: Is it sufficient to say that the similar and sharing are the prerequisites for relationship with the other? What do the similar and sharing provide the subject to allow this recognition of otherness and difference? Can one suggest a more underlying affect than a sense of the common to ground recognition?

One path to pursue an answer might look further at Benjamin's discussion of identification. For example, she writes, "I have to be able to accept the impossibility of incorporating otherness, but retain the ability to imagine it without being threatened or undone by it. Identification must be tolerated in order that the other's qualities not evoke intolerable envy or fear" (1998, 64). Thus, for Benjamin, otherness naturally appears threatening; it evokes "intolerable envy or fear." What basic emotion can mitigate this initial reaction and lead to recognition? I suggest that even for Benjamin one can accept and confirm the other, because there is a basic trust. This trust can be seen as overcoming the initial fear and sense of the threatening. However, does trust contest envy? If one looks at some common antonyms for envy—comfort, confidence, contentedness, good will, kindness, pleasure (*Roget's 21st Century Thesaurus* 2009b)—these seem to be emotions that are affiliated with trust.

There are some suggestive thoughts in Benjamin's later work that seem to touch on this question of trust. In her article on acknowledging failure in the intersubjective relationship, in reference to the "moral third," that is, the notion that there is a moral dimension to the intersubjective relation that guides the participation of the subjects, she writes:

> I use this ["moral third"] to designate the essential component principles of the *lawfulness* involved in repair—lawfulness begins 'primordially' with the sense that the world offers recognition, accommodation, and predictable expectations, and develops into truthfulness, respect for the other, and faith in the process of recognition.
>
> (2009, 442)

Benjamin states that in taking a relationship beyond rupture into repair, the participants are guided by a "primordial" sense. I do not think it is too bold to suggest that what this sense refers to is a trust in a moral grounding in the world, that the world offers more than just chaos and accident. One can trust that there is in the world some element of purpose and truth. In her words, "The world offers recognition, accommodation and predictable expectations, and develops into truthfulness, respect for the other, and faith in the process of recognition." Thus, at least here, there is the suggestion that what allows the process of recognition to proceed is a type of trust.

A new and potentially helpful way of looking at their dispute about similarity or difference is now possible. Both sides hold that individuals naturally find otherness difficult to honestly face. Benjamin argues that sharing and the same overcome this initial obstacle, while Buber sees this overcoming through the relationship to the divine. From this perspective, they have given us two different paths to speak about gaining that primary trust in the self, the other, and the world that allows an authentic and reciprocal relationship with the other to proceed. Benjamin holds that trust arises out of experiences of identification and sharing, and also through the respect for the "moral third." Buber finds that the relationship to God provides that trust in the self, the world, and consequently, in the other.

The second significant difference in their overall positions is Benjamin's presentation of the relationship to the mother as the initiation and foundation for intersubjectivity, while Buber attributes many aspects of this role to the divine. For Benjamin it is through the mother–infant relationship that the infant recognizes herself as a subject, with her own mind, that is, with feelings, thoughts, desires, intentions, and agency. Benjamin writes, for example, "The mother's dialogic ability stimulates the child's recognition of her subjectivity; as she represents and reflects back the child's own subjectivity, she initiates symbolic capacities" (1998, 53). Attunement with the mother is the first experience of sharing similar feelings. She is the first object of identificatory love as well as object love, that is, love of the outside other. Her holding the infant allows the intersubjective sequence of destruction, survival, recognition to be played out,[10] and in Benjamin's later work the mother's surrender to the needs of her infant initiates primordial or pre-symbolic thirdness (2002, 48). While experiences with other persons both build upon and impact these foundations, this first relationship continues to echo in later developments, as in the stage of post-Oedipal complementarity (1998, 69–70) as well as in erotic encounters.

For Buber the encounter with God, the "eternal Thou" (1970, 122), is seen as the initial basis for genuine relationships to others, and as an added dimension that fulfills these. The creature is initially opened to the other as the result of naturally possessing—that is, being given by God as Creator—what he terms an "innate Thou" (78). Further, God's "grace" is needed for ensuing I–Thou relationships to appear, and every such relation points to the divine, which perfects them (123).

Though there are fleeting references to the mother in Buber's writings, the absence of any substantial treatment is patent. Actually, the case appears to be more of an erasure than of mere absence. In *I and Thou* Buber directly refers to the birth and earliest adventures of the infant. However, he envisions this as:

> Every developing child rests, like all developing beings, in the womb of the great mother—the undifferentiated, not yet formed primal world. From this it detaches itself to enter personal life… But this detachment is not sudden and catastrophic like that from the bodily mother… The innateness of the longing for relation is apparent even in the earliest and dimmest stage.
>
> (1970, 76–77)

Here the concrete, "bodily mother," as it were, is displaced by the romanticized, illusory "great mother." The bodily mother is not a subject who initiates intersubjectivity, but an object identified with a catastrophe. The openness to relation is, fortunately in this scenario, innate, that is, given by the Creator.

In many places, Benjamin refers to the basic move of patriarchy, which is to deny the subjectivity of the mother. The mother becomes at most an object—the womb—and self and other relations focus on the father–son relationship (1988, 220). What are some of the ramifications of this disregard for pre-Oedipal experience, with its corresponding denial of the subjectivity of the mother and enshrinement of the classic father–son Oedipal scene? A few observations come to light. The disregard for the mother–infant relation means that the early basis or origins of both true subjectivity and intersubjectvity must either be consigned to a nonexistent *illo tempore*, as in the origin of Buber's innate Thou, or to a later revelatory event. It means that God will be exclusively set as male, as just assumed by Buber. We also see its impact in the neglect of gender—which always means that the male gender is made the norm, assumed to be neutral and universal—as an important element in understanding both the development and dynamics of human relationships.

While a number of examples of these general consequences may be explored,[11] there is a particularly intriguing illustration in Buber's work. Although *I and Thou* is often seen as the template for understanding the preeminent role of the other in individual development, there is a significant lacuna in its treatment. I–Thou relationships are shown to exist very early in life, but their maturation awaits the individual's fully developed I–consciousness or subjectivity. This occurs, according to Buber, at a particular moment:

> To be sure, for a long time it [I–consciousness] appears only woven into the relation to a Thou, discernible as that which reaches for but is not a Thou; but it comes closer and closer to the bursting point until one day the bonds are broken and the I confronts its detached self for a moment like a Thou—and then it takes possession of itself and henceforth enters into relations in full consciousness.
>
> (1970, 80)

Buber's account of this development is incompatible with his persistent theme of the relationality of human life, of becoming an I through a Thou. This strategic moment in the ripening of full I–Thou relations utilizes an extremely monological narrative about the I confronting itself and taking possession of itself. Benjamin's narrative of both subjectivity and intersubjectivity that places the decisive moments within the context of the mother–infant dyad is much more convincing and consistent, as well as allowing her to explore the often neglected relationship between mothers and daughters. Actually, for Benjamin, following D. W. Winnicott, it is the early relationship to the mother, and her continual inner presence, that even allows the individual to be alone with one's own feelings and thoughts (Benjamin 1988, 42).[12]

The remedy for this erasure is obvious. First, the mother as subject and the dynamics between the mother and infant need to be incorporated into Buber's work. Second, the dynamics of sex/gender differences must be addressed in his narrative. Third, as I have argued in other places, the divine must be envisioned as masculine and as feminine (Oppenheim 1997, 83–114). The feminist philosopher and psychoanalyst Luce Irigaray gives fine expression to each of these necessities, as well as the connection between them, in such writings as *Speculum of the Other Woman* (1985a), *This Sex Which Is Not One* (1985b), and in her reflections on the modern Jewish philosopher Emmanuel Levinas, "The Fecundity of the Caress" (1986) and "Questions to Emmanuel Levinas" (1991).[13]

Another question can be seen to arise from this examination. It concerns the overall meaning and significance of Buber's religious discourse. What beyond the erasure of the mother does the language about God contribute to Buber's portrayal of the interhuman? We have seen some of its powers in his discussion of that fundamental trust in self/world/others, in his affirmation that life has meaning, and, lastly, in his conviction that the individual's life is circumscribed and given direction by responsibility to others. The latter is depicted, once again, in terms of "God's address," which "permeates the events in all our lives… and turns it into instruction, into demands for you and me" (Buber 1970, 182). Buber also uses the language of mission to articulate this feature: "When you are sent forth, God remains presence for you; whoever walks in his mission always has God before him; the more faithful the fulfillment, the stronger and more constant the nearness" (164).

Buber's understanding of the powers of religious language stands in stark contrast to Benjamin's view of religion, at least until a hint of a change in her recent work.[14] The force of Benjamin's three major books puts her very much in agreement with the line of thought of Sigmund Freud's classic text *The Future of an Illusion* (1964), which concludes that religion is an illusion, a projection, and wish-fulfillment. The term "religion" does not appear in the indices of any of her books, but there are dramatic allusions to its being psychologically damaging. This attitude is most apparent in *Bonds of Love*, precisely in connection with the central theme of the book concerning the dynamics of domination/sadism and submission/masochism. The first pages feature a description of and her commentary on Fyodor Dostoyevsky's famous scene in *The Brothers Karamazov* between the Grand Inquisitor and Jesus. She begins with Jesus' question:

> Why has a free act of love been transformed into a practice of submission? The Inquisitor responds that people do not want freedom and truth, which only cause deprivation and suffering; they want miracle, mystery, and authority. The pain that accompanies compliance is preferable to the pain that attends freedom. The awesome nearness of the

> ultimate power embodied in the Church makes pain tolerable, even a source of inspiration or transcendence. This ability to enlist the hope for redemption is the signature of the power that inspires voluntary submission. We recognize it in a wide range of social phenomena—whether pope or political party—as the power that inspires fear and adoration simultaneously.
>
> (1988, 5)

Religion in this instance is identified with "submission." It is a support for those who do not have the courage to accept the "deprivation and suffering" of the life of "freedom." Instead, they choose the "miracle, mystery, and authority" of "pope" and "Church," which makes the "pain" of such freedom "tolerable." Ultimately, religion provides the "signature power" of the "hope for redemption" from the necessities and limits of the human condition, again, through "voluntary submission" to religious authority. More generally, Benjamin proposes that the masochist/submissive gains power through identification with the supremacy of the sadist or dominant figure. In patriarchal society, the male son identifies with and submits to the father, whether pope or God, and women submit to men.

In Benjamin's discussion of the classic bondage novel *The Story of O*, the themes of submission and religion are seamlessly brought together. She writes of O:

> Her lover is like a god, and her need for him can only be satisfied by obedience, which allows her to transcend herself by becoming an instrument of his supreme will. In this way, O's story, with its themes of devotion and transcendence, is suggestive of the surrender of the saints. The torture and outrage to which she submits is a kind of martyrdom, seeming "to her the very redemption of her sins"… But her desire to be known is like that of the sinner who wants to be known by God.
>
> (1988, 60)

Buber's understanding of mature religiosity stands in dialectical opposition to Benjamin's portrayal. He envisions religion, at least in terms of the I–Thou relation with the divine, as enhancing human agency and responsibility, and deepening the sense of meaning in life, rather than subverting these. This is well illustrated by a statement in which he explicitly rejects the notion of a one-sided domination in reference to the divine–human encounter:

> Where the Absolute speaks in reciprocal relationship, there are no longer such alternatives [between autonomy and heteronomy]. The whole meaning of reciprocity, indeed, lies in just this, that it does not wish to impose itself but to be freely apprehended. It gives us something to apprehend, but it does not give us the apprehension. Our act must be entirely our own for that which is to be disclosed to us to be disclosed, even that which must disclose each individual to himself. In theonomy the divine law seeks for your own, the true revelation reveals to you yourself.
>
> (1957, 98–99)

The Missing Buber

The argument that reference to Martin Buber is more than not present, but missing from the work of Benjamin has two stages. The first is that an expectation for such an appearance emerges from the comparison of the fundamental similarities in their positions, her use of his terminology, and references to Buber by other contemporary relational thinkers. The second stage considers the productive insights that the engagement between them brings to light.

The preeminent feature in the comparison of the works of Benjamin and Buber is the obvious similarity in their positions. Her discussions of intersubjectivity certainly warrant some reference to Buber, as in her insight that "intersubjective theory postulates that the other must be recognized as another subject in order for the self to fully experience his or her subjectivity in the other's presence" (1995, 30). Among the host of quotations from *I and Thou* that parallel this statement are: "Persons appear by entering into relation to other persons" (Buber 1970, 112), and "I require a Thou to become; becoming I, I say Thou" (62). There might be no better description of recognition than the lines from Buber (except for the gendered placeholders): "The basis of man's life with man is twofold, and it is one—the wish of every man to be confirmed as what he is, even as what he can become, by men; and the innate capacity in man to confirm his fellow men in this way" (1999, 12). Equally, Benjamin's description of mutual recognition as "the reciprocity of giving and taking, acting and having an impact, communicating and negotiating difference" (1995, 195), fits perfectly with Buber's I–Thou relation. Even recognition's inevitable breakdown is well-expressed in Buber's assertion that "the sublime melancholy of our lot [is] that every Thou must become an It in our world" (1970, 68). Benjamin's view of omnipotence and Buber's description of the I–It relation overlap in many areas, especially in terms of the self's control, appropriation and objectification of the other. Additionally, these types of relations evade "presence," either through the self's fantasy or desire rooted in the past. Dramatic affinities are palpable in their discussions of the transpersonal dimension of the in-between/between and in their common appreciation for the boundless possibilities that are opened through genuine speech or dialogue.

In the recent "Afterword" to "Beyond Doer and Done To," Benjamin twice actually uses Buber's famous terms, as in "an orientation to a third that mediates 'I and thou'" (2012, 94) and "without obliterating the difference between *I* and *thou*" (97; her emphasis). She often makes reference to the notion of dialogue in conjunction with descriptions of the third: "the third… an interactive process that creates a dialogic structure" (2012, 106)—a term which indeed stands for Buber's philosophy, as evidenced by the title of Maurice Friedman's well-known text of 1955, *Martin Buber: The Life of Dialogue*. In Benjamin's later essays, the omission is even more glaring, with the deep correspondence, already noted, between her discussions of thirdness and the in-between and Buber's topic of the between.

Unlike Benjamin, some other relational psychoanalysts have seen the parallel between, or even influence of, Buber's philosophy on that psychoanalytic tradition. Lewis Aron has an extensive examination of Buber in his book with the subtitle "Mutuality in Psychoanalysis." He devotes a section of one of his chapters to him, which begins with the statement that "among all twentieth-century philosophers, Martin Buber elaborated a philosophy of dialogue that most closely resonates with the relational psychoanalytic approach and its emphasis on mutuality" (1996, 154). Aron's list of psychoanalysts who were influenced by Buber or who proposed concepts markedly similar to his include Emmanuel Ghent, Kenneth Gergen, D. W. Winnicott, and Hans Loewald, as well as some existential psychotherapists. He compares Buber's I–It and I–Thou relations to psychoanalytic notions of "instrumental part-object relations… and whole object relations" (155). Finally, Aron identifies similarities between some of his own types of mutuality and Buber's treatment of mutuality and reciprocity.

Donna Orange dedicates a chapter to Buber in her recent work *Thinking for Clinicians: Philosophic Resources for Contemporary Psychoanalysis and the Humanistic Psychotherapies.* She highlights Buber's perspicacious analyses of psychoanalytic practices in the last two decades of his life. Though acknowledging that the work of this "philosopher of dialogue… has gone largely unnoticed in the psychoanalytic world" (2010, 15), she insists that Buber's clinical insight should "embrace us and inspire us" (33).

In explaining the defining concept of her book *The Intimate Edge*, Darlene Ehrenberg briefly turns to Buber's contributions concerning dialogue. For her, the intimate edge identifies the area of dynamic contact and exchange between analyst and analysand. It refers to the space where the patient is given the opportunity to work through his or her fears, anxieties, and fantasies, but at the same time the integrity of the analysand and the boundaries between the two participants are respected (1992, 38–39). In this context Ehrenberg writes, "My emphasis on the importance of this kind of engagement is consistent with Buber's view that profound growth and change in the treatment situation occur in the context [of] what he labeled an 'I–Thou' relation, in contrast to an 'I–It' relation" (39).

Aron and Starr refer to many of the ways that Buber anticipated "the most significant themes of relational psychoanalysis," including his "concept of the 'interhuman,' his 'I–You' relation, his 'category of the between,' as well as his emphasis on dialogue and mutuality" (2013, 178). Finally, Steven Cooper mentions Buber's view of "the imagined real" and its similarity to his view of containment, which he characterizes as "among the most intimate ways in which two people can interact, open up, and excite possibility and limitation with each other" (2000, 117).

Much of the strength in this argument about the missing Buber should be evaluated in terms of whether it furthers the understanding and development of the ideas of both thinkers. In the course of what might be termed this "dialogue" with Buber, Benjamin has been asked to consider whether underlying the need for similarity, there is a fundamental role for trust in what she terms recognition, and also to reexamine her approach toward religion. On the other hand, Benjamin's encounter with

Buber has led us to demand a remedy for the erasure of the mother and sexual difference in the latter's ontogenetic narratives. Buber's position concerning the monologic step in the becoming of a self has been critiqued, and it can be suggested that the feature of a shared rhythm introduced by Benjamin might be incorporated into his depiction of the dynamics of the I–Thou relation.

I hope that these and other issues have been raised while respecting the distinctiveness or otherness of both thinkers. Benjamin once wrote that "the ongoing discussion about intersubjectivity in psychoanalysis should have a chance to inform contemporary theory outside psychoanalysis in a much deeper way than it has done so far" (1998, xii). Her important proposal should be answered with another appeal. Perhaps the work of Martin Buber can be used to heal Benjamin's lack of appreciation for the vibrant possibilities of religious language for revealing unanticipated dimensions of our intersubjective lives.

Notes

1 These are some of the synonyms for the term "missing" in *Roget's 21st Century Thesaurus*, Third Edition.
2 See, especially, his book *The Interpersonal World of the Infant* (2000).
3 In a later essay Benjamin emphasizes, "I see such engagement in reciprocal recognition of the other… as ultimately a pleasure" (2012, 92).
4 Hilary Putnam highlights this in his discussion of *I and Thou*, and makes the distinction between "*mere* 'I–It' relations and *transformed* 'I–It' relations" (2008, 63).
5 My reference to the third as referring to a respect for "the value of human life overall" is an interpretation of two statements by Benjamin. She writes of the "moral third" and "respect for human vulnerability" (2009, 447), and "respect for the other's common humanity" (2012, 98). The latter expression in particular is the basis for my interpretation.
6 In addition to the works discussed here, see Buber's essays "Dialogue" (1965, 1–39), "Elements of the Interhuman" (72–88), and "The Word that Is Spoken" (1999, 149–157).
7 The significance of this disagreement as to whether sameness or difference underlies authentic relationship is dramatically illustrated by Benjamin's reference to Emmanuel Levinas. She introduces her discussion:

> At issue here is whether the reduction of the other to the same is to be avoided by declaring the other to be absolutely other (Levinas), positing a radical alterity outside a knowledge which inherently strives to control it;

> or whether it is to be avoided by recognizing that the other must also be an alter ego, irreducible to my ego precisely because it is an ego.
>
> (1998, 100)

8 It might be good to acknowledge a possible reluctance on Benjamin's part to address Buber's work, or to expect that it could lead to anything substantial. In her *Like Subjects, Love Objects* she distinguishes between philosophical and psychological discourses. Benjamin holds that in discussing human relationships, for philosophy the question is about what the putative ideal is for individual or social life, while for psychoanalysis it is about what is (empirically?) required for health in the sense that its absence inevitably produces concrete, harmful effects in the individual (1995, 20–21).

9 Buber produced extensive reflections on therapy. In his article "Guilt and Guilt Feelings," he identifies some dimensions of "existential guilt" that are beyond the purview of the therapist, as they belong to the realm of "faith," or what I would term religious discourse (1999, 122–26).

10 Benjamin utilizes Winnicott's concept of "destruction" throughout her work. She discusses the relationship between destruction and recognition in *Like Subjects, Love Objects* (1995, 90–92), as well as in many other places.

11 For example, is this also reflected in enshrining difference (the inequality between father and son, God and man) in understanding authentic relations, with an accompanying rejection of sameness?

12 In Winnicott's pivotal essay he writes of the "paradox":

> Although many types of experience go to the establishment of the capacity to be alone, there is one that is basic, and without a sufficiency of it the capacity to be alone does not come about; this experience is that of being alone, as an infant and small child, in the presence of mother. Thus the basis of the capacity to be alone is a paradox; it is the experience of being alone while someone else is present.
>
> (1965, 30)

13 Irigaray's essays are examined in a number of the author's works (Oppenheim 1997, 53–82; Oppenheim 2006, 175–219). Irigaray's "Body Against Body: In Relation to the Mother" includes an insightful comment about "when the father refuses to allow the mother her power of giving birth and seeks to be the sole creator" (1993, 16).

14 Benjamin seems to express some appreciation for religious discourse in a recent discussion of the third. In becoming aware of Søren Kierkegaard's ideas about Christian love, and God as the third, she sees a connection between that concept and "surrender or faith." In this regard, she quotes from Marie Hoffman's recent *Toward Mutual Recognition: Relational Psychoanalysis and the Christian Narrative*: "The third, which thinkers would call the idea, is the true, the good, or more accurately the God relationship" (2011, 124). I am arguing that an acquaintance with Buber's work would have been an even more accessible and valuable resource.

References

Aron, Lewis. 1996. *A Meeting of Minds: Mutuality in Psychoanalysis*. Hillsdale, NJ: Analytic Press.

Aron, Lewis, and Karen Starr. 2013. *A Psychotherapy for the People: Toward a Progressive Psychoanalysis*. New York: Routledge.

Benjamin, Jessica. 1988. *The Bonds of Love: Psychoanalysis, Feminism, and the Problem of Domination*. New York: Pantheon Books.

—. 1995. *Like Subjects, Love Objects: Essays on Recognition and Sexual Difference*. New Haven, CT: Yale University Press.

—. 1998. *Shadow of the Other: Intersubjectivity and Gender in Psychoanalysis*. New York: Routledge.

—. 1999. "Recognition and Destruction: An Outline of Intersubjectivity." In *Relational Psychoanalysis: The Emergence of a Tradition*, edited by Stephen A. Mitchell and Lewis Aron, 181–210. Hillsdale, NJ: Analytic Press.

—. 2002. "The Rhythm of Recognition: Comments on the Work of Louis Sander." *Psychoanalytic Dialogues* 12 (1): 43–53.

—. 2007. "Intersubjectivity, Thirdness, and Mutual Recognition: A Talk Given at the Institute for Contemporary Psychoanalysis, Los Angeles CA." Institute for Contemporary Psychoanalysis. Accessed November 6, 2015. http://icpla.edu/wp-content/uploads/2013/03/Benjamin-J.-2007-ICP-Presentation-Thirdness-present-send.pdf.

—. 2009. "Psychoanalytic Controversies: A Relational Psychoanalysis Perspective on the Necessity of Acknowledging Failure in Order to Restore the Facilitating and Containing Features of the Intersubjective Relationship (the Shared Third)." *The International Journal of Psychoanalysis* 90: 441–50.

—. 2012. "Beyond Doer and Done To: An Intersubjective View of Thirdness." In *Relational Psychoanalysis Vol. 4: Expansion of Theory*, edited by Lewis Aron and Adrienne Harris, 91–130. New York: Routledge.

Buber, Martin. 1957. "Religion and Ethics," translated by Eugene Kamenka and Maurice S. Friedman. In *The Eclipse of God: Studies in the Relation Between Religion and Philosophy*, 95–111. New York: Harper & Row.

—. 1965. *Between Man and Man*. Translated by Ronald Gregor Smith. New York: Collier Books.

—. 1970. *I and Thou*. Translated by Walter Kaufmann. New York: Charles Scribner's Sons.

—. 1999. *Martin Buber on Psychology and Psychotherapy: Essays, Letters, and Dialogue*. Edited by Judith Buber Agassi. Syracuse, NY: Syracuse University Press.

—. 2003. *Two Types of Faith*. Translated by Norman P. Goldhawk. Syracuse, NY: Syracuse University Press.

Cooper, Steven H. 2000. *Objects of Hope: Exploring Possibility and Limit in Psychoanalysis*. Hillsdale, NJ: Analytic Press.

Ehrenberg, Darlene Bregman. 1992. *The Intimate Edge: Extending the Reach of Psychoanalytic Interaction*. New York: W. W. Norton and Company.

Freud, Sigmund. 1964. *The Future of an Illusion*. Translated by W. D. Robson-Scott. Garden City, NY: Anchor Books.

Friedman, Maurice S. 1955. *Martin Buber: The Life of Dialogue*. Chicago: University of Chicago Press.

Hoffman, Marie T. 2011. *Toward Mutual Recognition: Relational Psychoanalysis and the Christian Narrative*. New York: Routledge.

Irigaray, Luce. 1985a. *Speculum of the Other Woman*. Translated by Gillian C. Gill. Ithaca, NY: Cornell University Press.

—. 1985b. *This Sex Which Is Not One*. Translated by Catherine Porter and Carolyn Burke. Ithaca, NY: Cornell University Press.

—. 1986. "The Fecundity of the Caress: A Reading of Levinas, Totality and Infinity section IV, B, 'The Phenomenology of Eros.'" In *Face to Face with Levinas*, edited by Richard A. Cohen, 231–56. Albany, NY: State University of New York Press.

—. 1991. "Questions to Emmanuel Levinas: On the Divinity of Love." In *Rereading Levinas*, edited by Robert Bernasconi and Simon Critchley, 109–18. Bloomington, IN: Indiana University Press.

—. 1993. *Sexes and Genealogies*. Translated by Gillian C. Gill. New York: Columbia University Press.

Mitchell, Stephen A., and Lewis Aron, eds. 1999. *Relational Psychoanalysis: The Emergence of a Tradition*. Hillsdale, NJ: The Analytic Press.

Oppenheim, Michael. 1997. *Speaking/Writing of God: Jewish Philosophical Reflections on the Life with Others*. Albany, NY: State University of New York Press.

—. 2006. *Jewish Philosophy and Psychoanalysis: Narrating the Interhuman*. Lanham, MD: Lexington Books.

—. 2013. "*Langue, Parole et Chanson*: On Language as Song in Psychoanalysis and Jewish Philosophy," *Pastoral Psychology*, 62 (4): 403–21.

Orange, Donna M. 2010. *Thinking for Clinicians: Philosophical Resources for Contemporary Psychoanalysis and the Humanistic Psychotherapies*. New York: Routledge.

Putnam, Hilary. 2008. *Jewish Philosophy as a Guide to Life: Rosenzweig, Buber, Levinas, Wittgenstein*. Bloomington, IN: Indiana University Press.

Roget's 21st Century Thesaurus, Third Edition. 2009a. "Missing." Philip Lief Group. Accessed October 2, 2015. www.thesaurus.com/browse/missing.

—. 2009b. "Envy." Philip Lief Group. Accessed November 6, 2015. www.thesaurus.com/browse/envy.

Stern, Daniel. 2000. *The Interpersonal World of the Infant: A View from Psychoanalysis and Developmental Psychology*. New York: Basic Books.

Winnicott, D. W. 1965. *The Maturational Processes and the Facilitating Environment: Studies in the Theory of Emotional Development*. London: The Hogarth Press and the Institute of Psycho-Analysis.

Chapter 3

The Presence of the Other

On Transformation

At the macro level there are parallel logics to psychoanalysis and religion. Both are systems of transformation. They present diagnoses of illness, provide processes of treatment, and promise states of health. What post-Freudian relational psychoanalysts and the Jewish philosophers of encounter feature in terms of this understanding is that transformation occurs by means of interpersonal processes. Significant engagements with other persons are the means for life-altering change.

The idea that psychoanalysis and religion are systems of transformation—essentially, that they are treatments—while sometimes overlooked, is well documented. Sigmund Freud, on the first page of his *A General Introduction to Psychoanalysis*, wrote: “One thing, at least, I may presuppose that you know—namely, that psycho-analysis is a method of medical treatment for those suffering from nervous disorders” (1969, 17). There are many other features to psychoanalysis, especially in terms of its theories about what Freud termed the “mind and its workings,” which for him included “the psychical apparatus,” “the theory of instincts,” “the development of the sexual function,” and a conception of psychopathology (1949, 5). However, these theoretical elements are the foundation and guide for its core activity, that method or technique of treatment. Despite all of the developments psychoanalysis has undergone, the basic components for effecting change remain: diagnosis, treatment, and a view of well-being or health. It is a technique for change, or as Thomas Ogden writes, “most fundamentally the analytic relationship exists for the purpose of helping the analysand make psychological changes that will enable him to live his life in a more fully human way” (2004, 109).

The argument that religion is essentially a system of transformation is possibly more problematic.[1] Still, it is clearly illustrated in the foundational four noble truths of Buddhism, that begin with a diagnosis (“life is suffering"), present a method ("the eightfold path"), and speak of health as the extinguishing of "desire," that is, of an ultimate state of peace (Nirvana). Surveying the panorama of religions, one sees depictions of such significant transformations as those from sin to salvation, ignorance to wisdom, bondage to liberation, and illusion to enlightenment.[2] Religions offer a variety of means from sacred texts to rituals, moral instruction, discipleship, and personal experiences of the transcendent. The common translation of both *Dao* and *Torah* is path or way.

This correlation of religion and change is highlighted in the contemporary theorist Frederick Streng's definition of religion as a "*means to ultimate transformation*" (1985, 2). Many philosophers have concurred with this view. Søren Kierkegaard has his pseudonym Anti-Climacus offer: "Everything essentially Christian must have in its presentation a resemblance to the way a physician speaks at the sickbed" (1980, 5). In this case, the patient is suffering from "sickness unto death" or despair (6), and health is defined as faith. Ludwig Wittgenstein in his conversations on religion speaks of religious instruction in these terms: "It would be as though someone were first to let me see the hopelessness of my situation and then show me the means of rescue until… I ran to it and grasped it" (cited in Putnam 2008, 27).

While it is not contentious to expect that the post-Freudian psychoanalysts in our study continue Freud's emphasis on transformation, this feature may not be obvious in terms of that other discourse in the pairing of the "two languages of love." However, as argued in the author's previous book, *Jewish Philosophy and Psychoanalysis*, the essential insights of Franz Rosenzweig, Martin Buber, and Emmanuel Levinas can be envisioned as "narratives of the interhuman" (Oppenheim 2006, 25–50), which depict the individual's movement from an existence of alienation to a life of meaningful human interaction and authenticity. This view of their work is well-illustrated in the "little book" that Rosenzweig crafted as a popular summary of his forbidding text *The Star of Redemption*, titled *Das Buchlein vom gesunden und kranken Menschenverstand* (the little book of healthy and sick human understanding).[3]

What is distinctive to the understandings of the post-Freudians and the Jewish philosophers is that the key or catalyst for transformation is the other, the presence of the other. This precept follows the discussions in the earlier chapters that showed these two streams shared the position, enunciated by Stephen Mitchell, that to speak of "an individual human mind is an oxymoron; subjectivity always develops in the context of intersubjectivity" (2000, 57). If the prevailing perspective is that persons are fundamentally and developmentally intersubjective, that the human is essentially interhuman, then transformation must follow the same logic. The psychoanalysts see analysis as a "two-person" process; the distinct personality of the therapist is as much in play as that of the patient, and the crucible of change is that "in-between" or "third" which transcends both. Buber, Rosenzweig, and Levinas are, of course, universally recognized for their insights into the dynamic effects of "dialogue" or encounter. Two "persons" consistently linked together are ubiquitous in their reflections, the transcendent One (God) and the next one or neighbor.

The argument about transformation adumbrated here will be elucidated in three parts. The first section will, beginning with a brief "return to Freud," turn to the psychoanalysts and their understanding of transformation, through the general rubrics of diagnosis, treatment, and health. Specifically, it will detail contemporary views of the nature of the patient's sufferings, the role of the analyst, the dynamics of analysis, and the goals of the process. A brief examination of the special contributions of four theorists will conclude the section. The second part explores the Jewish philosophers' discussion of transformation, principally through a review of their understandings of what corresponds to the phases of diagnosis, transformation, and health. There will also be a few vignettes from the three philosophers that provide depth to their positions. The last section brings the two sides into a dialogue. It commences with Buber's discussion of the dynamics and goals of analysis, and concludes with Freud's remark about the psychoanalyst as a "secular pastoral worker" (cited in Hoffman 1998, 5).

The Psychoanalysts

The classical Freudian model of analysis is built upon notions of the nature of the psyche and an understanding of development, pathology, and treatment. For Freud, in terms of his later structural model of id, ego, and superego, the mind is a battleground of forces. The id is at the origin of mind and is the seat of those powerful drives expressing the libido (Eros) and aggression (Thanatos). The superego is a later psychic development, the outcome of the Oedipal stage, which is a counter-force of both societal norms and vindictive moralism pressing against the desires of the id.

The ego, or I, is the partially conscious and partially unconscious mediator between fantasy and reality, the infantile and the mature. The therapist, on the side of the ego, works to bring the unconscious to consciousness, or in Freud's phrase, "where id is there ego shall be."

The neurotic patient turns to the therapist and the ordeal of analysis as a last resort. The liberator is insight provided by the therapist's interpretation. Through insight into the nature and etiology of the neurotic symptoms, which have their source in infantile fantasies and desires, the analyst gives more strength to the ego. Of course, this process is very difficult; there is resistance by the patient to abandoning her or his old, worked-out compromises, even if these are at some level deeply unsatisfactory.

The material for analysis, that is, for the unearthing of the libido's attachment to parental images and infantile wishes for gratification, includes dreams, free association, and the transference—that is, the patterns of infantile interactions that have been projected upon the therapist. The therapist must be a kind of blank slate, without encouragement or support, so that the transference will be uncontaminated. The therapist's attitude is one of abstinence, neutrality, and objectivity. This ability to interpret but not respond to the patient's transference, whether positive or negative, is built up from having undergone their own analysis and training. Mitchell summarizes the classical view of the therapeutic process: "The ultimate aim of psychoanalysis is to overcome the resistance, to flush out the beast [expressing the fantasies and desires], to 'track down the libido… withdrawn into its hiding place' (Freud), to tame the infantile wishes by uncovering them through memory" (1988, 281).

As with so many other developments in psychoanalysis, the recent shifts in the understanding and practice of analysis both continue and transfigure the presentation of its founder. In terms of this continuity, Freud's "talking-cure" always focused on the interaction between analyst and analysand as the key to transformation. In *A General Introduction to Psychoanalysis*, as one example, he describes the "dialogue which constitutes the analysis," that is, the process for "psycho-therapy." Freud points especially to the importance of words and emotions. He addresses the question that shadows the early history of his movement—how "mere talk can possibly cure anybody." In answer he speaks of the "magic power" of words, that they "are universally the means by which we influence our fellow-creatures."[4] He also highlights emotions, in stipulating the necessity that the patient establishes "a special affective relationship to the physician" (1969, 19).

There is a wider intellectual context to recent developments that should be addressed.[5] The discipline of psychoanalysis has been affected by long-term perspectival changes in the natural sciences, social sciences, and humanities. This is true particularly in terms of Freud's model of the analyst as a blank slate. While the need for a commitment to abstinence in terms of specific ethical practices is still seen as unbreachable, the principles of neutrality and objectivity, which Freud took from the scientific establishment of his day,[6] have been put into question in terms of their feasibility as well as their desirability. Among the most important factors in relation to the former is the famous 1927 uncertainty principle of Werner Heisenberg.[7] While it technically concerns the possibility, actually the impossibility, of determining both the position and momentum of a particle, its impact goes far beyond quantum physics. It has come to mean that it is impossible to abstract the observer from whatever is being observed, or, from the other side, that the object of study is always affected by the investigator and her or his theories and methods. This lesson has been deepened by feminist standpoint theory and post-modernism more widely. Thus, over a vast panorama of disciplines today, especially those which focus on human subjects as social creatures, there is tremendous skepticism about neutrality and objectivity.[8]

These precepts, and the underlying approach termed objectivism, have been replaced with views such as perspectivalism and constructivism. In general, these theories speak about the ways that reality is deeply affected by the approach one takes to a matter, and about how experience is never passive, since the subject naturally constructs and fashions what comes to constitute experience. Many psychoanalysts have also been influenced by hermeneutical theory, which emphasizes the paramount role of interpretation as well as the ambiguity and multiple facets of one's object of study. What Mitchell terms the "hermeneutic/constructivist perspective" (1993, 57) and Irwin Hoffman's "dialectical–constructivist view" (1998; the subtitle of his book) are good illustrations of this position. While Jacques Derrida and deconstructionism pushed issues of ambiguity and instability very far, Lewis Aron's succinct reference to him provides a good summary of the foregoing. For Derrida, meaning, and one might also say "reality," is seen as "multiple, unstable, and open to interpretation, relative to particular social, political and historical contexts" (Aron 1996, 256).

Starting with the changed diagnostic focus, the departure from the classical model of psychoanalysis in the theorists under study here is dramatic.[9]

This change is noted in the title of one of Mitchell's chapters, "What Does the Patient Need: A Revolution in Theory" (1993, 13). Mitchell sees the very subjectivity of the patient as the problematic issue. It concerns basic and everyday feelings about and experiences of oneself, others, and the world. Referencing especially D. W. Winnicott, he writes, "What the patient needs… is a revitalization and expansion of his own capacity to generate experience that feels real, meaningful, and valuable" (1993, 24). Thomas Ogden was quoted earlier in terms of seeing the analytic task as helping the patient live her or his life in a "more fully human way" (2004, 109). There is an existentialist cast to this understanding of the patient's "illness" in this focus on existence and meaning. Added is the need for a human life that includes liveliness, that is, spontaneity, intensity, and even creativity, play, and fantasy.

Obviously, given the different nature of the diagnosis, amounting to nothing less than a drastic change in register, there must be a corresponding revolution in treatment. The missing fullness of life could not be treated through the paradigm of the classical analyst, who withdraws to observe and only returns to offer interpretations. A blank slate and paragon of neutrality and objectivity cannot address issues of meaning and value. So here it is not a question of the possibility of neutrality and objectivity, but of their desirability, given the patient's situation. It would be the very humanness of the analyst, the interlocutor, and the quality of the environment created by the two partners that would provide what is missing. These could offer experience of what human fullness, as well as real stagnation, distress, conflict, and struggle feel like. The person—character rather than personality—of the analyst in relation to the specific analysand will be central to the process. Of course, the analyst's training, experience, and technique[10] are also important. Finally, following this thread, since the focus is on the meaning of a life and of life in general, there is no pat, specific answer. Both persons must be collaborators in this elusive quest.

Thus, the interaction between analyst and analysand has come to be viewed as the foundation for transformation. As Hoffman writes, "In the last several decades… we've seen increasing attention to the role of the relationship itself as a factor, even as the crucial factor, in the therapeutic action of the analytic process" (1998, 3). What is supposed to take place in this setting is seen in various ways. For some, especially from the Object Relations and Self Psychology schools, the setting of analysis provides an opportunity for the patient to freely develop his or her natural drive for self-expression and development. In that sense, the setting is a "holding environment" where the patient is protected from impingement and domination from the outside. Self-psychologists favor the notion of the therapist as encouraging and supporting the analysand.[11]

In Relational Psychoanalysis the focus is on the crucial give and take of the process. Descriptions of this exchange between patient and analyst often speak of how positive movement in the relationship arises after serious periods of stasis or times of tension and conflict. Darlene Ehrenberg introduces the concept of the "intimate edge" to emphasize the fabric of the interchange:

> Attending to the most subtle aspects of what goes on *interactively* in the analytic relationship, in an almost microanalytic way, increases the dimensions of the immediate experience and actually transforms it, generating a unique trajectory of evolving experience at what in effect becomes the "intimate" edge of the relationship.
>
> (1992, 33)

While the raison d'être of the process is always the treatment of the analysand, notions of mutuality, of at least the interchange of two partners, have become omnipresent. In this light, Aron finds that "the language of contemporary psychoanalysis is replete with words with the prefixes co, inter, and bi," offering as examples such terms as "coparticipant, coconstruction, coinvestigator, interactional, intersubjective, interpersonal, interrelational, interaffectivity, bipersonal, bidirectional" (1996, 138).

This is the discourse of "two-person" therapy or analysis. The almost exclusive concern with the patient's transference in the classic model has given way to discussions about the ongoing cycles of transference and counter-transference. With Winnicott's famous statement as a background, that "there is no such thing as a baby" outside of the mother–infant dyad, Ogden writes, "There is no such thing as an analysand apart from the analyst" (2004, 159). The steps in the conversational dance express unacknowledged motives and desires by both parties. It is replete with each side's projection and enactment of unconscious scenarios upon the other. In reaction to this understanding of what is inevitably taking place, there is even a general move in the literature to be wary of the terms transference and counter-transference, because they propagate the illusion that these unconscious projections and enactments are both circumscribed and infrequent.[12]

Discussions of "two-person" therapy and the mutuality of the encounter also point to changes in the relative power positions of both sides. The patient position has been enhanced with the recognition of him or her as a subject, partner, or collaborator. Jessica Benjamin is not hesitant to speak of this collaboration as a "dialogic process" (1999, 204), where dialogue serves as both means and end. This has also brought some theorists to question the supposed superiority of the analyst in this relation. For example, as cited by Aron, Heinrich Racker speaks of "'the myth of the analytic situation'... that analysis is an interaction between a sick person and a healthy one." This is in reference to Racker's acknowledgment that "each personality has its internal and external dependencies, anxieties, and pathological defenses; each is also a child with his internal parents" (Aron 1996, 255). Still, there are differences between the two sides, starting with the responsibility of the analyst for the process and her or his overall therapeutic position. Aron's characterization of the relationship as mutual and asymmetrical is appropriate here.

There is a clear development away from seeing the pivotal role of the analyst in terms of interpretation of the analysand's dreams, free associations, transference, and neurotic symptoms. This does not mean that these expressions are not explored, but again the context is of an interactive process. The patient's dreams, free associations, and transference are seen as part of a dialogue, conscious and unconscious (Ogden 2004, 132–33). These expressions and others both of the patient and the therapist are thus understood to be impacted by and contribute to the ongoing intense relationship in the present.

The genuineness of the person of the analyst is a fundamental feature in the literature. Hoffman writes, for example, "It is important for the analyst, within the constraints of the analytic role, 'to be himself or herself,' acting and speaking with a certain quality of personal authenticity" (1998, xxvi). In a more technical vein, in terms of the transference, Mitchell characterizes the analyst as both an old and new object (1988, 151–58). The relationship to the analyst must be similar enough to that of a significant person in the patient's early history for the transference to take hold. On the other hand, only by offering novel and fuller types of interactions can new models of relationship be carried into the future by the patient.

The most symptomatic issue that arises out of the focus on the specific makeup of the therapist is the question of how much of the therapist's feelings and life-experiences should be disclosed to the patient. It is seen as helpful to reveal to the analysand that this figure of authority is human, that she or he has a wide range of feelings, concerns, and emotions. While not everything that the analyst feels should be expressed, there has to be a sense of honesty as well as spontaneity. Among other considerations, the view that some of the feelings and emotions of the analyst should be expressed also stems from an understanding that patients have a desire to know and to care about those with whom they have a relation.

Summarily, the movement from focusing primarily on the analyst's mastery of technique to seeing as crucial her or his character or very being as a person comes through clearly in Mitchell's reflection on the significance of the analyst's presence. He writes:

> Sometimes [in the midst of analysis], when language itself has proved treacherous and corrupt, the analyst can say nothing; affirmation through continued *presence* is the only solution.
>
> (1993, 214; my emphasis)

> What may be most crucial is the process of negotiation itself, in which the analyst finds his own way to confirm and participate in the patient's subjective experience, yet over time establishes his own *presence* and perspective in a way that the patient can find enriching rather than demolishing.
>
> (cited in Aron 1996, 139; my emphasis)

Finally, it seems that more contemporary attention and a wider panorama of features are given to the analytic task or the goals of analysis than in earlier periods. Freud, for example, provided only schematic allusions to these in terms of making the unconscious conscious, the movement from id to ego, dispelling the neurotic symptoms, or his well-known statement cited by Erik Erikson, about the ability "to love and to work" (Erikson 1968, 136). In describing the analytic task, Steven Cooper lists such terms as "freedom, autonomy, a capacity for intimacy, truthfulness, authenticity, a capacity to bear solitude, responsibility, courage" (2000, 267). Analysts often refer to Ogden's phrase, to "become human in a fuller sense" (2004, 15). Among the most prominent notions in the literature is the term "meaning." Mitchell speaks of the development of the patient's "capacity to generate experience that feels real, meaningful, and valuable" (1993, 24). Meaning points, in turn, to such characteristics as a life of purpose or direction, interest and passion, and, finally, a sense that what one has done and is doing is valuable.[13]

Another goal often cited is a sense of spontaneity, creativity, play, or fantasy. The earlier theorist Winnicott has an important influence in this area. He makes play a central ingredient in the development of a person's true self. In a significant chapter on "Playfulness," Ehrenberg cites Winnicott's statement: "It is in playing and only in playing that the individual child or adult is able to be creative and to use the whole personality, and it is only in being creative that the individual discovers the self" (1992, 116).

Four Analysts

This section will detail a few of the significant contributions of four contemporary analysts to the developing understanding of transformation. It will augment the more general treatment above that described the special attention given today to the nature of the analytic interaction and the role and person of the analyst. These features will be explored through the lenses provided by Aron's discussion of mutuality, Hoffman's examination of the dynamic between ritual and spontaneity, Ogden's reflections on reverie, and Cooper's analysis of hope.

Lewis Aron's *A Meeting of Minds: Mutuality in Psychoanalysis* is a rich and intricate exposition of the background and current discussions regarding mutuality in the psychoanalytic process. There is an important reflection in terms of the analysand's formerly unrecognized participation. As background, Aron discusses the emerging importance given to the notion of affective attunement, which is the human need "to connect with others, to attach, to know and to be known" (1996, 120). He cites a famous article by Harold Searles, with the provocative title of "The Patient as Therapist to the Analyst," to discuss, more specifically, the patient's desire to help the analyst as a person. It is through therapeutic efforts toward the analyst that patients "can make reparation, lessen their guilt, become sure of their 'symbolic worth,' and therefore feel fully human" (135). Thus, there is significant curative value in recognizing and allowing the patient's concern and help for the analyst.

While mutuality is, once again, a persistent theme in Irwin Hoffman's *Ritual and Spontaneity in the Psychoanalytic Process: A Dialectical–Constructionist View*, it does not efface the other element in the analytic dialectic, asymmetry. The relationship between the participants is asymmetrical in that the analyst knows more about the life of the patient, and the patient perceives the "analyst as *a person with superior knowledge, wisdom, judgment and power*" (1998, 203). Hoffman offers an illuminating example of the way that mutuality and asymmetry build upon each other. He writes:

> The asymmetry, the hierarchical arrangement, makes our participation in the spirit of mutuality *matter* to our patients in an intensified way, one that helps to build or construct our patients' views of themselves as creative agents and as persons ultimately deserving of their own and other people's love. (204)

The dialectic of ritual and spontaneity refers to the analyst's stance defined by a particular role as well as by his or her make-up and training as a unique person. The ritual side of her participation draws upon the authority and "mystique" of the analyst's role as well as her maintaining some distance for reflection. Times of spontaneous participation by the analyst reveal that she or he is a person like the patient, with the strengths and weaknesses that all exhibit.

Hoffman gives expression to other trends in the wider literature, but always in a distinctive way. He discusses the need to confront the tragic side of life, the patient's inevitable experiences of sacrifice and loss. To this he adds a view about the pervasiveness of the "death anxiety and adaptation to mortality" (1998, xx). The overall flavor of Hoffman's treatment, demonstrating many of the foci and features detailed above, is well-summarized in one of his statements about the task of the analyst:

> It entails for the analyst an integration of being with the patient as a fellow human being, sharing the same kind of personal vulnerability, and being, *ironically*, the very one who is idealized as authorized by the culture and by the patient himself or herself to bestow upon the patient a sense of personal significance and worth. (243)

Another pair of analytic concepts is given prominence in the title of Thomas Ogden's work *Reverie and Interpretation*. He defines reverie as "our ruminations, daydreams, fantasies, bodily sensations, fleeing perceptions, images emerging from states of half-sleep, tunes and phrases that run through our minds" (2004, 158). These are obviously deeply personal but at the same time, and especially significant in the analytic context, intersubjective events. The concept of reverie is from one perspective Ogden's primary illustration of that interactive, mutually choreographed dance that takes place in analysis. From a second perspective it is more than the sum of the two sides, for it is an example of what is a unique, independent dimension. Ogden's influential phrase "the analytic third" involves "a jointly but asymmetrically constructed and experienced set of conscious and unconscious intersubjective experiences in which analyst and analysand participate" (110). The analytic third is constituted by those flavors or tones that permeate the to-and-fro of sessions, which belong to neither participant. Above all else, this third is a powerful forum for transformation.[14]

Hope is the prism that Steven Cooper uses to explore the subjectivity of the analyst and analysand as well as the dynamic between them.[15] The topic of hope also reflects the wider shift we have seen from focusing on "the *content* of our [analysts'] interventions to the *process* of inquiry, explanation, and even rhetoric and suggestion" (2000, 215). The author begins *Objects of Hope* by asking "Indeed, what is a theory of therapeutic action if it is not a theory of hope?" (xiii).[16]

Cooper insightfully utilizes the difference between being a subject who places hope in the other and being the object of another's hope. Mutuality is expressed here, as the two participants are alternately subjects and objects of hope. The patient's hope in the ability of the therapist is one of the key asymmetrical features of the overall relationship. This gives power to the analyst's ability to initiate change, and it is part of the analysand's own transference syndrome, drawing upon the earliest hopes that the child felt toward the parents in shaping his or her development (2000, 156–57). The therapist also has hope in the therapeutic development of the patient, but must guard against illusions concerning the patient's situation or the therapist's own capacity to help. The dynamic features of hope surpass even these interchanges, because hope is also carried by the analytic dyad together.

The possibilities, limits, and dangers in psychoanalysis are also explored through the medium of hope. The analyst's hope gives the patient the power to enter into treacherous new ground, unraveling old compromise formations and opening up to unexplored avenues. Yet, the inevitable limits must also be faced and borne. These range from the limits of time, in terms of the therapeutic hour and all of the factors that can affect the duration of analysis itself, to the acknowledgment and grievance over the patient's lost possibilities and lapsed relationships. Additionally, hope is not necessarily a positive factor, since there are "magical and omnipotent fantasies" that haunt both sides (Cooper 2000, 221). To place hope in another also means that the other may be an object of "disappointment, destruction, danger, competition, and envy" (xii). Finally, even Cooper's examination of health utilizes this fascinating effect, in writing that "the ability to create, resurrect, challenge, modify, and even renounce our hopes is as good as any other definition of health that I have come across" (73).

The Jewish Philosophers

As suggested earlier, religions as systems of transformation offer a wide variety of vehicles to bring about change, including myths, rituals, sacred texts, intense and exceptional personal experiences, and legal and moral codes. The Jewish philosophers of our study are especially committed to one of these vehicles, personal meeting or encounter.[17] Authenticity and meaning arise out of full human relationships, and both draw upon and are expressed through love/responsibility for the neighbor. Earlier chapters in this book have already examined the central insights of Buber, Rosenzweig, and Levinas. The first part of this presentation will therefore be abridged, but the rubric of diagnosis of illness, treatment, and health used to order their understandings will shed a distinct light on this material. The section will conclude with a few characteristic selections from their texts.

The notion of illness fits well within the narrative of transformation of the Jewish philosophers. A crisis, that is, the recognition of a fundamental sickness, may arise at a distinct moment, although it can also slowly simmer and then erupt. It is fundamental in the sense of being tied to the very foundation of a human life. The symptoms of the illness are feelings of meaninglessness, purposelessness, and a lack of direction/orientation. The cause of meaninglessness could generally be described as an inescapable self-centeredness or egoism, with its accompanying isolation from others.

For Buber, the I–It realm defines one of the two-fold ways (I–It and I–Thou) through which humans traverse their world. In that world of

I and It, the individual takes an instrumental or functional attitude toward the other, and the other, whether animate or inanimate, is regarded as just the object of that goal-directed desire. In this way, the individual is partial (defined by a vocation, for example), as a teacher or artist. Buber resists the urge to romanticize any vocation or wider attitude toward the other as object or thing, despite whatever kindness there may be in one's action. As long as the individual's life is defined by goals, by "goal-directed verbs" (1970, 54), it is a shadow life. In truth, the other is merely an extension of the self, and the self is just one who experiences and uses. What is indisputable for him is that meaning does not appear in this realm of "the having of things." While the basic attitude of I and It is appropriate to many areas of life, Buber believes that what today seems to be paramount is "that false drive for self-affirmation," which turns the world into a collection of objects colored by one's limited desires (126).

Rosenzweig presents a different frame to speak of human isolation and self-centeredness, with the accompanying sense of meaninglessness. Humans are born into a world of isolation, a life defined and circumscribed by the confrontation with death. In Rosenzweig's words, "death, his [the self's] own death, has become the event that dominates his life" (2005, 85). In the register of the everyday, where the individual is a creature or simply a piece of the world, one is confronted with the natural round of birth, growth, decay, and death. Within that parameter, as Martin Heidegger saw, the future is defined by the possible impossibility of one's extinction. However, unlike Heidegger, who saw death as opening up meaning, Rosenzweig saw the overwhelming fear of death as closing out everything.[18] There is neither the possibility of aid to the other nor someone there to give comfort to the self. In Attic tragedy this condition only allows for the soliloquy of the self with itself, a speech-act pervaded with defiance.

Levinas, a student of Heidegger, departs from him in many ways, but one of the most interesting critiques he offers in terms of his teacher is that there is a missing sense of enjoyment in the latter's description of life. Levinas sees humans as not just living life, but attempting and often succeeding in enjoying it, writing: "Life is *love of life*, a relation with contents that are not my being but more dear than my being: thinking, eating, sleeping, reading, working, warming oneself in the sun" (1969, 112). This defines the egoist I, a creature dominated by natural self-interest, *conatus essendi*. However, to just follow one's desires is not meaningful, even if it includes contact with, or more precisely implicates, those in one's path. Freedom is not fulfillment, but in this case is arbitrary and unjustified in respect to others. The inevitable outcome is that haunting "ennui… the enchainment to itself, where the ego suffocates in itself due to the tautological way of identity, and ceaselessly seeks after the distraction of games and sleep in a movement that never wears out" (1981, 124).

Under the second rubric, of treatment, there are two scenes of transformation, one with human others and one with the divine partner. The two relationships have many similarities, grounded in the notion that God is experienced as a person. We will see that there are important differences in the portrayals of the three thinkers, but the underlying view that purpose and direction arise out of transformative meetings is deeply shared.

Buber views the I–Thou relation as the only path toward human fullness. For him, "I require a Thou to become; becoming I, I say Thou" (1970, 62). It is a life punctuated by relations of mutuality and reciprocity with the natural world, other humans, and artistic creations that forms a person. These relationships culminate in the confrontation with the divine. He writes, "Extended, the lines of relationship intersect in the eternal Thou" (123). In different words, it is the training or *Bildung* that comes from myriad I–Thou relations that serves as a platform to address God. While each I–Thou relation has transformative effects, it is the exchange with God that opens up a new dimension of living. "When a man steps before the countenance, the world becomes wholly present to him for the first time in the fullness of the presence, illuminated by eternity" (157). Through this encounter with the divine, that is, revelation, the individual's unique meaning and direction are illuminated.

In Rosenzweig's narrative, transformation from one's initial alienated state of affairs requires a divine catalyst. He writes, "For it is only in the love of God, pouring into the rock of the Self that the flower of the soul begins to grow" (2005, 183). Significantly, the call from God to the individual is mutually transformative. Not only is the human partner now able to escape the cage of the self to love and to speak, but God also becomes fully manifest. Rosenzweig expresses this as: "The I… can become audible only with the discovery of the You" (189), which for him means that only in the discovery of the other is it possible to fully be an I, an actual I.

For Levinas, the face-to-face relation, the very definition of the ethical realm, affords the dynamic to dissolve the self's attachment to itself. The face of the other issues the command, from an ethical height, that "Thou shalt not kill." One is singled out, elected. Ultimately, the command is not literally only about killing, or even allowing the other to die alone; it represents every aspect of a concern for the other that annihilates self-regard. Thus, it is ethics, the relationship to the other built upon responsibility, that is fundamentally transformative. The role of God in the process is indirect. For example, in *Ethics and Infinity*, the divine appears only as a reference, through one's ethical testimony. In Levinas' words, "When in the presence of the Other, I say 'Here I am!', this 'Here I am!' is the place through which the Infinite enters into language, but without giving itself to be seen" (1985, 106).

How is health or the fullness of life understood by the three Jewish philosophers? Buber insists that revelation is not a private experience pointing to itself, of a life dedicated solely to the divine partner, but leads back into the everyday world. The unique meaning that was received in revelation "wants to be demonstrated by us in this life and this world" (1970, 159). Following the encounter with the divine, everything now lives "in the fullness of the [divine] presence, illuminated by eternity." One lives with "the power of loving responsibility for the whole unexplorable course of the world" (157). Buber also portrays this fullness as one where the individual is open to the ethical demands woven into each moment, along with the requisite sacrifice and risk.

Rosenzweig is similarly critical of the notion that the encounter with God is sufficient in itself for a life of human fullness. While God's transformative word is embodied in what is equally an expression of God's love and a directive, the commandment to love the Lord, this is then followed by the second of the two foundational precepts, which is the obligation or responsibility to love the neighbor. It is this neighbor-love which confirms the meaningfulness of the individual's unique path and directs the person into the world in the deepest way. *The Star of Redemption* concludes with a biblical *midrash* on Micah 6:8 that portrays a full life in terms of the attributes of humility, trust, faith, hope, and love (2005, 447). It is humility that is particularly revealing, and perhaps surprising, in this list. Rosenzweig sees humility as the transformed effect of defiant pride discussed earlier. He defines humility as "conscious of being what it is through the grace of a Higher Being," and adds that "it knows nothing can happen to it. And it also knows that no power can rob it of this consciousness" (181). Thus, this defining, enduring feature of health is an attribute fully dependent on the Other.

For Levinas, health is grounded in one's responsibility for the other. This may seem a narrow sense of human fullness, but one of the tasks of *Totality and Infinity* is to demonstrate the truth of this insight. Thus, one finds, "the establishment of this primacy of the ethical, that is, of the relationship of man to man—signification, teaching, and justice—a primacy of an irreducible structure upon which all the other structures rest… is one of the objectives of the present work" (1969, 79). Responsibility is the anchor of language itself, in that what allows speech to flourish is the separation and difference of the two partners, as well as the directed openness or "exposure" of the subject to the other. It is the only possible source for the new, since a life that develops, grows, and is creative comes through the relation to the "transcendent" other who is not me. Additionally, responsibility is connected to love. In Levinas' words, "The metaphysical event of transcendence—the welcome of the Other, hospitality—Desire and language—is not accomplished as love. But the transcendence of discourse is bound to love" (254). Concluding actually a partial inventory of fullness, for Levinas, the individual's uniqueness is not some enigmatic quality that adheres to a self, nor the subject of a judgment about what is comparable or incomparable about different persons. He writes, "Exposedness ["exposure to the other"] is the one-in-responsibility, and thus the one in its uniqueness" (1981, 56).

All three Jewish philosophers recognize that there is a necessary communal and political dimension to the notion of human fullness. In many different writings, Buber critiques the modern view that divides life between the private and public arenas. In the one there is intimacy and love, and in the other there are duties and politics.[19] Drawing on the Bible, Buber insists that it is morally wrong to differentiate these platforms, the life in one directed by love and in the other ruled by the will to power. Those who live before the divine countenance find God's calling evident in both. Communal life arises when there is some type of shared approach to the divine, even if not expressed through the language of religion. He writes, "True community" emerges when persons "stand in a living, reciprocal relationship to a single living center" and also "stand in a living, reciprocal relationship to one another" (1970, 94).

For Rosenzweig and Levinas, the effects of love of and responsibility for the neighbor build to a communal portrait. Rosenzweig finds that although various types of communities, animated by God's love, are today limited, they hold the promise to include everyone. The limited "we," growing out of the dual, builds to an "all" (2005, 253–55). In opposition to Thomas Hobbes, Levinas sees responsibility as the very justification and most important characteristic of true community. For him, a great deal is at stake in this opposition. He writes, "It is then not without importance to know if the egalitarian and just State in which man is fulfilled (and which is to be set up, and especially to be maintained) proceeds from a war of all against all, or from the irreducible responsibility of the one for all" (1981, 159). There already exists the model for this in the divine call first given to the patriarch Abraham, which animates the promise of the people of Israel. In a reading in harmony with classic rabbinic commentaries, Levinas insists that Israel ideally is to stand as both the historical Jewish people and as the place-name for the whole of humanity (1990, 22).

A Few Vignettes

The concluding section of this treatment of the three Jewish philosophers will examine a few vignettes from their work. These will either look in more depth into their distinctive presentations or illustrate common themes that the three share. In relation to Martin Buber, this will include his rather esoteric "waking dream" and one of his autobiographical fragments, "A Conversation." The waking dream (1970, 120–122) is a polysemous vision that appears at the end of Section II of *I and Thou*, after his discussion about the modern increase of the I–It world and the resulting distortions of the self. The dream follows under our rubric of "diagnosis." The focus is the individual "overcome by the horror of the alienation between I and the world," "without direction" (120). Buber insists that the individual knows "the right direction" to alleviate this situation, which is of "return that leads through sacrifice." However, this knowledge is rejected as "mystical." Instead, the individual "summons thought" to fix the situation, which it attempts to do by suggesting that the alienation is an illusion, either because "man" is actually a small aspect of the greater world ("the I is contained in the world") or the world is merely an expression of the greater "soul" (the "I is stuffed full of world"). Both views affirm the truth of "One and all." However, at some inevitable point, the person will see both "pictures at once," and will be "seized by a deeper horror" (121).

Although this is a somewhat ambiguous vision, there are some guideposts. Alienation here points to a life of I and It, where no true relation to the other, whether person or world, is found. It is without direction, because direction, or meaning, only issues from true relation. Buber insists that people know in their depths how to overcome this situation. The true direction is "through sacrifice," which is one of the main characteristics that Buber attaches to the path of I and Thou. In this connection he speaks of I and Thou in terms of sacrifice and risk (1970, 60). There is sacrifice in the sense that the relation to any particular Thou is exclusive, and all else must be put aside. It is risky because the relation is not determined by the past—neither time nor causality hold sway—and one comes out of the relation different than when one entered into it. Buber frequently describes this as a path of return, playing off the Hebrew word *teshuvah*—return or repentance (168).

However, this authentic return that alleviates "the horror of alienation" is usually discounted. It is not substantial enough, that is, deliberate, analytical, sensible, objective, and all of those other synonyms for rational. Over-relying on reason and the objective order, the individual tries to take a safe, sane path. Reason is up to the task by proving that one's feeling of alienation is mistaken. It reports that the individual is not actually isolated from the other, because the self and other are "in reality" One. The story ends with the inevitable failure of reason's artifice, which leaves the individual in a state of "deeper horror."

The segment "A Conversation" is an account of what in another context Buber describes as a "mismeeting or misencounter" between himself and a young man who came to speak with him (2002, 22). Its significance for us is that there is a brief allusion to how presence can be transformative. Buber recollects that although the meeting was "friendly," he failed to recognize the unspoken question of that destined hour. He asks, "What do we expect when we are in despair and yet go to a man? Surely a presence by means of which we are told that nevertheless there is meaning" (54). When an individual is in the midst of despair, perhaps haunted by a sense of the hollowness of life, what can the other offer? Buber's answer appears to be that the authentic offering is not some type of advice, a formulated answer. Engaged presence itself embodies an answer. Welcoming and being there for the other communicates directly that they matter, that life matters, that is, that beyond the chaos of the moment there is meaning. This is the gift that true presence bestows.

Franz Rosenzweig's *Understanding the Sick and the Healthy* was written in 1925 in conjunction with courses taught by him at his adult educational institute, the *Lehrhaus*. The booklet presents the treatment of a person stopped dead, as it were, in the midst of life. The fear of death overcame the will to participate in the stream of life. Our interest in the patient's "diary" concerns its outlook on health. Health does not mean that the fact of death is denied, but that it is lived with, with others. One finds direction, relationship, meaning in the course of everyday life. Rosenzweig writes:

> God, man and the world… the three of them constantly joining and interweaving and separating. The undulations of beseeching and receiving, receiving and thanking, go on incessantly. Man asks, God gives, the world receives and thanks—and then man asks anew.
>
> (1999b, 96)

What allows a person to "go on incessantly" is trust. A trust in the source of life and the world, that is, in God, opens the way to participate fully and meaningfully in the everyday. Rosenzweig writes, "To avail himself of today, man must, for better or worse, put his trust in God" (1999b, 93). One trusts that what presents itself is not just happenstance, nor ultimately evanescent. It is not accident, because one is directed by the command to love the neighbor, and each next one who is encountered "represents the whole world and the very next instant may represent eternity" (89). While eternity is sown through each individual's responsive acts, it can also be experienced communally in the round of holidays celebrated by religious communities. In the end, death is not ignored; in Rosenzweig's words, "There is no remedy for death; not even health. A healthy man, however, has the strength to continue towards the grave… In health, even death comes at the 'proper' time" (103).

"Substitution," the chapter which is the core or "germ" of Emmanuel Levinas' second major work, *Otherwise Than Being or Beyond Essence* (1981, 193), provides a good synopsis of the three stages of diagnosis, transformation, and health (99–129). The diagnosis concerns the portrait of subjectivity or identity that is dominant, especially in the modern West. There, "to be" means "to do," to produce, enforce, express, possess. The I is synonymous with consciousness, which moves out toward the other, but then returns to itself. It is the story of the ruling sovereign, traversing his or her kingdom and then retiring to the throne. This journey, exemplified by the outreach of knowing, is safe and secure; no danger or surprise is allowed to interfere (99).

Substitution is a trope for the transformation that rends the ego, that "*for oneself*," and transforms it into a "for the other" (Levinas 1981, 118). It refers to a calling (assignation), that is, passivity, and the being for the other. In responsibility, the individual becomes "forgetful of itself" (115), finds itself, or is remade into a true self. "I am 'in myself' through the others" (112). Finally, in terms of health, as devastating to the triumphal ego as substitution is, the individual is not left bereft or alienated (105). Meaning arises out of responsibility. To give to the other opens the way for a person to actually bring about the good. Such acts, for Levinas, are unequivocal and indelible. Things in the world can change, effects can be unforeseen, but the acts of sacrifice themselves have a sense of being permanent, at least in that register that is "otherwise than being," the realm of the good. This even takes on that greatest challenge to human meaning. Levinas writes, "Contrary to the ontology of death this self opens an order in which death can be not [sic] recognized" (115); and, in one of the concluding pieces in the section: "The approach, inasmuch as it is a sacrifice, confers a sense on death… We can have responsibilities and attachments through which death takes on a meaning" (129).

A Conversation

In this final section the two discourses on transformation will be juxtaposed or brought into a conversation. Initial steps in this direction have already occurred. Buber critiqued in some detail aspects of the therapeutic relationship as it was practiced in his later years. Also, as discussed at the end of the previous chapter, his philosophy has already impacted the ways that some relational psychoanalysts understand and practice analysis.

Unlike the other two Jewish philosophers, Buber discusses at length how his philosophy of dialogue illuminates the therapeutic relationship. Over a range of essays, and a dialogue with Carl Rogers (1999, 246–270), Buber anticipates many developments in both the theory and practice of psychoanalysis that are only recently fully coalescing. In a seminar of 1957 he comments:

> In the last ten years or so I have the impression of a certain change in psychotherapeutic practice in which more and more therapists are not so confident that this or that theory is right and have a more 'musical', floating, relationship to their patient. The deciding reality is the

> therapist, not the methods… He knows that at a certain moment the incomparable person of the patient stands before the incomparable person of the doctor… and accepts the unforeseeable thing that goes on between therapist and patient.
>
> (1999, 236–237)

The quotation touches upon some of the central features of what is now seen as "two-person" therapy, in the full intersubjective mode: that analysis is fundamentally about two persons in an encounter, that the analyst sees the other as a unique person and draws upon themselves as a person, that there are often "unforeseeable" events in the encounter that must be accepted and faced with little guidance from theory or technique.

Another long quotation about the task of the analyst, this time from an earlier essay of 1951, "Healing Through Meeting," reinforces and augments these reflections:

> What is demanded of him is that he draw the particular case out of the correct methodological objectification and himself step forth out of the role of professional superiority… into the elementary situation between one who calls and one who is called. The abyss does not call to his confidently functioning security of action, but to the abyss, that is to the self of the doctor, that selfhood that is hidden under the structures erected through training and practice, that is itself encompassed by chaos, itself familiar with demons, but is graced with the humble power of wrestling and overcoming, that is thus ready to wrestle and overcome ever anew… The psychotherapist… will return from the crisis… as a changed person in a changed situation.
>
> (1999, 18–19)

These lines bring out further themes in the discipline: the questioning of the analyst's supposed "superiority," the nature of the analyst's response which combines training, experience, and familiarity with her or his own "demons," along with the humble power to confront, and finally, that beyond the transformation of the patient there is the reality of the analyst herself being changed by the encounter.

Another piece to be added concerns what Buber sees as the key feature of the patient's experience of the analyst, that which allows analysis to be transformative. Buber names it as trust, ultimately a trust that widens to encompass life itself. This idea appears in the context of his dialogue with Rogers. In discussing the analyst's approach to the patient, Buber distinguishes between acceptance and confirmation. Acceptance, which has been seen as an important element of the analytic relationship since Freud, means that the analyst must hold back from making moral judgments and accept the patient/other as he or she is. Confirmation goes beyond that. It is, "first of all, accepting the whole potentiality of the other and making even a decisive difference in his potentiality" (1999, 266). It also includes the aforementioned feature of a fundamental trust. What is required of the analyst, Buber answers to Rogers, is "a being that gives him [the patient] now certitude. 'There *is* a soil [under his feet]. There *is* an existence. The world is *not* condemned to deprivation, degeneration, eh, destruction. Eh, the world *can* be redeemed. *I* can be redeemed *because there is this trust*'" (268).

The issue of Buber's prescience is significant. It indicates that from the point of view of his fundamentally dialogic philosophy he is able to critique elements in the classical model of analysis, to understand contemporary developments, and to suggest areas where further progress is required. Since the positions of the other Jewish philosophers share many essential features with his, Buber's proven insight itself provides a warrant for this comparative examination concerning the issue of transformation. From another angle, developments in the theory and practice of analysis—that patients suffer from feelings of meaninglessness and hollowness, that the human presence of the analyst is the fundamental catalyst for change, and that health is understood in terms of a full human life—have brought the stream of relational psychoanalysts closer to the Jewish philosophers' understanding of transformation. In light of the vast material presented here, only a few of the most productive areas will be highlighted in the discussion of diagnosis, treatment, and health.

Mitchell's diagnostic observation, i.e. "What the patient needs... is a revitalization and expansion of his own capacity to generate experience that feels real, meaningful, and valuable" (1993, 24), sets the stage for the whole exchange between the two streams of theorists. Its accuracy is confirmed by Ogden: "Most fundamentally the analytic relationship exists for the purpose of helping the analysand make psychological changes that will enable him to live his life in a more fully human way" (2004, 109). Levinas provides an analogous depiction of illness, of that "ennui... the enchainment to itself, where the ego suffocates in itself" (1981, 124).

His reflection also identifies the underlying cause specific to the Jewish philosophers' portrayal, the obsession with oneself—what Rosenzweig characterizes as "defiant pride" (2005, 180), and Buber sees as "the false drive for self-affirmation" (1970, 126). The psychoanalysts trace the illness back to the pre-Oedipal period, especially faults in the initial mother–infant relation. Many would agree with Hoffman that the patient also suffers from the effects of experiences of suffering and loss as well as anxiety about mortality.

Following the change in diagnosis between classical and contemporary analysis, the understanding of treatment obviously undergoes a revolution. Hoffman speaks of the "increasing attention to the role of the relationship itself" (1998, 3). More precisely, there is a coming realization that human *presence is transformative*. In the context of a rupture in the analytic situation, Mitchell finds that "affirmation through continued presence is the only solution" (1993, 214). This insight is mirrored in the writings of the Jewish philosophers. Buber, reflecting back on a mismeeting, understands what was missing in these terms: "surely a presence by means of which we are told that nevertheless there is meaning" (2002, 54). Further, one feature that is distinctive to the position of the Jewish philosophers in this context is that the presence of the other immediately brings to the fore the ethical realm. Significantly, the self earlier preoccupied with itself becomes, through responsibility, "forgetful of itself" (Levinas 1981, 115).

Three features of the healing relationship are prominent in the two discourses: mutuality, asymmetry, and what is characterized as "the third" or "the between." Aron foregrounds this first feature in the subtitle of his book, "*Mutuality in Psychoanalysis*." The choice and appeal of the word "dialogue" is another dramatic sign of the importance of mutuality for the analysts. Recent acknowledgments that both the patient and the analyst are flawed and that they both are changed through their encounter underscores this dimension. Another major—and innovative—step in the examination of mutuality is the discussion of the patient's concern for the therapist. Aron cites Searles' "The Patient as Therapist to the Analyst" concerning the analysand's desire to know and to help the therapist (Aron 1996, 135). This acutely revisions not only that specific dynamic of mutuality, but also our understanding of human nature itself.

Mutuality along with its cognate reciprocity are the hallmarks of Buber's I and Thou relation. Rosenzweig believed that in the midst of dialogue, we become "dependent on the other for what is ours" (1999a, 87). For him and Buber, mutuality even pervades the relationship to the divine. Thus, Rosenzweig depicts God's emerging only after the call to the human, and Buber writes of God needing the individual for what is his or her task in the world. While Levinas insistently rejects mutuality as an element in the ethical relation, there is an important insight that he shares with the other Jewish philosophers and even the psychoanalysts in this connection. In welcoming and giving to the other, the self is reconstituted—as a full, unique self—through responsibility. Along with other analysts, Edgar Levenson has indicated that "cure becomes a mutual process, and the patient is not only the interpreter of the analyst's experience, but a collaborator in the therapist's cure" (cited in Aron 1996, 135).

The notion of asymmetry figures in different ways in the two discourses. For the therapist, the patient's growth or health is the central concern of the whole encounter. Correspondingly, there are responsibilities that the analyst has toward the analysand that are not shared. Hoffman offers an intriguing insight about the dynamic between mutuality and asymmetry. He sees the authority of the position of the analyst in conjunction with moments of mutuality experienced in the therapeutic dialogue as enhancing the patients' sense "as creative agents and as persons ultimately deserving of their own and other people's love" (1998, 204). For Rosenzweig, the relation between God and the soul is asymmetrical in a number of ways, as is that particular I–Thou relation for Buber. Asymmetry plays an even stronger role in Levinas' portrayal of the subject's responsibility to the other in the face-to-face, not to mention the notion of substitution! He portrays this in terms of the height and vulnerability of the other. In a wider sense, all human relationships feature different combinations of mutuality and asymmetry; the two discourses we are examining making this case in their particular arenas.

Finally, Ogden's and Benjamin's descriptions of the emergence of "the third" and Buber's depiction of "the between" suggest that there can be a quality to human relationships that transcends the prior limits and powers of the participants. A therapeutic *novum* emerges from out of those dialectics between mutuality and asymmetry, ritual and spontaneity, vulnerability and responsibility. It is from experiences of this *novum* that the Jewish philosophers are, in the words of Levinas, brought to speak of "the traces of the coming of God to mind" (1998, ix).

There is a significant congruity between the psychoanalysts and the Jewish philosophers in their views about the constituents of health, the third stage or dimension in our examination of transformation. Some common elements would include meaning, trust, hope, and the ability to affirm life in the face of sufferings, loss, and death. There are also particular emphases distinctive to each discourse, such as spontaneity and play in the analytic discussions, and responsibility, community, and, of course, the relationship to the divine in the Jewish descriptions. Since a number of these features characterizing a full human life are extensively treated in other places in this book, only a few will be examined in detail here.

It is noteworthy that the psychoanalysts do not usually discuss the nature of health as an independent topic. Rather, relevant features are examined in the context of understanding the constituents of productive analytic treatments. This is fully appropriate, since the therapeutic relationship is understood to both model and provide the patient with authentic experiences of that living "in a more fully human way" (Ogden 2004, 109). Cooper is able to depict therapeutic action as well as health overall through the spectrum of hope. In terms of the latter he writes, "The ability to create, resurrect, challenge, modify, and even renounce our hopes is as good as any other definition of health that I have come across" (2000, 73). Especially intriguing is his account of the analyst and the patient as both subjects and objects of hope. These designations might also be used to provide another dimension to the Jewish philosophers' discussion of the exchange between God and the soul. God is obviously the object of hope for the soul. However, in giving a direction/task/mission to the soul, clearly the individual becomes equally an object of God's hope. Following in this vein, while the traditional religious view of the soul sees it as the partner that carries hope, Cooper can be used to suggest that hope is also one of God's essential attributes.

Additionally, Cooper recognizes that extravagant hope can be an obstacle to health, even something pathological. He writes, "Sometimes the patient's omnipotent fantasies for change or cure implicate interpretation as magical and substitutive for his need to solve the conflicts and problems he confronts in the analysis" (2000, 222). This insight is something that the Jewish philosophers can equally affirm in terms of the illusory hope in some magical divine intervention in a time of crisis.

Cooper's effort to examine health through the lens of hope might find its equivalent in Rosenzweig's treatment of humility. In a way, humility encompasses for Rosenzweig many other attributes of health, such as love, trust, faith, and hope (2005, 447). For him it is the result of God's initial love for the soul, being the transformed configuration of defiant pride. Its definition, "conscious of being what it is through the grace of a Higher Being," equally describes faith. Trust might be referenced in Rosenzweig's statement that the humble soul "knows nothing can happen to it" (181). Lastly, since in the *Star* it is walking humbly with God that leads one into the future, "into life," hope is drawn in. The distinctive intersubjective platform of the Jewish philosophers comes through in that the other who graces the soul is here a "Higher Being."

Both the analysts and the philosophers share the understanding that human health must include the recognition of life's inevitable sorrows and limits. As Hoffman expresses this, "the psychoanalytic situation is a particular instance of the effort to construct meaning and affirm worth in a highly skeptical, unstable, and uncertain world" (1998, xviii). The analysts discuss the inescapable loss of persons and of opportunities. The Jewish philosophers also engage with the topic of death. Rosenzweig's *Star* seeks for what might be as "strong as death" and finds the answer in love (2005, 169). His *Understanding the Sick and the Healthy* acknowledges that "there is no remedy for death," but attributes to that health buttressed by faith "the strength to continue towards the grave" (1999b, 103). There is also Levinas' subject who, in forgetfulness of her or his own death, is obsessed with the responsibility of not letting the other die alone.

In terms of characteristic differences in the treatment of health, the analysts' discussions of spontaneity, play, fantasy, and creativity are significant. These are those life ingredients missing from patients suffering from the sense of deadness, hollowness, and hopelessness. One of the challenges of analysis is to provide experiences of play and creativity, which allow repressed or unacknowledged aspects and experiences to be reintegrated. Ehrenberg's *The Intimate Edge* highlights play. She cites intriguing statements of Winnicott that "*psychotherapy is done in the overlap of the two play areas, that of the patient and that of the therapist*" (1992, 117; emphasis in the original), and that "it is only in being creative that the individual discovers the self" (116).

The Jewish philosophers include a communal dimension, which is missing in the literature of their dialogic partners. They hold that the full life is not made alone, nor even with one's partner or family; it requires a dedication to community. There are responsibilities to one's community(ies) before the divine. As with the love of the neighbor, which is non-exclusive, the community is seen to eventually encompass everyone. A full life requires that, as far as one can, none are left behind. The Jewish philosophers' insistence that each person is entrusted by the divine with a particular mission also refers to this wider purview concerning health.

Still, the overall similarities in the writings of the psychoanalysts and the philosophers, especially about health, may bring one to reminisce about a comment once made by Freud. Hoffman writes, "Freud identified the role of the analyst as that of a 'secular pastoral worker,' someone who serves as a guide to people as they struggle to find their way in life on the basis of personal, individual experience" (1998, 5). Hoffman noted that Freud was wary about taking up this authority, and really wanted analysts to limit their influence to that of helping patients confront the realities of life (80). The psychoanalysts whom we have explored certainly have gone beyond the Freudian limits in writing about their hope for the patient. To see them as offering a secular response to the struggle for personal authenticity and meaning is actually quite an accurate observation. Despite all the departures from the discipline's founder, many have a tragic view of life that mirrors Freud's understanding of the possibilities given the "objective" truth about reality. Death as the transcendent gives life its vitality but also its final end. We are not surprised that the philosophers have a vocabulary that opens "reality," without ignoring its obvious limits. They trust that there is a different register that respects this world but envisions other possible levels of meaning that are ineffable but also indelible—confirmed in that everyday world of human encounters and overseen by a sense of a divine presence. In Buber's words, "When a man steps before the countenance, the world becomes wholly present to him for the first time in the fullness of the presence, illuminated by eternity" (1970, 157).

Notes

1 The issue of the purpose of religion can be viewed from many different perspectives. For example, in *God in Search of Man* (1955) Abraham Heschel sees Judaism as a means for giving thanks, appreciating life's meaning, and maintaining an awareness of God's presence.

2 One way of describing this movement in Judaism is from ignorance and meaninglessness to a life of direction and purpose. In this sense, Torah is that guide that takes one from the naïve life of the *am ha-aretz*, or man on the street, to the person who has appropriated or become Torah, the *talmid chacham*.

3 Eric Santner discusses this transformation in Freud and Rosenzweig in terms of the movement out from "the structured undeadness that keeps us from

opening in the midst of life and the neighbor/stranger who dwells there with us" (2001, 23).

4 Aron and Starr examine Freud's uneasiness concerning the analyst's power of suggestion, and also detail how that issue became a shibboleth in the differentiation between psychoanalysis and psychotherapy (2013, 201–203).

5 Many psychoanalytic theorists discuss this wider intellectual background, including Mitchell (1993, 18–21), Aron (1996, 20–30), and Orange (2010).

6 Aron and Starr provide an additional framework in understanding Freud's insistence on these analytic features. They write, "Freud's response to his culture's anti-Semitism, including his insistence that the 'subjective factor,' i.e. his Jewishness, had nothing to do with his theories, contributed significantly… to his stress on the analyst's anonymity and neutrality" (2013, 259).

7 Although Einstein was certainly no fan of quantum physics (Kumar 2008, x), along with Heisenberg, his work demonstrated that "the position of the observer and the acts of observation influence the nature of the data gathered" (Aron 1996, 256).

8 The feminist and postmodern critique of the concepts of neutrality and objectivity in classic psychology is well discussed in *Religion and Psychology: Mapping the Terrain* (Jonte-Pace and Parsons 2001, 43–56, 110–126, 129–146).

9 There is much recent interest in the work of Sándor Ferenczi, an influential friend and collaborator of Freud. According to Aron, he "set the agenda" for contemporary questions about the Freudian model, which now explore the relative significance of "technique versus metapsychology; experience versus insight; subjectivity versus theory; empathy versus interpretation; a 'two-person psychology' versus a 'one-person psychology'" (1996, 162). See also Ferenczi's *The Clinical Diary of Sándor Ferenczi* (1988).

10 In light of these changes in understanding the role of the analyst, there is much discussion concerning what constitutes the analyst's expertise. See, for example, Aron (1996, 262–263).

11 There are fine presentations of the history and recent views of both the dynamic within analysis and the place of the analyst throughout Aron's book *A Meeting of Minds* (1996).

12 For example, Aron quotes James McLaughlin that "the term countertransference particularly cannot accommodate the intrapsychic range and fullness of the analyst's experience vis-à-vis the patient" (1996, 77).

13 In Chapter 5, "Revisiting an 'Illusion,'" there is a more detailed discussion of the concept of meaning in the works of the post-Freudians and the Jewish philosophers.

14 In addition to reverie, Ogden regards language as a pivotal catalyst for change. See Chapter 4, "*Langue, Parole, et Chanson*," of the present work.

15 Also see Mitchell's *Hope and Dread in Psychoanalysis*, which has been frequently cited in this chapter.

16 In Freud's corpus there is little to say about hope, and it is often viewed by those who followed him as an obstacle rather than a support to the therapeutic effort (Cooper 2000, 13–15).

17 There are other vehicles that these philosophers find effective for transformation. Buber put together groups of Hasidic stories and worked with Rosenzweig on what became a famous bible translation. Rosenzweig's *Star* shows his appreciation for Jewish ritual and law, and Levinas has written and presented many Talmudic commentaries.

18 See Karl Löwith's famous early essay of 1942, "M. Heidegger and F. Rosenzweig or Temporality and Eternity."

19 Buber's discussions of politics and true community can be seen in *I and Thou*, (1970, 96–100, 157), as well as in the essays "Hebrew Humanism" (1959, 457–463), and "The Question to the Single One" (1965, 65–71).

References

Aron, Lewis. 1996. *A Meeting of Minds: Mutuality in Psychoanalysis*. Hillsdale, NJ: Analytic Press.

Aron, Lewis, and Karen Starr. 2013. *A Psychotherapy for the People: Toward a Progressive Psychoanalysis*. New York: Routledge.

Benjamin, Jessica. 1999. "Recognition and Destruction: An Outline of Intersubjectivity." In *Relational Psychoanalysis: The Emergence of a Tradition*, edited by Stephen A. Mitchell and Lewis Aron, 181–210. Hillsdale, NJ: Analytic Press.

Buber, Martin. 1959. "Hebrew Humanism." In *The Zionist Idea: A Historical Analysis and Reader*, edited by Arthur Hertzberg, 457–63. New York: Temple Book.

—. 1965. *Between Man and Man*. Translated by Ronald Gregor Smith. New York: Collier Books.

—. 1970. *I and Thou*. Translated by Walter Kaufmann. New York: Charles Scribner's Sons.

—. 1999. *Martin Buber on Psychology and Psychotherapy: Essays, Letters, and Dialogue*. Edited by Judith Buber Agassi. Syracuse, NY: Syracuse University Press.

—. 2002. *Meetings: Autobiographical Fragments*. Translated by Maurice S. Friedman. New York: Routledge.

Cooper, Steven H. 2000. *Objects of Hope: Exploring Possibility and Limit in Psychoanalysis*. Hillsdale, NJ: Analytic Press.

Ehrenberg, Darlene Bregman. 1992. *The Intimate Edge: Extending the Reach of Psychoanalytic Interaction*. New York: W. W. Norton and Company.

Erikson, Erik H. 1968. *Identity: Youth and Crisis*. New York: W. W. Norton and Company.

Ferenczi, Sándor. 1988. *The Clinical Diary of Sándor Ferenczi*. Edited by Judith Dupont. Translated by Michael Balint and Nicola Zarday Jackson. Cambridge, MA: Harvard University Press.

Freud, Sigmund. 1949. *An Outline of Psychoanalysis*. Translated by James Strachey. New York: W. W. Norton.

—. 1969. *A General Introduction to Psychoanalysis*. Translated by Joan Riviere. New York: Clarion Books.

Heschel, Abraham Joshua. 1955. *God in Search of Man: A Philosophy of Judaism*. New York: Harper Torchbooks.

Hoffman, Irwin Z. 1998. *Ritual and Spontaneity in the Psychoanalytic Process: A Dialectical–Constructivist View*. Hillsdale, NJ: Analytic Press.

Jonte-Pace, Diane, and William B. Parsons, eds. 2001. *Religion and Psychology: Mapping the Terrain: Contemporary Dialogues, Future Prospects*. London: Routledge.

Kierkegaard, Søren. 1980. *The Sickness Unto Death: A Christian Psychological Exposition for Upbuilding and Awakening*. Edited and translated by Howard V. Hong and Edna H. Hong. Princeton, NJ: Princeton University Press.

Kumar, Manjit. 2008. *Quantum: Einstein, Bohr, and the Great Debate about the Nature of Reality*. New York: W. W. Norton and Company.

Levinas, Emmanuel. 1969. *Totality and Infinity: An Essay on Exteriority*. Translated by Alphonso Lingis. Pittsburgh, PA: Duquesne University Press.

—. 1981. *Otherwise Than Being or Beyond Essence*. Translated by Alphonso Lingis. The Hague: Martin Nijoff Publishers.

—. 1985. *Ethics and Infinity: Conversations with Philippe Nemo*. Translated by Richard A. Cohen. Pittsburgh, PA: Duquesne University Press.

—. 1990. *Difficult Freedom: Essays On Judaism*. Translated by Seán Hand. Baltimore, MD: Johns Hopkins University Press.

—. 1998. *Of God Who Comes to Mind*. Translated by Bettina Bergo. Stanford, CA: Stanford University Press.

Löwith, Karl. 1942. "M. Heidegger and F. Rosenzweig or Temporality and Eternity." In *Philosophy and Phenomenological Research*, 3: 53–77.

Mitchell, Stephen A. 1988. *Relational Concepts in Psychoanalysis: An Integration*. Cambridge, MA: Harvard University Press.

—. 1993. *Hope and Dread in Psychoanalysis*. New York: Basic Books.

—. 2000. *Relationality: From Attachment to Intersubjectivity*. Hillsdale, CA: Analytic Press.

Ogden, Thomas H. 2004. *Reverie and Interpretation: Sensing Something Human*. Lanham, MD: Jason Aronson.

Oppenheim, Michael. 2006. *Jewish Philosophy and Psychoanalysis: Narrating the Interhuman*. Lanham, MD: Lexington Books.

Orange, Donna M. 2010. *Thinking for Clinicians: Philosophical Resources for Contemporary Psychoanalysis and the Humanistic Psychotherapies*. New York: Routledge.

Putnam, Hilary. 2008. *Jewish Philosophy as a Guide to Life: Rosenzweig, Buber, Levinas, Wittgenstein*. Bloomington, IN: Indiana University Press.

Rosenzweig, Franz. 1999a. *Franz Rosenzweig's "The New Thinking."* Edited and translated by Alan Udoff and Barbara E. Galli. Syracuse, NY: Syracuse University Press.

—. 1999b. *Understanding the Sick and the Healthy: A View of World, Man, and God*. Translated by Nahum Glatzer. Cambridge, MA: Harvard University Press.

—. 2005. *The Star of Redemption*. Translated by Barbara E. Galli. Madison, WI: University of Wisconsin Press.

Santner, Eric L. 2001. *On the Psychotheology of Everyday Life: Reflections on Freud and Rosenzweig*. Chicago: University of Chicago Press.

Streng, Frederick J. 1985. *Understanding Religious Life*. Belmont, CA: Wadsworth Publishing Company.

Chapter 4

Langue, Parole, et Chanson

On Language

While the semiotic and discursive aspects of language are significant and intriguing, it may well be that other dimensions of this global phenomenon we call language reveal more about the depth and possibilities of human living. At least, this appears to be the conclusion shared by some post-Freudian psychoanalysts and modern Jewish philosophers of encounter. The main figures participating in this dialogue are the American psychoanalysts Hans Loewald, Stephen Mitchell, and Thomas Ogden, and the German Jewish philosophers Franz Rosenzweig and Martin Buber, as well as the French Jewish philosopher Emmanuel Levinas. Particularly on the psychoanalytic side, a number of other thinkers will be introduced.

These thinkers can be seen to suggest that Ferdinand de Saussure's famous discussion of language as *langue* and *parole*, that is, as system and performance, fails to capture its sensory, affective, formative, dialogical, ethical, and even metaphysical dimensions, which come to the fore in human relationships. Many of these elements are evoked by the metaphor of "song" (*chanson*).

This exploration of the promises and actualities of language will be pursued by way of a dialogue between the psychoanalysts and philosophers. They represent two very different approaches or discourses, but in terms of this particular study they neither contest nor conflict. The inexhaustible features of language allow sometimes overlapping and sometimes diverging insights to augment each other. Just as a single song calls for another rather than silencing the next, the insights of these thinkers build upon one another. Since the scope of this topic in the two discourses is so vast that a systematic treatment would necessitate tomes, using a lighter touch, the following discussion will introduce and play with striking illustrations that hopefully build into a song, a *duet*.

This dialogue is grounded in the shared insight that persons cannot be understood as either autonomous minds or isolated individuals. Stephen Mitchell writes that "an individual human mind is an oxymoron; subjectivity always develops in the context of intersubjectivity" (2000, 57), and Franz Rosenzweig sees conversation as illustrating the truth that we are "dependent on the other for what is ours" (1999a, 87). More poignantly both the psychoanalysts and the philosophers insist that the intersubjective or interhuman grounds identity, growth, meaning, and authenticity. Perhaps more than any other human activity, language exemplifies the fullness of humans' lives together.

We will begin by briefly putting this discussion into the context of the wider linguistic turn identified in so many of the contemporary human sciences. The foray will continue and narrow by examining why the psychoanalysts and the philosophers see language as the key to understanding persons. The treatment of the psychoanalysts will progress through the themes of the sensory, affective, and formative dimensions of language, as well as the linguistic ambience of analysis. The tour of the philosophers' terrain will include the dynamics of dialogue, ethics, and the divine, finishing with an exegesis on scripture/text. The concluding section will compare the powers and limits of each of the two contributions to our understanding of the place of language in our existence. We will come to see (or is it hear?) that intersubjectivity, as emphasized by both the psychoanalysts and the philosophers, is the indispensable ground that allows these vibrant features of language to resound.

A major theoretical development throughout the twentieth century, with no hint of cessation today, is what has been termed the "linguistic turn." Initially identified in terms of the discipline of philosophy, the impact of the recognition of the embeddedness of all human activities in a linguistic matrix has extended to the humanities, the social sciences, and, in the widest sense, the natural sciences.[1] Some of the thinkers most identified with this illuminating approach are the linguist Ferdinand de Saussure and the philosophers Ludwig Wittgenstein and Jacques Derrida. A statement by Jean-Paul Sartre provides a striking overview that is particularly appropriate in our context:

> Language cannot be separated from the world, from others, and from ourselves. It is not an alien enclave that can outwit me or subvert my purpose; it is me, so that I am nearer to being myself when I am farther

> away—with others and among things; it is the indissoluble reciprocity of men and their struggles together embodied by the internal relations of this linguistic whole that has neither door nor window, where we can neither go in *nor* come out, where we are.
>
> (cited in Mitchell 1993, 95)

Sartre highlights themes that ground as well as punctuate our treatment. He contests the Romantic view that language is a clumsy instrument standing in the way of the immediacy and fullness of experiencing others, things, and even ourselves. For Sartre, rather than being an "alien enclave," it is as natural to human life as the air we breathe. It is not a "door" or "window" to things; it structures, or better, permeates all of our experiences, including of ourselves. A cumulative gift from generations past and persons present, it is a continual reminder of our lives and "struggles" together.

Saussure is often mentioned as a prominent early figure in this intellectual advance, initiating Structuralism and leading to post-Structuralism. His influence can be traced to student notes pieced together to form the text *Course in General Linguistics* (1906–1911). He began by distinguishing two approaches to language, one of which focuses on *parole*, and the other on *langue*. His contribution lay with the latter, language as systematic structure, rather than the former, the activities of speech. Saussure looked at the individual linguistic sign and its two constituents, the concept or "signified" and the sound-image or "signifier." His most important and intriguing insight was that language is built upon oppositions or differences. He wrote, "In the linguistic system, there are only differences" (cited in Tracy 1987, 54). There is a series of differences of sound combined with a series of differences of ideas. By themselves the particular signs are "arbitrary," but in playing upon each other a system of meaning is produced.[2]

The Place of Language in Human Life

How basic is language to our lives? The psychoanalysts and philosophers concur that language is more formative and fertile than any of our other cultural activities. As we will see, there is even more to it than this, and, paraphrasing a comment soon to appear, language is the very stuff of life. While many psychoanalysts could be cited, especially those within the Relational tradition, the matter is best put by Stephen

Mitchell. The fact that the first chapter in his most important statement, *Relationality*, about the background and nature of that tradition, is titled "Language and Reality" is absolutely telling about his view of the significance of language. Early on he notes that psychologists, philosophers, social scientists, and others interested in various aspects of the panorama of mental activities and cultural life have been more and more deeply engrossed in the study of language. As Mitchell sees it, "Increasingly over the course of the 20th century, language has become understood as the material out of which adult mentation is generated, *the very stuff of mind*" (2000, 5; my emphasis). He cites Wittgenstein and Gilbert Ryle, who saw thinking as "interiorized" speech, and Jacques Lacan, who famously offered the polymorphous anagram "The unconscious is structured like a language." Later in his work, Mitchell interjects an additional perspective, one from evolutionary biology, in stating that language is "an emergent property of the human brain" (106). To explain this, he quotes Steven Pinker, from *The Language Instinct*, who suggests that humans do not *choose* to speak to others, as it were, but are wired to do so: "People know how to talk in more or less the sense that spiders know how to spin webs… spiders spin spider webs because they have spider brains, which give them the urge to spin and the competence to succeed" (cited in Mitchell 2000, 106).

Another of Mitchell's works, *Can Love Last?*, offers further frames of reference to make the point that, here paraphrasing Sartre, language is us. The first comes from Martin Heidegger and is the notion of individuals being born or "thrown" into an already constituted situation as humans. For Heidegger, as for Mitchell, the linguistic aspect of this situation is especially important. Mitchell affirms that "in the beginning, we might say, is the relational, social, linguistic matrix in which we discover ourselves" (2003, 76).

For Rosenzweig, Buber, and Levinas, language and the human are synonymous. In Rosenzweig's *The Star of Redemption*, which seeks to portray the meetings between "God, man, and world," that is, the fundamental features of one's path through life, language necessarily constitutes "the central part" of the entire book (2005, 188). Rosenzweig contrasts mathematics with language. The former only outlines the world of possibilities, while language opens up the world's fullness as experienced in everyday life. It holds for both the species and for the individual that through language one becomes human. Thus, he writes, "Language is… the seal of humanity in man. It is whole from the beginning: man became man when he spoke" (120), and: "The I discovers itself at the moment where it affirms the existence of the You" (189).

In Martin Buber's philosophical-poetic *I and Thou*, language carries most of his message. This is true even structurally, from its opening lines, tying the "twofold attitude" of humans toward the world with the basic "word pairs" "I–Thou" and "I–It" (1970, 54), to the panoramic conclusion, where he surveys all human history in terms of the succession of ages in which "the living word appears" or the "decomposition of the word" occurs (168). Paralleling Rosenzweig's approach, Buber also ties the phylogenetic development of the species and the ontogenetic development of the person to the acquisition and use of language. In his most extended essay on this topic, "The Word That Is Spoken," we find: "The mystery of the coming-to-be of language and that of the coming-to-be of man are one" (1999, 154). In *I and Thou* he attends to the individual: "I require a Thou to become; becoming I, I say Thou" (1970, 62). We will soon come to see what lay behind Buber's statements, but at least one notion has already appeared. Buber disputes the instrumental view of language as a tool, replacing it with an understanding that language is the very platform for experiences and actions, particularly evident in creative endeavors—what he calls the life of the spirit: "In truth language does not reside in man but man stands in language and speaks out of it—so it is with all words, all spirit" (89).

The issue of language occupied Emmanuel Levinas' attention throughout his authorship, at times emerging, in the words of one critic, as the "central issue" (Wyschogrod 2004b, 344). Even a cursory statement about the role of language in human life is a complex matter in terms of Levinas' challenging philosophy; still, the topic of the "original language" of humans allows an initial sense of his stance. Of course, at the heart of Levinas' work is the obsession with ethics, with the infinite responsibility for the neighbor. For him, this is "First Philosophy" (1985, 77), and his examination of language is fully in accord with this concern. The concept of the "original language" does not refer to some primordial spoken or written words, but to what is the ethical presupposition and foundation for all speech and writing. For Levinas, the approach to the other is thus "the very essence of language prior to every particular language" (1987, 122) and, at the same time, nothing less than "the secret birth of thought itself" (125).

Psychoanalysis: Themes and Dimensions

For many of the psychoanalysts the discussion of language first turns to an analysis of the infant's early development as well as to unconscious processes, which at times highlight the sensory dimension of this phenomenon. One of the most prominent examples of this approach comes from the influential essay on language by Hans Loewald "Primary Process, Secondary Process, and Language" (2000). Loewald distinguishes between two fundamental ways of organizing experience: primary process and secondary process. The first originates out of the infant's earliest environment, where it and the mother, while physically separate, form a single mental system or dyad. In this state there is no differentiation between what belongs to the mother and what belongs to the infant or between self and other, inner and outer, or even before and after. Over time, the mental operations of infant and mother begin to separate. Differentiation or duality characterizes the second mode of experiencing—distinguishing between self and other, inner and outer, before and after, fantasy and reality. Events and experiences are processed consciously and rationally. Consonant with all of the psychoanalytic approaches today, Loewald believes that individuals function simultaneously at both of these levels, the unconscious and conscious.

However, unlike many other analysts and theorists, Loewald does not limit language to later developments, in this case, to secondary process activity.[3] There is a significant place for language in the infant's first experiences,[4] and words continue to touch this chord, to exhibit this dimension even after they take their place in the overall signifying system. Loewald writes about the earliest linguistic events between mother and infant:

> She speaks with or to the infant, not with the expectation that he will grasp the words, but as if speaking to herself with the infant included… He does not apprehend separate words—words separate one from the other and separate from the total experience—but he is immersed, embedded in a flow of speech that is part and parcel of a global experience within the mother–child field.
>
> (2000, 185)

Or again: "The mother's flow of words does not convey meaning to or symbolize 'things' for the infant… but the sounds, tone of voice, and rhythm of speech are fused within the apprehended global event" (187).

While in everyday adult experience words have meaning, do "symbolize 'things,'" they also continue to carry what Loewald terms "evocative-magical qualities," which are the elements most pertinent for this study (2000, 186). The first encounter of a new term spoken by another has a lingering impact, as a feature of its underground vibrancy, on subsequent encounters with that word.[5] There is also a "power of words," which extends beyond their abstract function as rational sign (200). Words are actions; they may shake the hearer's body, soul, or both. Obscene jokes as well as insults are good examples of word–actions impacting the recipient's body, while great poetry has the capacity even to elicit reverie. Words as names also exhibit these qualities. A name can, as if magically, evoke or summon the person or thing named. All of these examples touch upon the perennial hidden density of the primary process activity of mind. At the end of his essay, Loewald submits that together the signifying and visceral dimensions of language are needed for life to have meaning and depth:

> Language… in its most genuine autonomous function is a binding power. It ties together human beings and self and object world, and it binds abstract thought with the bodily concreteness and power of life. In the word primary and secondary process are reconciled. (204)

Our discussion of the next feature of language, its creative affective/effective dimension, will focus upon some aspects of the prior discussion, particularly the notion of language as action[6]—actually here it is language as events—introduced by Loewald. Thomas Ogden's *Reverie and Interpretation* represents one of the most engaging presentations of language's active properties. In the chapter "On the Use of Language in Psychoanalysis" and, in particular, in the section "Creating Effects in Language," he is interested not in language as it points to, reflects, or expresses something else, but in its power to itself produce unallied or independent emotional experiences.[7] He often turns to poetry and literature to illustrate this idea. Poetry, which is always meant to be transformed into speech, has the outstanding power to go beyond trying to recreate an experience. A new experience is fashioned by the words. In this sense, the key to understanding this aspect of language is not to look "behind" it, but "into it," which includes the way something is said (2004, 202). Ogden writes, "Meaning is *in* the language and the effects created by it" (214).

As is the case with all of the psychoanalytic writers treated here, Ogden's insights into and examples of these more subtle but powerful elements of language often draw upon the interactions between therapist and patient. Still, such analytic experiences are not *sui generis*, but reflect what readily occurs in intense exchanges with significant others, as well as, perhaps in a more muted way, in everyday, more mundane settings. Ogden notes that the literature about the analytic encounter has increasingly explored the total situation, "the life in words," of the exchange between analyst and patient. Here, experience is not brought to light, but "brought to life" (2004, 201). He holds that the goal of the analytic meeting or conversation is to enhance the ability of the patient to feel and experience in the present, to become more fully human:

> The analytic discourse requires of the analytic pair the development of metaphorical language adequate to the creation of sounds and meanings that reflect what it feels like to think, feel, and physically experience (in short to be alive as a human being to the extent that one is capable) at any given moment. (208–209)

Ogden's concerns brought him to reject the view that language is most productive when it is used with the greatest possible clarity and precision. Rather, he values language's ambiguity, its resonances, its "slippages" and echoes (2004, 157). If words and sentences are to engender living experiences, they cannot be seen as fixed, crystallized elements of meaning. Meaning is always contextual, produced and understood in the ever-changing emotional flow of the dialogue. It is at this point that Ogden introduces the metaphor of music: "Words, when they are living and breathing, are like musical chords" (4), and "We must attempt in our use of language… to be makers of music, rather than players of [single] notes" (4–5).

The next theme, the formative dimension of language, referring here to language and identity, utilizes a number of different authors/musicians (Stephen Mitchell, Roy Schafer, Jessica Benjamin, and Thomas Ogden). One approach reflects the recent interest in narrative. Many thinkers recognize that it is through story that we make sense and give direction to past memories, current experiences, and future hopes. To be a person, in the sense of having an identity, requires a narrative format to organize experience around oneself as a self. Mitchell illustrates this well:

> We are our stories, our accounts of what has happened to us... To have a self, we need a protagonist, someone who does things and to whom things happen. The past needs to be organized into a narrative, or several alternative narratives. *No stories, no self.*
>
> (2003, 145; my emphasis)

The classic expression of the insight that the self emerges through narrative is found in Roy Schafer's *Retelling a Life*. He writes:

> So-called self-concepts, self-images, self-representations, or more generally the so-called self may be considered to be a set of narrative strategies or storylines each person follows in trying to develop an emotionally coherent account of his or her life among people. We organize our past and present experiences narratively.
>
> (1992, 34)

Schafer argues that the general notion of the self is embedded in or completely dependent upon narrative. The "self" is a figure, the subject or agonist, in a story, often a silent story pulsing through the mind. It is a term that provides a way of organizing experience, of making past and present "emotionally coherent." It provides a pivot for past events and actions as well as for expectations for the future.

A remarkable view of analysis naturally follows from this insight. Analysis is the endeavor of patient and therapist to understand the dynamics of the manifest and latent stories that run through the mind of the patient and to then jointly construct, co-create, or retell more productive accounts. The particular version will be influenced by the patient's experiences and needs, as well as by the general storyline provided by the school or schools—Freudian, Kleinian, Lacanian, Self or Relational Psychoanalysis—that the analyst utilizes. For Schafer, the criteria for determining what constitutes a more helpful version might include "improvements in the patient's quality of life, the patient's vision of reality, and his or her adaptation-enhancing integration of personal life-historical narratives" (1992, 184).

A corollary of this way of linking language and identity is discussed by Thomas Ogden. If Schafer explores the constructive and re-constructive ways that language affects identity, Ogden's interest includes the ability of language to destabilize identity narratives. Clearly, much of the effort of the analyst must be directed to problematizing unhelpful patient stories. He writes:

> The analyst relies on language to upset (unsettle, decenter, disturb, perturb) the given—the given of the patient's conscious beliefs and narratives by which he creates illusions of permanence, certainty, and fixity of the experience of self and of the people who occupy his internal and external worlds.
>
> (2004, 218–219)

Proceeding further with the connection between language and identity, Jessica Benjamin in *The Shadow of the Other* examines various intersubjective facets of identity. In this context, she utilizes D. W. Winnicott's influential concept of "transitional space" (Benjamin 1998). In studying early development, Winnicott writes of a period when the child moves from a position characterized by inner illusion and fantasy, where persons and things are basically extensions of the self, to a more realistic interaction with the world, where these objects can be recognized in their independence. He is especially interested in the role of the mother, or other significant caretakers, in this transition. They must give the child the space to engage with the dynamics of inner and outer, self and other, by supporting the child's play with these oppositions. In this context, a blanket often takes the role of a "transitional object," something both part of and distinct from the child, a magical comforter (Winnicott 1986, 254–271).

Benjamin sees language and especially dialogue as providing "transitional space." Here language, or more appropriately speech, is not something possessed by or in the "mental control" of a single person, but constitutes that space or "third" which appears as the product of the two in relation. In her words, "Speech no longer figures as the activity of a subject empowered to speak, but as a possibility given by the relationship with a recognizing other" (1998, 28). Dialogue provides the opportunity for each person to open the way for the other to express herself, to develop, to become a self. As the reference to Winnicott indicates, this ever-recurring possibility draws upon early interactions between mother and infant.[8] Through the evolving recognition of each other, the infant comes to see the mother as separate and, at the same time, arrives at the first sense of self, of identity and separation. This is well summarized in Benjamin's lines:

> In the intersubjective conception of recognition, two active subjects may exchange, may alternate in expressing and receiving, cocreating a mutuality that allows for and presumes separateness. The arena for this catching and throwing is the intermediate in-between space, the dialogue which becomes the "third term." (29)

We have seen that the psychoanalysts are particularly interested in the intricacies of language revealed in the analytic situation. A brief reference to what Ogden terms "dramatic speech" provides a final example of the insights that have been drawn from that experience. Ogden finds that poetry, that genre that stands mid-way between speech and song, illustrates an important feature of what ideally occurs in the analytic dialogue. The poet both creates something deeply personal and gives it over to another. He writes:

> "Dramatic" speech (quite the opposite of being staged) is a highly revealing and intimate use of language in that one has offered and entrusted to another person something that one has made *for him* to use as he will. It is a use of language that is risk-taking in that it asks something of the listener in the process of making something for him.
>
> (2004, 13)

In the analytic context, in every human dialogic context, the possible blossoming of interchange may be aborted. It may be that the gift was not given with sincerity and out of fullness, or there may be a failure for the words to be honestly and fully received. However, whenever and wherever speech is given and then accepted and taken up, that which emerges is nothing less than two human presences.

The psychoanalysts have shown that language is both the "very stuff of mind" (Mitchell 2000, 5) and the ground for "the indissoluble reciprocity of men and their struggles together" (Sartre, cited in Mitchell 1993, 95). Much more than tool or sign, vibrating between self and other, unconscious and conscious, emotion and reason, fantasy and reality, language is the very essence of… "us."

Jewish Philosophy: Themes and Dimensions

For Franz Rosenzweig, Martin Buber, and Emmanuel Levinas the terms language, speech, and dialogue are usually interchangeable, and refer to the whole gamut of relations between persons, the fullness of the social dimension of existence. Since for them the social is at the heart of human nature, language is the very foundation of the life of persons. We will look at portraits of the dynamics of dialogue, the ethical dimension that permeates all linguistic exchanges, the place and contribution of interaction with the "divine" partner, and their reflections on scripture. While all of these topics echo in the works of the three philosophers, only the most compelling examples will be illustrated here.

The subject of the dynamics of dialogue, or more widely of encounter, is the emblematic feature of this stream of modern Jewish philosophy: Rosenzweig's treatment of "speech-thinking," Buber's "I and Thou," and Levinas' "face-to-face." Rosenzweig's most elaborate presentation of the concept of "speech-thinking" is in what is probably his most important essay, "The New Thinking."[9] The main argument is that the discipline of philosophy has conceived of thinking as a solitary activity, and has looked to logic and mathematics as models for its understanding of timeless and unchanging truth. The essay argues that, on the contrary, when thinking is concerned with human living, truth emerges out of dialogue with others. This view of truth, which finds its paradigm in language, both takes time seriously and "is in the need of an other" (1999a, 87). Rosenzweig reveals the creative power of language that arises out of the intricate exchange in conversation or dialogue:

> In actual conversation something really happens. I do not know beforehand what the other will say to me, because I do not even know beforehand what I will say; perhaps not even whether I will say anything at all… To need time means: not to be able to presuppose anything, to have to wait for everything, to be dependent on the other for what is ours. (86–87)

There are two points of importance to us here. The first is that something new actually occurs in the linguistic exchange. Since it is not choreographed in advance, it can be creative and take both persons to a place that neither had envisioned. The second is that speech is endowed with the ability to blur the lines between self and other, between what is from me or mine and from you or yours. For example, in a conversation a word may arise that colors and contours much that follows from both partners. In such cases, which are actually not at all rare, we essentially become "dependent on the other for what is ours." In this enigmatic phrase, Rosenzweig incisively captures part of the power and mystery of language.

Martin Buber, truly the master of dialogue, if this can be attributed to any philosopher, exposed the dynamics of this phenomenon in many of his writings over the decades. I would like to look briefly at the book *I and Thou* and also at a late essay, "Distance and Relation." In the former he begins by outlining the two distinct ways that a person addresses the world (actually, exists in the world) "in accordance with the two basic words [or "word pairs"] he can speak" (1970, 53). One of these pairs is "I–It" and the other "I–Thou." The first describes an approach where the other, whether person, animal, or thing, is treated as an object. The second word pair denotes an interaction, true relation, characterized by mutuality and reciprocity. Buber writes, "Between you and it there is a reciprocity of giving: you say Thou to it and give yourself to it; it says Thou to you and gives itself to you" (84).

The link between the I–Thou relation and language is reinforced by the notion that while speech is not absolutely necessary for this type of interaction—since, among other reasons, such relationships can be with nature and also artistic creations—it is through language and with other persons that it is fully developed. According to Buber, when the I–Thou exchange within the human sphere occurs, "the relation is manifest and enters language. We can give and receive the Thou" (1970, 57).

Two further features of the I–Thou encounter are germane to the present discussion. First, in addressing another as a Thou, both the self and the other stand in their entirety. Thus, it is primarily through dialogue that each person emerges whole, instead of existing partially, defined solely by one's vocation, interests, background, or other features. Additionally, this preeminent form of dialogue, even if only lasting in its abundance for "instants," stands above the intrigues of manipulation and power as well as the restraints of time and causality (Buber 1970, 59). Only this is "actual life" (62); only this is partaking of the present.

Buber's essay of 1950 "Distance and Relation" follows through with earlier themes but expresses them with a new clarity. The interplay of distance and relation allows him to underscore some of the major features and dynamics of human existence and of language in particular. He writes, "The principle of human life is not simple but twofold... I propose to call the first movement 'the primal setting at a distance' and the second 'entering into relation'" (1999, 4). The primary insight is that the depth of relation is only possible when each person stands in their distinctiveness. While this process includes even a person's attitude to the world, it is especially significant in the meeting of persons, where it is embodied in the "great characteristic of men's life with one another, speech" (12). It is in conversation that the distance between persons, their individual distinctiveness or "otherness," comes to the fore. The great secret of speech, its realization, occurs when two individuals approach each other without holding back and confirm the integrity of one another. "Genuine conversation, and therefore every actual fulfillment of relation between men, means acceptance of otherness," Buber declares (13). As the other is affirmed in his or her individuality, one oneself becomes a distinct individual. The authenticity of each can be realized only in this way. He concludes, "It is from one man to another that the heavenly bread of self-being is passed" (16).

Briefly, as already acknowledged, the dynamics of speech are synonymous with the "face-to-face" for Emmanuel Levinas. As he writes, "Meaning is the face of the Other, and all recourse to words takes place already within the primordial face-to-face of language" (1969, 206). The presuppositions that allow speech to emerge hold true for every authentic meeting between persons. However, the overall encounter with the other person, and specific elements within the flow of language, are much different for Levinas than for Buber. Levinas contests the view that the highest encounter is characterized by mutuality and reciprocity.[10] Instead, in turning to the face of the other, the priority of that other is first and foremost. The face shakes the foundation of one's self-love, *amour propre*, and even one's right to be: the "face… *ordains* me to serve him" (97). The face stands in its height, its ethical priority over oneself, and concurrently reveals its vulnerability to one's designs. This translates into one's infinite responsibility for the other.

Dialogue or speech is not just a matter of two persons in relation; the philosophers also recognize a communal dimension in language. In Rosenzweig's writings it is in dialogic partnership with the divine that language and community are featured. As is true for the individual, who becomes an "I" as the result of the interaction with the divine, communities of persons also require this dynamic in order to fully form. Characteristic of Rosenzweig, who was fascinated with the creative powers in calling to the other and in names, he brings together calling, names, and the emergence of a community. He writes, "He [God] bears a name for our sake, so that we may call Him. It is for our sake that He permits Himself to be named and called by that name, *since it is only by jointly calling upon Him that we become 'We'*" (1999b, 91; my emphasis). The activity of calling to the divine/other creates a community out of previously unconnected persons.

The topic of human community is also very striking in Buber's thought, and although not entirely missing from Levinas' repertoire, the individual face-to-face is his central concern. Buber sees community as augmenting and not conflicting, as it were, with his model of the dialogue of I and Thou; in his words, "The communal speaking… begins in the midst of speaking to one another" (1999, 106). Language or speech not only brings people together in the present, but as the custodian of words spoken over generations, it is that astonishing bond that unites people past and present. Buber writes of this with a grand flourish:

> Speech in its ontological sense was at all times present whenever men regarded one another in the mutuality of I and Thou; whenever one showed the other something… All this flowing ever again into a great stream of reciprocal sharing of knowledge—thus came to be and thus is the living We, the genuine We, which, where it fulfills itself, embraces the dead who once took part in colloquy and now take part in it through what they have handed down to posterity. (107)

The next cluster of topics is dramatically prefigured in Levinas' portrayal of the major constituents of his treatment of language: ethics and the divine. With Rosenzweig, ethics, the discourse of obligation and responsibility, is grounded in his understanding of religious commandments. In fact, both the coming to be of the individual and the life with others take place under the canopy of the dual love commandments to love God and to love the neighbor. This is clearest in *The Star of Redemption*. The catalyst for Rosenzweig's chapter on revelation is the biblical commandment to "love the Eternal your God with all your heart" (2005, 190). This love demand tears the individual out of her or his previous isolation and self-concern. In linguistic terms, which is how Rosenzweig sees it, this is the move from soliloquy to dialogue. The divine call of obligation, to "love me," is transformative, changing a self into a "soul." The second commandment, "to love the neighbor," widens the person's life to engage with other persons. The neighbor is, in German, the next or closest one, *das Nebenmensch*.

The person is thrust into the world, responsible to bring the transformative words of love to whomever stands nearest. The individual's dialogues are thus not accidental, but are a calling and mission that extend God's love, ultimately pointing to redemption: "The one who is chosen by God's love loses his own will… by taking upon his shoulders the yoke of the mission… In this way he leaves the magic circle of Revelation and enters into the Kingdom of Redemption" (269).

Buber is also not averse to seeing the I–Thou encounter in terms of obligation and responsibility: "Love is responsibility of an I for a Thou" (1970, 66). However, by this time it is obvious that the topic of language and ethics is paramount for Levinas. The connection is manifest in Levinas' essay "Language and Proximity." The term "proximity," which is used as synonymous with the face-to-face relation, is joined with two other words, "substitution" and "obsession." Together, the three terms "proximity," "substitution," and "obsession" dominate Levinas' later discussion of ethics,[11] as well as permeating through and through this essay on language. As he details it:

> Language, contact, is the obsession of an I "beset" by the others. Obsession is responsibility… Responsibility as an obsession is proximity… Language is fraternity, and thus a responsibility for the other, and hence a responsibility for what I have not committed, for the pain and the fault of others.
>
> (1987, 123)

And: "The I… in a permanent sacrifice substitutes itself for others and transcends the world. But this is the source of speaking, for it is the essence of communication" (124).

In the above quotations, Levinas' fundamental teachings about language are abridged in a few terse lines. The responsibility each person has for others, for all others ("fraternity"), is not a consequence of some prior choice or action. It exists as the ground for our humanity. As with an obsession, responsibility for the other haunts a person at every moment, referring not to one's freedom, but to a condition of passivity and powerlessness. Additionally, the responsibility for the other can be seen as a matter of substitution. The self sacrifices itself, in the sense of its right to self-preservation, and places the concern for the other above self-concern. This sacrifice, substitution, is the basis for human transcendence, indicating the ability of individuals to rise beyond that law that holds for all other living things. Levinas expresses the feature of transcendence in an earlier text: "The calling into question of the I, coextensive with the manifestation of the Other in the face, we call language" (1969, 171).

Together, proximity, obsession, and substitution are nothing less than "the essence of communication" (Levinas 1987, 124). This insight also typifies Levinas' later writings, encapsulated in his distinction between the "saying" and the "said." In this context, the said is the situation of language in the everyday world. Language produces meaning through a system of signs. It both identifies things and, as human interchange, reflects and expresses power relations. Here language is executed, as one commentator concludes, "as a relation of word and being" (Wyschogrod 2004a, 407).[12] In contrast, the saying is the pre-existing ideal or "essence of communication," which allows for the possibility of everyday speech. This is the ethical dimension of language, the very "source of speaking." Saying reveals our "proximity," that language is fundamentally ethical: Its core is address and response.

More than Buber or Levinas, the topic of the divine dimension of language is omnipresent in the thought of Rosenzweig. He sees language as both totally human and totally divine. The two sides cannot be separated. *The Star of Redemption* affirms this in two contexts. The first statement is part of Rosenzweig's narrative about God's creation. Creation includes, in particular, both humans and language. He describes language as "the wedding gift of the Creator to humanity," which is "the mutual possession of the children of men" (2005, 120). Being a gift implies that:

> To trust it [language] is easy, for it is in us and around us, and when it comes to us from the "outside," nothing other than it echoes from our "inside" toward the "outside." The spoken word is the same, whether it is listened to or said. The ways of God and the ways of man are different, but the word of God and the word of man are the very same. What man feels in his heart as his own human language is the word that has come from the mouth of God. (163)

The second context is Rosenzweig's discussion of the biblical Song of Songs. This poem is the model for revelation, for the relation of God to humans and ultimately the relation between humans. Life with others, as we have seen, lives off God's prior love for each person. In this quote, Rosenzweig moves from love to language, and in the end both are merged:

> It is not possible for love to be "purely human." When it begins to speak—and this it must do, for there exists no other utterance spoken besides itself than the language of love—so when love speaks, it is already changed into something superhuman; for the sensuous character of the word is full to the brim with its divine supra-sensuous meaning; like language itself love is at once sensible and supra-sensuous.
>
> (2005, 216)

Buber uses the expression "God's address" to affirm that there is divine meaning to be found at every moment in one's life. If one is open to this sphere within the everyday, life is found to have purpose and direction. As Buber states:

> God's address to man penetrates the events in all our lives and all the events in the world around us, everything biographical and everything historical, and turns it into instruction, into demands for you and me. Event upon event, situation upon situation is enabled and empowered by this personal language to call upon the human person to endure and decide.
>
> (1970, 182)

The metaphor of God's "address" or "word" allows Buber to draw upon features of human dialogue, of being personally addressed and obligated to respond. For Buber it teaches that this "word" is not far off, not further away than one's intimate partner, friend, or neighbor—and who is not one's neighbor?

Levinas is more sparing in his use of the term "God," especially in his philosophical writings. In reference to the face-to-face relation he speaks of a trace of God, that is, out of the vulnerability of the face of the other comes the divine proclamation "Thou shalt not kill!" (1985, 89). However, it is in connection to the next topic, language and scripture, that he most powerfully portrays the relationship of the divine to language.

Rosenzweig and Buber worked on a new translation of the Bible from the spring of 1925 until Rosenzweig's death at the end of 1929.[13] Rosenzweig's essay "Scripture and Word" reiterates his many-leveled sense of the spoken-ness of scripture and of its interweaving of divine and human. He saw scripture as arising out of three-fold dialogues between persons. He writes, "But the essential content is precisely what escapes the specifying and distancing power of *Schrift* [text or writing]: the word of God to man, the word of man to God, the word of men before God" (Buber and Rosenzweig 1994, 41). For him, scripture records God's presence, His address, in the undertakings of individuals and the events that envelop them.[14] Thus we find: "In this moment of theirs God is what acts immediately in them and speaks immediately through them" (42).

Rosenzweig's treatment of the biblical book the Song of Songs is perhaps his most passionate appeal to the divine depth present in language (2005, 213–219). He rejects the "modern" view that has "scientifically" determined that this biblical text is solely a "worldly" love song that has been inexplicably included in the canon. His retort is that readers of the text have known for centuries that the inclusion was not an error, but the natural acknowledgment that language as well as love exhibit two-fold dimensions. He writes:

> The Song of Songs was recognized as a love song, and at the same time immediately as a "mystical" poem. One simply knew that the I and You of the inter-human language are also quite simply the I and You between God and man. One knew that in language the difference between "immanence" and "transcendence" is extinguished. (214)

Levinas' "Foreword" to some of his well-known Talmudic commentaries in *Beyond the Verse* is a short ode to the divine aspect of language. Its primary focus is the unending nature of interpretation or "exegesis" of "Holy Scriptures." This is Levinas' referent for the famous Talmudic dictum "The Torah speaks the language of men." For him, this refers to the insight that God's infinite Word is miraculously "maintained in the spoken language" of humans. The "contraction" of the infinite divine word into the finite words of humans obviously results in an "enigmatic surplus of meaning," which necessitates the need for continual exploration and analysis of the text by the reader (1994, x).

Levinas plays out another theme in his *midrash* on language and text, utilizing a double reference to the Hebrew prophets. On the one hand, the divine infusion can be described in terms of "the prophetic dignity of language" (1994, x). Just as the prophet was inspired by the divine Word to give voice to a message not his own, exegesis is an event "where man listens, amazed to what he utters" (xi). On the other hand, the definitive message of the prophets permeates both scripture and every human writing. The prophets voiced God's command to be responsible for the other, tearing the hearer out of his or her customary "self-care." Levinas insists, "My co-ordination with the other in language is the expression of commandments received: writing is always prescriptive and ethical, the Word of God which commands and vows me to the other, a holy writing before being sacred text" (xii).

Holy Scripture is thus for Levinas "language *par excellence.*" Its message of responsibility, of standing before the face of the other, is implied in all speech, regardless of what is said. This is the perennial "prophetic essence" of language, alive whether "the Word of God… is already audible or still muffled in the heart of every act of speech" (1994, xii).

Finally, Levinas sees exegesis as both confirming the uniqueness of each person and placing the individual within the wider flow of generations who have listened and responded to the holy text. Every person, out of his or her singularity, contributes to the growing prophetic "message," to that "revelation which is forever continued" (1994, x). Thus, through exegesis the irreplaceable quality of each human life is affirmed. Further, while each contribution is unique, there is a "pluralism of persons and generations" who stand before the text. Tradition is precisely that heightened dialogue bridging individuals and periods. The leitmotif of Levinas' treatment is a quotation from Amos 3:8: "The Lord God has spoken; who can but prophesy?" (xiii).

Levinas' panegyric on scripture provides a fitting conclusion to the treatment of the three Jewish philosophers. It includes many of the themes that we have been pursuing in their thought: scripture as the prototype for all human speech, the abiding divine dimension of language, the ethical feature of language, language embodying the "pluralism of persons and generations" (1994, xiii), and the axiomatic insight that the authentic person emerges out of dialogue, whether with the divine, other persons, or texts.

Continuing the Dialogue

The post-Freudian psychoanalysts and the Jewish philosophers offer two impressive discourses that detail some of the startling powers or features of language. There are common elements and distinctive insights, as well as areas of possible cross-fertilization. Most importantly, the two discourses can be seen to build upon each other, to provide supplementary approaches to appreciating the richness of language. Jane Flax, in *Disputed Subjects*, noted the need for such multiplicity, explaining that "each discourse tries to order the heterogeneous components of subjectivity within one master narrative or category… We will need multiple stories in a variety of styles to appreciate its complexity" (1993, 98). In the context of language and intersubjectivity, her judgment is especially salient.

Both discourses remark on the fabric of language's density. They celebrate the ambiguity of language, which indicates to them that language resonates with connections, overflows with meanings. The precise, isolated, strictly defined word is not archetype but aberration. Ogden appreciates language's "slippage" and echoes since words, like musical chords, take on different meanings according to context, in the total give and take of communication (2004). Levinas writes of the compression of the infinite divine word into the finite speech and texts of persons, which requires that the word be endlessly pursued/interpreted (1994). This ambiguity points to the dynamic depth of language, conscious and unconscious, rational and emotive, sensuous and formative, for the psychoanalysts, and to its endless associations, dialogical, ethical, and religious, for the philosophers.

The creative possibilities inherent in language are highlighted in both approaches. In particular, the psychoanalysts and the philosophers see the wider linguistic exchange between partners as having a life of its own. The psychoanalysts refer to this phenomenon, first described by Ogden, as "the analytic third," which offers a fresh opening for the subject to break out of well-trodden and often destructive patterns. Buber speaks of this dynamic as "the between," which nurtures the life of the spirit and is expressed in art, religion, and other human activities. Thus, each of the two discourses acknowledges language as a trusted means to the new, as an effective tool for transcendence.

Language and dialogue are also tied to identity. Benjamin focuses on "intersubjectivity," that is, the ways that recognition of the other as subject, and becoming a subject, are simultaneously given and received—gift given and reciprocated at the same time. Rosenzweig and Buber track the emergence of the self through dialogue; the first concludes that "we are dependent on the other for what is ours" (Rosenzweig 1999a, 87) and the latter that "it is from one man to another that the heavenly bread of self-being is passed" (Buber 1999, 16). Yet, even within these similarities, different emphases are apparent. The psychoanalysts feature the role of narrative in identity—Mitchell's "No stories, no self" (1993, 145)—and the philosophers allude to wider fields that impact identity, including community and tradition.

Among the most distinctive elements in the two disciplines are the psychoanalysts' focus on the unconscious and early development, as well as the analytic experience, and the philosophers' treatment of the divine dimension of language and its carry-over into ethics and scripture. Loewald's discussion of the infant's first encounter with language underscores a perennial feature within psychoanalytic treatments (2000). He is deeply interested in the mother–infant dyad, this "cosmos" in which words, as sounds or notes, orbit. Significantly, he holds that this unconscious, "primary process" dimension of language continues to reverberate throughout one's life. Psychoanalysts have always insisted that health requires a living bridge between unconscious and conscious, and for Loewald this is one of language's primary powers.

Many post-Freudians, probably starting with Melanie Klein, saw the interactions in analysis as mirroring, and hopefully augmenting and correcting, those between the infant and the earliest caregiver, usually the mother. This forum—the "analyst's couch"—is probably the most appropriate synecdoche, as it is the unique experimental chamber for many of the psychoanalysts' most impressive insights. The intensity and multi-layered depth of that conversation, in words and silences, and in bodily signs, is the platform for what Loewald identifies as language's "evocative-magical qualities" (2000, 186) and Ogden refers to as "reverie" (2004).

The most distinctive feature of the Jewish philosophers' repertoire is compressed into the term the "divine," as the origin and recurrent dimension of language. They expose the ethical undercurrent that flows through language, what Levinas terms its "prophetic dignity" (1994, x). The term "divine" allows them to highlight the community of speakers past and present that resonates in every word, sentence, or command. These themes are especially prominent in the three Jewish philosophers' discussions of the nature of the scriptural text. The Bible is for them the model for all language, written or spoken. In Levinas' words, scripture is "language *par excellence*" (xii). What is true for scripture—a miraculous origin, an ethical core, a transformative potential—is also fully applicable to all human language.

Among the many possible areas of cross-fertilization coming from the side of the psychoanalysts are the references to the mother–infant dyad and to the unconscious. While the philosophers' narratives about the divine dimension of language are fecund, these should not be allowed to erase or substitute for an acknowledgment of the first human relationship, usually between mother and infant. The significant features of this relationship for a person's development are eloquently detailed by Benjamin as well as by Loewald. Equally compelling is the warning of many feminist theorists, including the psychoanalyst and philosopher Luce Irigaray, that the erasure of the mother is often accompanied by the repudiation of the body, nature, and women overall.[15] Certainly some features of the three philosophers' work, in terms of dialogue, ethics, and the divine, are not immune to Irigaray's general admonition.

There is nothing similar to Benjamin's intricate dialogical choreography of intersubjectivity between mother and infant in any of the works of the Jewish philosophers. Rosenzweig replaces this primary relationship with the exchange between God and the soul. For Buber, the child emerges from a disembodied "womb of the great mother" with a natural readiness for relation already at hand (1970, 76–77). The Levinasian first encounter with the other which restructures the self is not with a specific other, and there is no direct or indirect reference to a mother. Additionally, while all three Jewish philosophers have sophisticated discussions of the use and meaning of anthropomorphic metaphors, God is always depicted as a "He." This raises an obvious suspicion about a male/God substitution for the primary female/mother figure.

Earlier it was demonstrated how Loewald's psychoanalytic treatment of the mother–infant dyad was tied to an appreciation for the sensuous and unconscious dimensions of language. In light of this, acknowledgment of the pivotal role of the mother in early development might introduce these elements into the philosophers' overall examinations of dialogue. Such a development would be very helpful, especially in terms of what are at times somewhat abstract portraits of dialogue, particularly in Buber's I–Thou exchange and in Levinas' face-to-face.

Additionally, the psychoanalytic discourse in terms of the unconscious can be seen as a reminder to the philosophers that language continually touches upon repressed elements of which the speaker and hearer are not aware. The philosopher Hilary Putnam describes Rosenzweig, Buber, and Levinas as moral perfectionists (2008, 59, 72–73). He means by this, that they are tremendously eloquent in detailing the highest demands and possibilities of human living. However, the other side—or underside—of this perfectionist perspective is that the frailty or negative features of the human are not given enough attention.[16] Thus, the psychoanalysts' awareness that, either consciously or unconsciously, words may be used to cover over unacknowledged aspects of a person's life can be seen to supplement the philosophers' portrait of language.

A possible lesson for the psychoanalysts coming out of this dialogue with the philosophers relates to the profound ethical texture of language. The three Jewish philosophers are in agreement that ethics permeates the very structure of language—the word spoken and the response/responsibility that ensues. For them, the responsibility to the neighbor grounds the word passed between persons. While the psychoanalytic discourse is certainly not totally allergic to the term "responsibility," even a cursory review of the books used in this essay demonstrates that it usually appears in only limited forms. Of course, Freud wrote of the responsibility of the analysand to express all that came into her or his mind—Freud's "fundamental rule"—and there are extremely sensitive discussions about the analyst's responsibility to the patient. Yet, rarely do the psychoanalysts take up the topic of responsibility for the other as a fundamental feature of relationships and as part of what constitutes the patient's, and every human's, basic health.

It is especially in terms of the philosophers' discussion of identity that the issue of responsibility might supplement the psychoanalysts' repertoire. For the former, identity is not constituted by the self or for itself, but through the call of the other. All three philosophers—through Rosenzweig's love of neighbor, Buber's I and Thou, and Levinas' face-to-face—correlate the very uniqueness of the self to the uniqueness of one's responsibility, the sense that only I am called at this time and in this manner, and that only I can respond as such. One of the interesting consequences of this perspective is that the self is turned away from itself, away from self-concern to an active concern for the other. When this is given practical and concrete meaning in the analytic environment, it opens the patient to real possibilities of accomplishment and satisfaction. In Lewis Aron's words, paraphrasing Harold Searles, patients "can make reparation, lessen their guilt, become sure of their 'symbolic worth,' and therefore feel fully human," if their concern for the therapist's own health is respected (1996, 135). Finally, since it is both a fundamental aspect of relationships and a basic feature of a self, the element of responsibility could also be explored as an important constituent of meaningful self-narratives or stories.

How appropriate is the metonym of "language as song" in the discourses of the post-Freudian psychoanalysts and the Jewish philosophers? The insight that language can be compared to song, or is a type of song, appears directly or indirectly in a number of places, including Ogden's statement that "words… are like musical chords" (2004, 4), in Loewald's description of the infant's being "immersed, embedded" in the mother's "flow of speech" (2000, 185), and in Rosenzweig's turning to the biblical love poem the Song of Songs as the prototype of speech (2005). Speech or speaking, as well as song, is an event, a performance that, while it may refer to something outside, is a creation with its own "evocative-magical qualities" (Loewald 2000, 186). Language, like song, has the capacity to evoke all the dimensions of human life: unconscious and conscious, fantasy and reality, affective and rational, ethical, communal, and religious. What of the human or interhuman is not captured in language/song? There is voice, body, rhythm, melody, and message—embodied emotion, of relationships missed or consummated, conjuring up the passionate systole and diastole of identity, suffering, and love.

Notes

1 An important early signpost, first published in 1967, was the anthology edited by Richard Rorty, *The Linguistic Turn* (1992). See Steven Kepnes' *The Text as Thou* for a discussion of "the linguistic turn in Jewish philosophy" (1992, ix–xv).
2 See David Tracy's discussion of Saussure's statement in *Plurality and Ambiguity* (1987, 52–60).
3 See Mitchell (2000, 8–10).
4 Mitchell brings up the example of words having an impact even on a fetus *in utero* (2000, 8–9).
5 Mitchell and Black note in *Freud and Beyond* that the psychoanalyst Harry Stack Sullivan also spoke of "the meaning of words" being "embedded in the original interpersonal contexts in which they were learned" (1995, 72).
6 Ogden in *Reverie and Interpretation* quotes Robert Frost as referring to poetry as "words that have become deeds" (2004, 242).
7 Of course, it is Freud's creation of psychoanalysis, "the talking cure," which is the best example of an understanding of language as event, of the transformative feature of words. The expression itself came from Josef Breuer's famous patient Bertha Pappenheim.

8 The parallel between the foundational mother–infant interaction and the remedial analyst–patient relationship, an omnipresent trope in relational psychoanalysis, is particularly important in Benjamin's *Shadow of the Other* (1998, 28–29).

9 Rosenzweig saw this writing as providing a summary of *The Star of Redemption*, and he permitted it to stand as the Introduction to its second edition.

10 There is a good overview of Levinas' criticisms of Buber's views of relation in Robert Bernasconi's "'Failure of Communication' as a Surplus" (1988).

11 This shift in terminology, from the face-to-face to substitution, is one of the most pronounced differences between Levinas' two works *Totality and Infinity* of 1969 and the later *Otherwise Than Being or Beyond Essence* of 1974.

12 Edith Wyschogrod's essay "From Ethics to Language: The Imperative of the Other" presents a fine discussion of the saying and the said. It is especially important as it places this in the context of Levinas' critique of Martin Heidegger.

13 Buber completed the translation in 1961. A book of essays about translating the Bible and the issues the two philosophers encountered, *Scripture and Translation: Martin Buber and Franz Rosenzweig* (1994), first appeared in German in 1936. For a treatment of Buber's "dialogical hermeneutic," see Kepnes' *The Text as Thou* (1992), especially pp. 41–60, 78.

14 The divine dimension of the Bible, particularly in relation to biblical law, is the topic of one of Rosenzweig's most important letters, which has been titled "Divine and Human" (1961, 242–247).

15 Irigaray's essay "Divine Women" explores the issue of portraying the divine as a woman (1993, 57–72).

16 This critique is more accurately directed to Rosenzweig and Levinas than it is to Buber. See, for example, Buber's essay "Guilt and Guilt Feelings" (1999).

References

Aron, Lewis. 1996. *A Meeting of Minds: Mutuality in Psychoanalysis*. Hillsdale, NJ: Analytic Press.

Benjamin, Jessica. 1998. *Shadow of the Other: Intersubjectivity and Gender in Psychoanalysis*. New York: Routledge.

Bernasconi, Robert. 1988. "'Failure of Communication' as a Surplus: Dialogue and Lack of Dialogue Between Buber and Levinas." In *The Provocation of Levinas: Rethinking the Other*, edited by Robert Bernasconi and David Wood, 100–135. New York: Routledge.

Buber, Martin. 1970. *I and Thou*. Translated by Walter Kaufmann. New York: Charles Scribner's Sons.

—. 1999. *Martin Buber on Psychology and Psychotherapy: Essays, Letters, and Dialogue*. Edited by Judith Buber Agassi. Syracuse, NY: Syracuse University Press.

Buber, Martin, and Franz Rosenzweig. 1994. *Scripture and Translation: Martin Buber and Franz Rosenzweig*. Translated by Lawrence Rosenwald and Everett Fox. Bloomington, IN: Indiana University Press.

Flax, Jane. 1993. *Disputed Subjects: Essays on Psychoanalysis, Politics and Philosophy*. New York: Routledge.
Irigaray, Luce. 1993. *Sexes and Genealogies*. Translated by Gillian C. Gill. New York: Columbia University Press.
Kepnes, Steven. 1992. *The Text as Thou: Martin Buber's Dialogical Hermeneutics and Narrative Theology*. Bloomington, IN: Indiana University Press.
Levinas, Emmanuel. 1969. *Totality and Infinity: An Essay on Exteriority*. Translated by Alphonso Lingis. Pittsburgh, PA: Duquesne University Press.
—. 1981. *Otherwise Than Being or Beyond Essence*. Translated by Alphonso Lingis. The Hague: Martin Nijoff Publishers.
—. 1985. *Ethics and Infinity: Conversations with Philippe Nemo*. Translated by Richard A. Cohen. Pittsburgh, PA: Duquesne University Press.
—. 1987. *Collected Philosophical Papers*. Translated by Alphonso Lingis. Pittsburgh, PA: Duquesne University Press.
—. 1994. *Beyond the Verse: Talmudic Readings and Lectures*. Translated by Gary D. Mole. Bloomington, IN: Indiana University Press.
Loewald, Hans W. 2000. *The Essential Loewald: Collected Papers and Monographs*. Hagerstown, MD: University Publishing Group.
Mitchell, Stephen A. 1993. *Hope and Dread in Psychoanalysis*. New York: Basic Books.
—. 2000. *Relationality: From Attachment to Intersubjectivity*. Hillsdale, NJ: Analytic Press.
—. 2003. *Can Love Last?: The Fate of Romance Over Time*. New York: W. W. Norton and Company.
Mitchell, Stephen A., and Margaret J. Black. 1995. *Freud and Beyond: A History of Modern Psychoanalytic Thought*. New York: Basic Books.
Ogden, Thomas H. 2004. *Reverie and Interpretation: Sensing Something Human*. Lanham, MD: Jason Aronson.
Putnam, Hilary. 2008. *Jewish Philosophy as a Guide to Life: Rosenzweig, Buber, Levinas, Wittgenstein*. Bloomington, IN: Indiana University Press.
Rorty, Richard, ed. 1992. *The Linguistic Turn: Essays in Philosophical Method*. Chicago, IL: University of Chicago Press.
Rosenzweig, Franz. 1961. *Franz Rosenzweig: His Life and Thought*. Edited by Nahum N. Glatzer. New York: Schocken Books.
—. 1999a. *Franz Rosenzweig's "The New Thinking."* Edited and translated by Alan Udoff and Barbara E. Galli. Syracuse, NY: Syracuse University Press.
—. 1999b. *Understanding the Sick and the Healthy: A View of World, Man, and God*. Translated by Nahum Glatzer. Cambridge, MA: Harvard University Press.
—. 2005. *The Star of Redemption*. Translated by Barbara E. Galli. Madison, WI: University of Wisconsin Press.
Schafer, Roy. 1992. *Retelling a Life: Narration and Dialogue in Psychoanalysis*. New York: Basic Books.
Tracy, David. 1987. *Plurality and Ambiguity: Hermeneutics, Religion, Hope*. San Francisco: Harper and Row.

Winnicott, D. W. 1986. "Transitional Objects and Transitional Phenomena." In *Essential Papers on Object Relations*, edited by Peter Buckley, 254–271. New York: New York University Press.

Wyschogrod, Edith. 2004a. "From Ethics to Language: The Imperative of the Other." In *Emmanuel Levinas: Critical Assessments of Leading Philosophers Vol. I*, edited by Claire Elise Katz, 402–414. London: Routledge.

—. 2004b. "Emmanuel Levinas and the Problem of Religious Language." In *Emmanuel Levinas: Critical Assessments of Leading Philosophers Vol. III*, edited by Claire Elise Katz, 339–363. London: Routledge.

Chapter 5

Revisiting an "Illusion"

On Meaning

While scholars conceptualize "religion" in a wide variety of ways (Saler 1993), certainly the ability to provide a meaning scheme for individual and social life is one of the most prominent features in their presentations. This inquiry will spotlight the appreciation of religion by the important post-Freudian psychoanalyst Hans Loewald. It will be presented as an example of how the emergence of the issue of meaning as central to psychoanalytic theory and practice can open the way for a deeper understanding of and engagement with that phenomenon (religion), which Freud famously condemned as an "illusion" (1964). Loewald's reflections will also be placed in the context of discussions by a group of contemporary psychoanalysts concerning the issue of meaning and the value of religion. Following this, in consonance with the comparative focus of this book, Emmanuel Levinas' "Notes on Meaning" will be used as a template to explore the treatment of meaning in the Jewish philosophers of our study.

The term "meaning" takes on multiple casts in different studies of religion, and appears to be almost omnipresent in important scholarly inquiries of at least the last half-century. I hope that the following examples do more than just confirm this statement, one which it seems to me is hardly controversial, but that they provide some considerations of the range of overlapping concerns that coalesce around the term in the context of the study of religion. The sociologist Peter Berger highlights the challenge of secularism to traditional religious notions of order and meaning in his work *The Sacred Canopy* (1967). The key enterprise of society according to Berger is "world-building," that is, imposing "a meaningful order, or nomos" upon reality (19), and religion is the power that sacralizes this order. From a slightly different angle Berger writes, "In all its manifestations, religion constitutes an immense projection of human meanings into the empty vastness of the universe" (100). A more contemporary sociologist, Colin Campbell, expands on Berger's reflections, describing three dimensions of the "meaningfulness" of religious systems taken in the widest sense: a descriptive account of reality, what persons are meant to feel about the portrait of reality presented, and the reasons why things are the way they are (2001, 75–76).

The influential anthropologist Clifford Geertz focuses on the feature of meaning in his definition of both culture and religion. He speaks of culture as "an historically transmitted pattern of meanings embodied in symbols, a system of inherited conceptions expressed in symbolic forms by means of which men communicate, perpetuate, and develop their knowledge about and attitudes toward life" (1973, 89). Without explicitly using the word "meaning," Geertz more or less characterizes an understanding of it in his definition of religion:

> (1) A system of symbols which acts to (2) establish powerful, pervasive, and long-lasting moods and motivations in men by (3) formulating conceptions of a general order of existence and (4) clothing these conceptions with such an aura of factuality that (5) the moods and motivations seem uniquely realistic. (90–91)

A bit less abstractly, and more helpfully for us, Geertz sees religious symbols as responding to the "problem of meaning," that is, the "suspicion that perhaps the world, and hence man's life in the world, has no genuine order at all—no empirical regularity, no emotional form, no moral coherence." Such symbols respond to this suspicion by relating "man's sphere of existence to a wider sphere within which it is conceived to rest" (108).

The connection between religion and meaning is prominent in the work of many Religious Studies scholars. Jonathan Z. Smith in *Map is Not Territory* describes the task of the historian of religions in the following way:

> What we study when we study religion is one mode of constructing worlds of meaning, worlds within which men find themselves and in which they choose to dwell. What we study is the passion and drama of man discovering the truth of what it is to be human… Religion is the quest, within the bounds of the human, historical condition, for the power to manipulate and negotiate one's "situation" so as to have "space" in which to meaningfully dwell.
>
> (1978, 290–291)

Finally, in *Plurality and Ambiguity*, David Tracy explores the enduring power of religious classics in the face of post-modern challenges (1987). He sees the "classics" as addressing "the fundamental questions that are part of the very attempt to become human at all" (86). Tracy describes these questions in terms of asking about "the meaning and truth of Ultimate Reality not only as it is in itself but as it is existentially related to us" (87). Included among those questions addressing our shared limit situations are:

> Questions provoked by radical contingency and mortality; questions evoked by the transience of all things human; questions attendant upon an acknowledgement of the historical and social contingency of all the values embraced and all the convictions lived by; the question of suffering… the question of the meaning of that ennui that can erupt into a pervasive anxiety, even terror… at certain moments… the question of why we sense some responsibility to live an ethical life… the question of the need to understand what possible meaning might be present in the profound love and joy we experience; the question of why I possess a fundamental trust… that allows me to go on… the questions provoked by the sense that in every act of resistance some strange and unnameable hope, however inchoate, betrays itself. (86–87)

Despite the diverse suggestions coming from scholars in these different disciplines, there are some "resemblances" shared by the "family." Meaning in the context of religion refers to an overall system that is expressed through foundational narratives, images, and symbols. These construct a portrait of the general order of existence, including Ultimate Reality, and the nature of the human condition. This speaks to both what constitutes this world and also why things are the way they are. Thus, the portrait is not just an objective description, but concerns the individual's particular place in the order of things. This order, significantly, includes a moral dimension. The portrait elicits, or alternatively fashions, powerful passions, moods, and motivations. It responds to some of humans' most elemental suspicions and fears: that there is no ordered universe, just chaos and vast empty space; that there is no moral coherence, that is, stable values, rationality and consistency to life, especially in the face of those limit situations such as suffering and death; finally, that there is no justifiable basis for either trust or hope.

The Psychoanalytic Concern with Meaning-Making

The significant changes in the ways that some psychoanalysts have come to view religion are concomitant with wider post-Freudian transformations—especially in British and American schools—in the last half-century or so. While there is some disagreement about the identification and description of these developments, there is a general consensus about their nature.[1] Critics point to what can be seen as four overlapping shifts in psychoanalytic theory and practice: from drive theory to object relations and the interpersonal, from the focus on the Oedipal dynamic to the mother–infant dyad, from analysis as objective and neutral to analysis as an interpersonal meeting where shared events occur and shared meanings are generated, and from psychoanalysis as a scientific discipline to psychoanalysis as a hermeneutical activity that offers a variety of narratives. Although a number of these changes have had some influence on the general re-evaluation of religion, it is primarily the last two enumerated that will be discussed here.

Sigmund Freud creatively utilizes perspectives, stories, and metaphors from many disciplines and areas to contribute to his psychoanalytic portrayal of human behavior, but his model of what it means to investigate and understand mental life is taken from science, and especially a nineteenth-century view of it. In his "Some Elementary Lessons in Psychoanalysis" of 1938, he speaks of psychoanalysis as a "natural science" (cited in Loewald 1978, 7).[2] He deeply admires the worlds uncovered by Newton and Darwin, which together evoke a strongly positivistic view of reality.[3] Both the world "out there" and "within" are constituted by set facts that may be deeply elusive, but are at least partially available through scientifically disciplined persistence. In terms of this background, two fundamental concerns for psychoanalysis in Freud's view were the description of the basic processes of mental life, metapsychology, and the identification and especially the investigation of the origin and development of the psychic illness, psychopathology. The first is ultimately described in terms of the instincts/drives and their structures (id, ego, superego), and the latter is told against the background of his psychosexual stages from infancy through adolescence.

In terms of religion, since neither the gods nor the monotheistic, patriarchal God partake of this circumscribed "reality"—as Laplace puts it well, the God-hypothesis is not needed in this account ("*Je n'avais pas besoin de cette hypothèse-là*")—Freud is left, or free, to label religion as an "illusion" (1964). The processes behind this projection and behavior are correspondingly described, much as dreams, in terms of wish-fulfillment and also obsessional neurosis. Put in another way, religion is a symptom of humans' mental immaturity, the need for parental protection from the existential challenges to life: suffering, instinctual privation, death. From *Civilization and Its Discontents*: "Its [religion's] technique consists in depressing the value of life and distorting the picture of the real world in a delusional manner" and thus, keeping its practitioners "in a state of psychical infantilism" (1961, 31–32). Consequently, in his *New Introductory Lectures on Psychoanalysis* Freud does not hesitate to state that for psychoanalysis, "religion alone is to be taken seriously as an enemy" (cited by Celia Brickman in Aron and Henik 2010, 27).

It is not a change concerning the ontological status of the gods, as it were, that characterizes many later post-Freudian directions, but a different view of humans and, correspondingly, the psychoanalytic enterprise itself. Actually, the hermeneutical turn demarcates a whole sea-change affecting scholarly work in all the social sciences and humanities. Tracy observes this "present interest across the disciplines in hermeneutics" (1987, 10), and attributes it to a crisis in the West in appropriating earlier foundational traditions and texts that are now experienced as profoundly riddled with "plurality and ambiguity" (8). More widely, Tracy argues that interpretation is a necessary platform for such quintessential activities as "experience, understanding, deliberation, judgment, decision, and action," for "to be human is to be a skilled interpreter." While Tracy ties hermeneutics to the quest for "meaningful action," the focus on meaning includes all of those human activities noted above (9).

For many psychoanalytic theorists, there is a shift from envisioning humans in terms of drives to seeing them in terms of constructing lives of meaning, as well as oriented toward objects/others. Meaning-making itself has come to be regarded as a fundamental human activity. As one critic, Anthony Elliott, states it, "The psyche is the launching pad from which people *make meaning*." This understanding has become so prominent that Freud's legacy is reformulated by Elliott, not without some justification: "Freud compels us to question, to endeavor to reflect upon, the construction of meaning—representations, ideas, affects, desires—and the mode of subjectivity implicated in the fabrication of signification" (1999, 7). Lewis Aron confirms this perspective on the master in his statement,

"For Freud... to interpret (*Deutung*) was to assign meaning (*Beduetung*) to the patient's material" (1996, 93–94).

Still, the new hermeneutical paradigm distances many analysts from part of the Freudian legacy. Instead of uncovering the structures of the mind and the repressed past of the patient, the various schools and streams are now seen as constructing alternative models of thinking and acting. As Stephen Mitchell sees it: "The analytic method is not archeological and reconstructive; it does not simply expose what is there. Rather, it is constructive and synthetic; it organizes whatever is there into patterns it itself supplies" (1993, 56).

Speaking from within the same broad relational stream of post-Freudian psychoanalysts, Lewis Aron and Adrienne Harris identify that "the core activity of psychoanalytic work," once again, is "meaning making" (Aron and Harris 2005, 311), and Karlen Lyons-Ruth writes about the patient and therapist working together to deconstruct old, limited meanings and "constructing more integrated, flexible, and hopeful ways of making meaning and being together" (342). Finally, Mitchell summarizes well the shift within psychoanalytic practice:

> What the patient needs is not a rational reworking of unconscious infantile fantasies... (but) a revitalization and expansion of his own capacity to generate experience that feels real, meaningful, and valuable. (1993, 24)
>
> [Adding that] The term meaningful here refers to a sense of personal value, importance, and devotion. (234)

Hans Loewald's Treatment of Meaning

The word "meaning" has a precise use and plays a very important role in Hans Loewald's thought. As we saw in previous chapters, he holds that the earliest experiences of the infant constitute the base of mental activity and are in various ways repeated in later, especially intense, relationships with others. Loewald labels the infantile and foundational psychic operations as "primary process" activity.[4] The primary process is unconscious and primitive, "unitary, non-differentiating, non-discriminating between various elements or components of a global event or experience." What are described as higher mental operations constitute Loewald's "secondary process" mentation. Here "*duality* and multiplicity are dominant, i.e. differentiation, division, a splitting of what was unitary, global, unstructured oneness" (2000, 196). These mental operations and behavior are ascribed by Loewald to the preconscious, his term is "*conscient*" processes (1978, 16), which are more than just ways of operation susceptible to conscious direction, but utilize distinctions, relations, self-reflection, and, ultimately, responsibility.

For Loewald, health and meaning arise from the creative interweaving of the two processes, of these two ways of addressing the world. In his words:

> It is this interplay between unconscious and consciousness, between past and present, between the intense density of undifferentiated, inarticulate experience and the lucidity of conscious articulate experience, that gives meaning to our life. Without such meaning-giving play we have no future of our own. Perhaps what we call man's symbolizing activity is that play.
>
> (1978, 49–50)

Loewald titles the third and final part of his famous Freud lectures at Yale University "Comments on Religious Experience." The connections between psychoanalytic concerns and religion, via the shared focus on meaning, are elaborated in two ways. In his words:

> Some aspects of religious experience are related to unconscious mental processes. Other aspects of religious life and thought can be approached by interpreting them in terms of the emergent dialectic between unconscious and conscient mentation, roughly speaking, between the irrational and the rational.
>
> (1978, 57)

The first connection, which is explored in a number of articles by James Jones (2001; 2002), points to the similarity between the realm of primary process mentation and "mystical and other timeless experiences" (Loewald 1978, 76). In both, there is what may be called "an experience of eternity" (62). It is the experience of a moment not of chronological or "objective" time, but of an instant of fullness. Here the total discrete elements of the life-history of the individual are condensed into this transient experience, with nothing lost. This may occur when an experience in the present triggers some powerful memories. Loewald writes, "These experiences take on a prototypical significance, as though they easily might stand for all experience, as though in them could be represented or fulfilled the essence, the sum total of our life, in archetypal form" (66). Through these events one gets in touch with the meaning of one's life; again in his words: "As experience augments and grows in an individual's life course, these instants, *in* time but not *of* time, contain more and more meaning which is poured into the *nunc stans*" (65). Thus, in this first instance, the psychoanalytic study of the unconscious highlights a particular type of experience of meaning, which is similar to the timeless oneness reported by religious mystics. It is in terms of this aspect that Loewald mentions Freud's reference to the author Romain Rolland, who maintained that the source of religion lay in what he described as an "oceanic" feeling (58–59).

For me, it is the second dimension that Loewald discusses that ties religion and psychoanalysis together in a most profound way. Above it was noted that he holds that "religious life and thought can be approached by interpreting them in terms of the emergent dialectic between unconscious and conscient mentation" (1978, 57). Similarly, at the very end of his *Lectures* he writes, "And the dialectic of id and ego/superego can be understood as paralleling the philosophical–theological or religious dialectic of eternity and temporality" (77). In religious terms this is the reflection and articulation (secondary process) of experiences of "eternity" (primary process), as well as the incorporating into one's everyday life or "temporality" (secondary process) the feeling and significance that is experienced in these undifferentiated instants (primary process). We saw before that it is in the context of this "dialectic" that Loewald writes about meaning.

In light of the significance that Loewald attributes to religious experience, reflection and life, toward the end of the lectures he speaks of the need for psychoanalysis to revise its traditional negative evaluation of religious experience: "We may be at the point where psychoanalysis can begin to contribute in its own way to the understanding of religious experience, instead of ignoring or rejecting its genuine validity or treating it as a mark of human immaturity" (1978, 73). Loewald's protest against Freud's standpoint, which he characterizes as "narrow and biased" (6), is clear.

There is a legitimate question of whether one can utilize Loewald's distinctive notions of meaning to exemplify contemporary developments in some areas of post-Freudian psychoanalysis, especially in any changed attitude toward religion. What are the referents and contexts for

Loewald's use of the term? Meaning refers to both a distinctive psychic process, this dialectic, and more broadly to an overall psychic organization characterized by integration, wholeness, comprehensiveness, and articulation, as well as responsibility. One of the *Lectures*, "Man as Moral Agent," focuses on this last feature, that effort "to own up to our own history, to be responsible for our unconscious" (1978, 21). Loewald sees as dangerous the exclusive reliance on or dominance of either primary process, as exhibited in psychosis, or secondary process, leading to neuroses. Meaning is also fashioned in a particular experience. In this experience the everyday ego is, in a sense, transcended. The individual's whole life is "poured" into one moment out of time. The meaning, however, is inexpressible. While this last, experiential context for the term "meaning" is probably distinctive to Loewald, at least within the post-Freudian stream, the discussion in terms of psychic processes and organization characterized by integration, wholeness, comprehensiveness, articulation, and, to some extent, responsibility is shared by many psychoanalytic theorists.

At this time, I would like to follow another rich vein in Loewald's reflections that clearly has many parallels within contemporary psychoanalysis. This is the connection between meaning and human relationality, that is, all of the different levels of the meeting of subjectivities/persons. Recounting some features of Loewald's reflections that highlight relationality, meaning arises from contact in the experience of the *nunc stans* with primary process mentation, and through the continual dialectic—what he terms "transference" (1978, 27)—between primary and secondary processes. We also saw that primary process activity is the individuation into the infant of the many-leveled processes of the mother–infant matrix. In addition, the mother's continual interactions and anticipations lead to the emergence of secondary process mentation, the infant's first sense of self and of its own mind. Further, secondary process reflection is itself depicted as a "*cons-cire*, a knowing-together… the internalization of an interplay originally occurring between the infant and his or her primary caretaker, mostly the mother, and then recurring in many other relationships" (13).[5] Finally, the analyst helps the patient to internalize this dialectic between primary and secondary processes in order to live-out a life of meaning and "responsibility" (21). In Loewald's words:

> [The analyst's] interpretation… brings the unconscious memory, reproduced in the here-and-now, into the context and on to the level

> of conscious thought. Under favorable circumstances, it enables the patient to connect or reconnect the two levels of mentation, to make the restructuring of the experience his own. (20–21)

The Place and Nature of Meaning in Relational Thought

In order to evaluate the wider relevance of Loewald's reflections concerning the issue of meaning and the possible tie to a re-evaluation of religion, we will now turn to some more recent post-Freudian expositions. The question that animates this exploration is: To what extent are contemporary psychoanalysts broadly identified with the relational tradition in accord with major elements of Loewald's position? This includes his view of the centrality of the issue of meaning in psychoanalysis, its relational dimension, the particular features of the term, and finally, his openness to or appreciation for religion.

A few additional statements about the recent prominence of the issue of meaning in psychoanalysis will convey the wide consensus concerning this development. Peter Fonagy and Mary Target write, "It is our premise that a crucial therapeutic aspect of psychoanalysis, for both children and adults, lies in its capacity to activate people's ability to find meaning in their own and other people's behavior" (see Aron and Harris 2005, 269). Steven Cooper ties the shift in psychoanalysis to his particular concern with the topic of hope in affirming that "psychoanalysis has moved from attempting to be a science of the retrospective (how wishes and compromise formations were forged in development and mediate experience) to being a way of understanding and making meaning of how wish and hope are influenced in the present" (2000, xvii). Jessica Benjamin's signature interest in intersubjectivity frames her view of this advance:

> In the past several years psychoanalytic work has undergone a radical change. The manifold ways in which we now try to grasp the meaning of the unconscious in terms of communication between ourselves and the other subject in the room have opened up the dialogic possibilities of intersubjectivity.
>
> (1995, 24)

Finally, Irwin Hoffman quotes the influential developmental psychoanalyst Daniel Stern: "Today we are most concerned with the emergence of meaning in experience that did not have meaning before, less and less concerned with what [Christopher] Bollas has aptly referred to as 'official psychoanalytic decoding'" (cited in Hoffman 1998, 21).

Many psychoanalytic theorists within the relational stream see the emergence of meaning as arising from various types of human interaction or "meetings," which is particularly clear in Mitchell's work. Mitchell believes that experience is always interpersonally mediated, and in particular that "the meanings generated by the self are all interactive products" (1993, 125). The particular focus on meaning in terms of a relational view of analysis is well elucidated by Aron:

> Meaning, in the analytic situation, is not generated by the analyst's rational (secondary) processing of the analysand's associations; rather, meaning is seen as relative, multiple, and indeterminate, with each interpretation subject to continual and unending interpretation by both analyst and analysand. Meaning is generated relationally and dialogically, which is to say that meaning is negotiated and coconstructed. Meaning is arrived at through "a meeting of minds."
>
> (1996, xii)

Benjamin's view that meaning is an essential gift from the other is clearly expressed in her words: "Recognition is that response from the other which makes meaningful the feelings, intentions, and actions of the self" (1988, 12).

At least in terms of the detail and extent that Loewald devotes to explaining his use of the term "meaning," his treatment is not characteristic of the contemporary psychoanalysts in our study. While the term plays a significant role in the latter's theories, it is not usually defined or explained in detail. A typical example of this appears in the "Introduction" to Lewis Aron and Karen Star's *A Psychotherapy for the People*, where a key sentence in their initial discussion of the central argument of the text begins, "While psychoanalysis continues to be the best promise we have for a humanistic, engaged therapeutic pursuit of meaning and relationship..." (2013, 12). However, this statement is not followed by an explanation of the term "meaning." Overall, as with the use of the term in most of our cases, it is just assumed that the reader understands what is meant. This approach is reinforced by another lacuna: The indices of this text and most of our other texts fail to list the term at all. Still, by weaving together fragments in the texts of five different psychoanalytic theorists—Mitchell, Benjamin, Aron, Ogden, and Hoffman, a portrait of their understandings of the term comes into view.

One of the main sources for examining Stephen Mitchell's view of the term "meaning" is the text *Relationality* (2000). What is particularly noteworthy about this treatment is that much of it occurs in the context of his discussion of, and clear concurrence with, Loewald's views about language, time, and memory. The integration of fantasy and reality into lived life is one of Loewald's key insights about meaning that Mitchell persistently explores. He concludes his chapter on "Language and Reality" with these words: "Meaning in human experience is generated in the mutual, dialectically enriching tension between fantasy and reality; each requires the other to come alive… For Loewald, only the enchanted life is a life worth living" (29).

Mitchell provides another glimpse of his understanding of the nature of meaning in a later reference to meaning and what might stand as its opposite, i.e., meaninglessness. This also occurs through a citation, in this case a quotation from Arietta Slade, about "listening for coherence, for the capacity to reflect upon and make sense of internal experience, and to listen for *incoherence*, of meaninglessness, of disorganization, and of disintegration, for moments when meaning cannot be made" (cited in Mitchell 2000, 86). For Mitchell, it is through interpretation, through putting an experience into a wider frame, that meaning is made. This is true although he recognizes that "experience is fundamentally ambiguous," that "its meaning is not inherent or apparent in it but… it lends itself to multiple understandings, multiple interpretations" (1993, 58).

The association Mitchell makes between meaning and the integration of different experiences and dimensions of mental activity is reinforced through an extended presentation in his text *Influence and Autonomy in Psychoanalysis* (1997). He writes:

> In my view, psychoanalysis has become a method for generating a certain kind of meaning, for fostering certain forms of experience and living… The way of life promoted by psychoanalysis operates in a matrix of dialectical tensions between conscious and unconscious thought and feelings; private sensations and public engagements; language and affect; past and present; actuality and imagination; verbal and nonverbal; bodily and psychical processes; social embeddedness

> and autonomous self-definition. These categories are not taken as polarities… but rather as interpenetrating and, in some sense, mutually creating each other. (24)

Overall, there is a clear and consistent use of the term "meaning" in Mitchell's work. Meaning points to the connection between "certain forms of experience and living." He highlights, as did Loewald, fantasy and reality, and the unconscious and conscious, but includes many other forms. Meaning's opposite, meaninglessness, refers to mental dimensions and lived experiences that cannot be creatively brought together in a wider system or order—actually, in a person's life. The phrase "matrix of dialectical tensions" is significant. It indicates that these diverse features, while often seen as opposite, as in "past and present; actuality and imagination," do not cancel each other out, or fight for prominence in a life. For example, health and maturity, that is, in some sense meaning, does not favor actuality or reality over imagination and fantasy. Additionally, their integration does not lead to some type of reductive, harmonious synthesis, but to a dialectic of tensions that allows each to sustain their integrity and also to have their proper time. Finally, Mitchell also sees meaning as related to experiences, and a life, that are intense, alive, vital. This comes across in the quotation cited earlier where "revitalization," "real," "valuable" seem to be synonymous with meaningful, as in "what the patient needs is a revitalization and expansion of his own capacity to generate experience that feels real, meaningful, and valuable" (1993, 24).

It is within the context of "recognition" that Benjamin discusses that important but often evanescent term in the psychoanalytic lexicon, i.e., meaning. For her, meaning, as in the meaning of a life, is a grant from the other. Through recognition of another as a subject in her or his own right, a person gives that other a sense of integrity and power. She writes in *Bonds of Love*, "Recognition is that response from the other which makes meaningful the feelings, intentions, and actions of the self. It allows the self to realize its agency and authorship in a tangible way." Importantly, Benjamin adds to this the dual nature of recognition, that is, that acknowledgment of oneself can only be substantial if the self regards that giving other as significant herself. Thus, we have: "But such recognition can only come from an other whom we, in turn, recognize as a person in his or her own right" (1988, 12). In the text, a particular interaction between infant and mother illustrates the creation of meaning: "Now, when the infant reaches excitedly for a toy, he looks up to see if mother is sharing his excitement; he gets meaning when she says, 'Wow!'" Here, meaning concerns recognition and confirmation through a sense of sharing feelings, and contacting the other's mind (30).

Benjamin draws upon elements in Hegel's discussion of the master–slave relationship for her view that meaning arises from the recognition of a self by the other. She elaborates that in Hegel's scenario, the subject "must be able to find himself in the other. The self can be known by his acts—and only if his acts have meaning for the other do they have meaning for him" (1988, 32). For Hegel, this proposition leads to a situation of conflict, where both the self and the other struggle for dominance, but also, paradoxically, require each other. Benjamin disputes Hegel's conflict scenario through her specific view of the mutuality of recognition:

> It is certainly true that recognition begins with the other's confirming response, which tells us that we have created meaning, had an impact, revealed an intention. But very early on we find that recognition between persons—understanding and being understood, being in attunement—is becoming an end in itself. Recognition between persons is essentially mutual. By our very enjoyment of the other's confirming response, we recognize her in return.
>
> (1995, 33)

In more recent presentations, Benjamin reaffirms her understanding of the creation of meaning through the terminology of "thirdness."[6] The third and thirdness refer to that dynamic, intersubjective space between persons where there is both respect for difference and a shared experience of recognition (2007, 3, 5). In this context, she offers: "Thirdness is felt as mental space to negotiate meaning. I am free to confer meaning, I respond out of my own sense of agency and authorship, rather than feeling myself merely acted upon, impinged upon, having to react" (6).

For Lewis Aron the term "meaning" is often tied to narrative and interpretation. He agrees with many theorists, including Mitchell, who see the practice of psychoanalysis as "fundamentally a study of meanings" (Aron 1996, 37). Meanings are generated as the analyst and patient co-construct compelling stories about the patient's life. In his words, "The analyst assembles, on the basis of psychoanalytic theory, a coherent picture of the patient's life that takes on a 'narrative truth' rather than being a 'historic truth'" (37). He stresses that interpretation, placing experience into these wider contexts and stories, is not just verbal. The whole interaction between analyst and patient, which would include conscious and unconscious, conceptual and affective, "*is* itself interpretative, which is to say that it conveys meaning" (214). The passionate, bodily component of meaning in the psychoanalytic context is also introduced through his expression of "felt meaning," as in the statement about psychoanalysis' "primary concern with felt meaning, significance, purpose and value" (2004, 444).

Thomas Ogden's discussion of meaning in *Reverie and Interpretation* reflects the originality of his perspective and insights, while at the same time it can be seen to augment our developing portrait of the use of that term in psychoanalysis (2004). Following his overall interest in "reverie," he stresses the non-conceptual feature of psychoanalytic meaning, even as this is conveyed through words:

> Meaning is *in* the language and the effects created by it. We listen *to* the language, not through it. (214)
>
> When I refer to effects created in language, I am placing emphasis on a dimension of language usage in which the creation and communication of meanings/feelings is indirect, that is, relatively independent of what is being said (at the level of the semantic content of language). (225)

In his expression "meaning/feelings" the two are totally intertwined. Ogden is also very interested in the instability and flexibility of words, of meaning/s. Experiences must be open to multiple interpretations, and each of these can develop as well as change over time. He writes:

> It is important that words be used (and read) in a way that allows their accrued meanings to be altered by (and to affect) each new emotional context in which they are spoken or written or read. (4)
>
> It is essential that the analyst's language embody the tension of forever being in the process of struggling to generate meaning while at every step casting doubt on the meanings "arrived at" or "clarified." (218)

The chapter title "The Dialectic of Meaning and Mortality in the Psychoanalytic Process"[7] in Irwin Hoffman's *Ritual and Spontaneity in the Psychoanalytic Process* communicates both the significance of the term for the author as well as the overall theme in his treatment (1998). The extensive focus on meaning, as well as the philosophical nature of many of his reflections, are distinctive to this text. There is an existentialist cast to Hoffman's fundamental position that the meaning sought and constructed in analysis must be forged against the background of life's insecurity and human mortality. He expresses this as: "The psychoanalytic situation is a particular instance of the effort to construct meaning and affirm worth in a highly skeptical, unstable, and uncertain world" (xviii). A list of the constituents of meaning can be ascertained by examining what he sees as some of the goals of analysis. These would include those senses of integrity, completeness, personal responsibility, agency, and especially, of worth and being loved. For Hoffman, and most other psychoanalysts, the analytic relationship is also seen as readdressing problems that first arose in the relationship between infant and parents (11).

In summary, in terms of the psychoanalytic discussion of meaning, while some elements of Loewald's exploration are unique, at least two features are omnipresent in the other psychoanalytic writings that we have been following. First, he finds that "the interplay between unconscious and consciousness, between past and present… gives meaning to our life" (1978, 49–50). This theme of interplay, which also includes the rational and irrational or fantasy and reality, is repeated by all of the theorists. Meaning refers to both a distinctive dialectical psychic process and to an overall psychic organization characterized by integration, wholeness, comprehensiveness, and articulation. The understanding of meaninglessness as incoherence, disorganization, and disintegration confirms this finding. Still, as the word "dialectical" indicates, meaning is not equivalent to mental stasis or even some type of balance. Mitchell is representative in using the terminology of "dialectical tensions" to speak of the different areas of this integration, including such polarities as fantasy and reality, past and present, memory and immediate sensations, bodily and psychical processes, and the public and private spheres (1997, 24).

Second, Loewald's discussion of meaning as an intersubjective product, in particular, arising from the interaction between mother and infant or analyst and analysand, is echoed in the wider literature. In Aron's words, "Meaning [in analysis] is generated relationally and dialogically, which is to say that meaning is negotiated and co-constructed" (1996, xii). Benjamin's view of recognition makes explicit important facets of this insight. Meaning emerges through the confirming response of another, a response which provides a sense of authorship and agency, as well as contact with another's mind. All would wholeheartedly agree with Hoffman to add to this list a sense of being valued (1998, 11).

There are many additional features in the use of the term "meaning" spread across the literature. Theorists share the view that human experience is both ambiguous and open to multiple interpretations. Interpretation, or meaning, is created through incorporating particular experiences into wider narratives or self-stories. The bodily and affective dimensions of meaning are repeatedly taken into account, as Ogden emphasizes in his statement, "Meaning is *in* the language and the effects created by it" (2004, 214). This is especially significant because in contexts outside of psychoanalysis meaning is usually understood as exclusively conceptual. For the psychoanalysts, meaning is attributed to a life that is intense, alive, vital, and creative. Finally, Hoffman brings to the surface features that others also acknowledge in various ways. Especially important is the recognition that at least part of the background for the struggle for meaning are those existential features of insecurity, experiences of loss, and mortality.

A New Psychoanalytic Appreciation for Religion?

Finally, we will now ask whether any positive correlation can be established between the significance of meaning in Relational psychoanalysis and a deeper understanding or even appreciation of religious experience.[8] We will find that the question cannot be conclusively answered, since the evidence, as it were, is ambiguous.

Aron's position is quite clear in writing, "With its goal as the enhancement and revitalization of human experience, and in its primary concern with felt meaning, significance, purpose, and value, the sharp division between religion and psychoanalysis diminishes" (2004, 444). However, his strong view about the positive significance of religion is not necessarily the result of some recent psychoanalytic developments. Throughout his life he was deeply immersed in the Jewish tradition, and as indicated in his article "God's Influence on My Psychoanalytic Vision and Values," a belief in God was always central to his life and thought (2004).

The extent of openness to religious life and values is much more nuanced in other psychoanalytic theorists. Most of Mitchell's statements about religion are references to Freud's well-known opposition. In a chapter on

"Guilt and Self Pity," he suggests that religion provides problematic relief from the inescapable sufferings in life: "Thus a [religiously] contrived sense of guiltiness can serve as a psychological defense against a more genuine sense of pathos or sadness for oneself" (2003, 155). However, he also comments on Ludwig Feuerbach's view that God's attributes are just projections of dissociated human characteristics and powers as being "a highly oversimplified account of religion" (1988, 209). In a more extensive discussion of psychoanalysis and religion, Mitchell compares types of meaning in different discourses or "systems" (1997). He writes:

> Moral systems ground meaning in virtuous action; aesthetic philosophies find meaning in the interesting and diverting; religious traditions locate meaning in relation to a prime mover or designer of the universe. Psychoanalysis grounds meaning in the rich tapestry of experience. (25)

While this statement provides, through the lens of meaning systems, an interesting perspective, it makes no specific judgment about religion.

There seems to be an important development in Benjamin's approach to religion, as detailed in Chapter 2 of the present work. In her three main books, she characterizes religion in terms of two fundamental themes (1988; 1995; 1998). The first is that religion promises an illusory, utopian resolution to the exigencies of life. In reference to the Grand Inquisitor in Dostoyevsky's *The Brothers Karamazov*, she writes, "The Inquisitor responds that people do not want freedom and truth, which only cause deprivation and suffering; they want miracle, mystery, and authority" (1988, 5). Benjamin also identifies religion with submission to authority. She punctuates her analysis of the erotic novel *The Story of O* with religious allusions, writing:

> In this way, O's story, with its themes of devotion and transcendence, is suggestive of the surrender of the saints. The torture and outrage to which she submits is a kind of martyrdom, seeming "to her the very redemption of her sins"... But her desire to be known is like that of the sinner who wants to be known by God. (60)

However, in her later essays and presentations the approach to religion is more positive. She establishes a connection between the "third" and faith in her statement, "Historically the idea of the third has been connected to surrender or faith" (2012, 124) and quotes in this connection Marie Hoffman who writes, "The third, which thinkers would call the idea, is the true, the good, or more accurately the God relationship" (cited in Benjamin 2012, 124).

The portrait of religion in Hoffman's *Ritual and Spontaneity* is predominately negative (1998).[9] It follows in the wake of the previously explored themes such as his focus on human meaning, the challenge to this by mortality, and the constructivist view of both meaning and reality. In an eloquent philosophical exposition, Hoffman explains that a "psychobiological bedrock" is constituted by "the immutable, transcultural, transhistorical truth… that human beings create their worlds and their sense of meaning in the teeth of the constant threat of nonbeing and meaninglessness" (16). Death, however, is not just a threat to human meaning, it also creates the conditions for the significance and vitality that we attribute to our scarce, limited time on earth. In his words, death is "a kind of necessary boundary which gives impetus to the assignment of value and meaning to experience" (49). It is within this context that Hoffman equates religion with the illusory promise of immortality and the dichotomy of body and soul, which suggest an escape from death's clutches (41). The supernatural divine equally undermines the significance of life, as he states: "Once again, the attributes of the omnipotent and omniscient *supernatural* being, if they were somehow attached to a *human* being, would do violence to the very dimensions of living that they were intended to enhance" (248). Nevertheless, this is not the only stance Hoffman takes toward religion. Consistent with his view that meaning and reality are multi-layered and socially constructed, there is a minor thread in the text which suggests that religion is one system of meaning among others, one which provides some support to those facing adversity (255).

After the foregoing investigations, no consistent correlation can be documented between the prominent role of the concept of meaning in psychoanalytic discourse and an openness to and appreciation for religion. While the emergence of the issue of meaning is one factor that has introduced the possibility for psychoanalysts to reassess the value of religion, the possibility is not always realized. In the works of Mitchell, Benjamin, and Hoffman there are moments of breakthrough, but also a persistent, underlying, literalist suspicion concerning religious concepts and values. What distinguishes Loewald's approach to the issue of meaning is the unique connection he makes between the unconscious, or primary process, and "mystical and other timeless experiences" (1978, 76) or experiences of "eternity" (62). He also believes that conventional understandings of religious life and experiences are inadequate representations of some of its more "mature" insights and expressions.

The Jewish Philosophers' Treatment of Meaning

The theme of meaning, particularly in terms of the expression "the meaning of life," is explicit or implicit throughout the writings of the three modern Jewish philosophers Franz Rosenzweig, Martin Buber, and Emmanuel Levinas. This observation confirms the contention expressed earlier, that Religious Studies scholars have identified the ability to provide a meaning scheme for individual and social life as one of the most prominent features of religious systems. Reflections on this theme pervade the writings of these Jewish philosophers in the context of our examinations of the topics of loving the neighbor, intersubjectivity, transformation, language, and responsibility, i.e., the chapters of the present work. Rather than attempting a summation or amalgamation of these treatments, a particular lens will be utilized that reveals a specific but accurate constellation.

First presented in a series of university lectures in 1979 and later reworked as articles in 1981 and 1986, Levinas' "Notes on Meaning" admirably fulfills this task (1998, 152–171). The argument that traverses his essay includes all of the major contentions that define Levinas' work, underscoring the significance of the topic for his philosophy. He begins, typically, with a question: "Does thought have meaning only through the knowledge of the world?" An allusion to persons "preoccupied" with the issue of the "meaning of life" quickly indicates that his investigation extends beyond the arena of knowledge (152). However, the tone set by this reference is not without judgment, suggesting that these preoccupations are often only a matter of people posing, exchanging superficial talk about some topic of the day.[10] While the essay's early focus is on the problematic link between meaning and knowledge, this second concern is also of some importance. It foreshadows his insistence that meaning is not synonymous with simply being, that the question of meaning can only be answered through the recognition and acceptance of one's ethical indebtedness.

For Levinas, Edmund Husserl is "faithful" to both his philosophy and all of philosophy through the notion that "*all meaning begins in knowledge*" (1998, 161). Meaning in this case is totally circumscribed in a closed system. It is linked to consciousness, intentionality, knowledge, and presence. Meaning attends to that of which we are aware, to what can be placed into a fixed, all-inclusive network designated as knowledge. In this case the meaningful absorbs all difference; it defines all that can possibly exist within our present awareness—intentionality. Additionally, since it represents all that is, it is nothing less than an expression of Being itself. In Levinas' words:

> The notion of intentionality, when well understood, signifies at one and the same time that being commands the modes of access to being and that being *is* according to the intention of consciousness: intentionality signifies an exteriority in immanence and the immanence of all exteriority. (159)

Levinas again uses a question to underscore his underlying message, asking whether this is the true fate of meaning and the meaningful. Must one conclude that there is no "inner life" beyond reason, and that the dialogue between persons is limited to the exchange or "transmission of signs" (1998, 158)? Of course, his answer is that the "alterity" of "one I with another," that is, the realm of ethics, transcends this closed cognitive circle. In this case, it is not about observing the other, but in the presence of his or her face one is awakened or commanded in responsibility. This other meaning, "the meaningfulness of the face," is the "proximity of the other" (162).

The nature of my responsibility follows from those attributes expressed by the face. Its "nudity and destitution," "the defense-less itself" orders me (Levinas 1998, 162). It reminds me of my power over the other person, and also immediately evokes the command "Thou shalt not kill." The particularity of this command in turn "accuses me," "questions me, and lays claim to me," and most importantly, implies that I must do something, "as though, already, I were indebted" (163). To be in debt means that indifference is no longer (morally) possible. The other's vulnerability, that is, his or her mortality, is now "my affair." In other words, "The death of the other man implicates me… as if, by this death… I became the accomplice by way of my indifference" (162). Consciousness of the other's mortality is thus the fundamental sign of my loss of innocence, but it equally designates her or him as my "neighbor." At this point, part of that other category of meaning—unintentional and immemorial—becomes clear. As Levinas expresses this, "Death's meaning begins in the interhuman. Death signifies primordially in the very proximity of the other man or in sociality" (163).

The significance of the command not to kill in Levinas' unorthodox phenomenology of the face introduces the authentic meaning/use of the word "God." God is not a term expressed as a subject within a seamless discourse. Rather, "in the face of the other man," as the timeless—in the sense of out of time—source of that order and demand, the individual can recognize "a God who 'loves the stranger'… an invisible, unthematizable God." Responding to the other constitutes the true witnessing to the divine. Thus, the Infinite is only properly conveyed through a witnessing-to, an "*à*-Dieu." Levinas emphasizes the break out of temporality in his expression, "*A-Dieu,* for which diachronic time is its unique cipher, is at once devotion and transcendence" (1998, 166).

The section of Levinas' essay that directly addresses our issue is titled "The Meaning of the Human" (1998, 166). He holds that the meaning of human life does not reside in just living, but in being called and witnessing to one's responsibility for the other. Although phrased as a question, Levinas' declaration breaks through: "We are asking whether the humanity of man is defined only by that which man *is*, or whether in the face that *asks for me* a meaning other, and older, than the ontological one is in the process of becoming meaningful." The meaning of the human is mapped by the call to transcendence, to the possibility of "the unto-God-in-me" (167). In other words, "the meaning of life" only appears when "life awakens to humanity" (171). Levinas insists that this definition inscribes, is the guarantor of, the individual's identity and uniqueness as well. He writes, "This is an ethos of the irreplaceable going back to this responsibility. This identity of the I or of the 'oneself' signifies the character of the inalienable, attached to responsibility" (169).

In the course of elaborating this "regime" of that otherwise meaning of meaning—actually, Levinas believes that all uses of the term are derived from this original case—he directly takes issue with psychoanalysis (1998, 168). He characterizes psychoanalysis as a method "of seeing or knowing." It is about exploring another person's "own spontaneous and reflected consciousness." The problem in this for Levinas follows in the train of his main argument. Meaning, or alternately the health of the human, cannot be fathomed by way of an inquiry into the workings of consciousness.

He writes, "The meaning of the human is not measured by presence, not even by man's presence to himself" (167). As we saw, the quest for meaning opens to the ethical task of becoming human, to an "otherwise" dimension of our life that grounds or is the authentic meaning of living.

Through his own specific style and message, Levinas articulates the major themes concerning human meaning found in the philosophies of both Rosenzweig and Buber: Meaning emerges through the encounter between persons; this encounter also has a divine dimension; meaning is the basis for individual identity and uniqueness; it is expressed through a life of responsibility; speech is one of its carriers; and finally, meaning does not arise out of facing one's own death, it surmounts death. There are literally countless possible examples of these themes in Rosenzweig's and Buber's works, many of which punctuate this book as a whole, but only a few representative illustrations will be summoned at this time.

Levinas forcefully argues that meaning is not the attribute or adventure of the single person. It is not found, as commonly assumed, through some type of self-reflection, "even by man's presence to himself" (1998, 167). Meaning emerges through responding to the face of the neighbor and stranger. The interhuman principle behind Rosenzweig's and Buber's philosophies—in the former's "to be dependent on the other for what is ours" (1999a, 87), and the latter's "I require a Thou to become; becoming I, I say Thou" (1970, 62)—dictates that meaning is an interpersonal creation. Rosenzweig speaks in *Understanding the Sick and the Healthy* of uncovering meaning by way of "the voice of many callers," which, by summonsing the individual "to live his particular and unique present," points out the path to one's future (1999b, 83). Buber maintains that through the authentic encounter with another we find "a presence by means of which we are told that nevertheless there is meaning" (1965, 14).

The significant role of the divine, the *à-Dieu*, as in Levinas' "The face, as *à-Dieu*, is the latent birth of meaning" (1998, 168), is echoed in the two other Jewish philosophers. Although the individual is directed by "the voice of many callers," Rosenzweig holds that behind these "a single voice [of God] calls" (1999b, 83). Rosenzweig also uses the language of participating in the eternal truth or God's truth to express his view that meaning arises out of the relationship to the divine. We find in the *Star*: "Life verifies its own received and now shared truth as its share in the eternal truth" (2005, 439). In the third section of *I and Thou*, discussing the main features of revelation, Buber writes, "nor does the association [with the divine Thou] make life any easier for us—it makes life heavier but heavy with meaning… the inexpressible confirmation of meaning. It is guaranteed. Nothing, nothing can henceforth be meaningless" (1970, 158). Additionally, this divine dimension of meaning is often associated with trust. In *Understanding the Sick and the Healthy*, Rosenzweig writes, "To avail himself of today, man must, for better or worse, put his trust in God" (1999b, 93). Buber alludes to the two sides of this trust in his statement, "He [God] addresses me about something that he has entrusted to me and that I am bound to take care of loyally" (1965, 45).

All three philosophers understand meaning as confirming persons in their particular identity and uniqueness. Levinas discussed this above in the context of responsibility: "This identity of the I or of the 'oneself' signifies the character of the inalienable, attached to responsibility" (1998, 169). With Rosenzweig, following our source of *Understanding the Sick and the Healthy*, this is expressed as a summons by other persons to live in one's "particular and unique present" (1999b, 83). Buber's treatment of revelation in *I and Thou* includes the insight that "the meaning we receive can be put to the proof in action only by each person in the uniqueness of his being and in the uniqueness of his life" (1970, 159).

The connection between the meaning of being human and one's responsibility to the other is incontrovertibly the basis of Levinas' "Notes on Meaning." Rosenzweig expresses this understanding in terms of the commandment to love the neighbor, for it is this responsibility that delineates the uniqueness of one's path through the world (2005, 253–254). For Buber, the scope of this responsibility is even widened in the section "The Single One in Responsibility" (1965, 65–71). He writes, "And he, the Single One, must answer, by what he does and does not do, he must accept and answer for the hour, the hour of the world, of all the world, as that which is given to him, entrusted to him" (66).

The insight that human meaning is carried or even embodied in speech or language is common to these philosophers. Levinas sees the essence of speech, just like the ultimate expressiveness of the face, as grounded in the call of the other. He states this as: "Is this not the very significance of the face and of the original speaking that asks for me… awakes me or gives rise to my response or my responsibility?" (1998, 167). For Rosenzweig, language has a more than human origin and confirmation. The human word is permeated by the orienting word of God; as he states this, "The world is real only insofar as it enters into this process [the course of world events], a process which brings all of it within the context of the human word and God's sentence" (1999b, 74). Buber has a very vibrant notion of God's speech addressing each person at every moment in writing, "It [creation] happens… as speech directed precisely at him… But the sounds of which the speech consists… are the events of the personal everyday life" (1965, 16). In another place he writes of this address: "To man as man belongs the ever renewed event of the entrance of meaning into the living word" (1999, 104).

Does meaning arise through the confrontation with one's own death? The Jewish philosophers dramatically reject the positive reply to this question, as exemplified in the philosophy of Heidegger.[11] Levinas argues that if death's challenge is just about my death, if it is a matter of the self's right to be, then the issue of meaning is left in abeyance. For him, meaning ensues when a person rises beyond the concern with the self to attend to the neighbor and stranger. As Levinas expresses this, "Death's meaning begins in the interhuman. Death signifies primordially in the very proximity of the other man or in sociality" (1998, 163). The capstone of Rosenzweig's *The Star of Redemption* is the statement that "love… is as strong as death" (2005, 217). Initially this refers to abiding in God's love, but it is immediately transformed into the love of the neighbor. For, Rosenzweig reminds his readers, "as he (God) loves you, so shall you love" (220). For his part, Buber repeats the biblical insight about love's prowess:

> A *great* relation [the I–Thou relation or love] exists only between real persons. It can be strong as death, because it is stronger than solitude, because it breaches the barriers of a lofty solitude, subdues its strict law, and throws a bridge from self-being to self-being across the dread of the universe… for [the sake of] the perfect realization of the *Thou*.
>
> (1965, 175)

Two features of Levinas' "Notes" are inconsistent with the treatments of meaning by Rosenzweig and Buber. They concern the seemingly one-to-one correlation Levinas establishes between responsibility for the other and meaning, and the limited scope of meaning when the focus is entirely on "the face" and "proximity." While the two other philosophers concur that responsibility to the other is a central element in the meaning of a life, they do not see these as synonymous. In *Understanding the Sick and the Healthy*, Rosenzweig raises the questions of "life's purpose" and "*my* purpose" (1999b, 45). However, these questions are not given a specific answer. Rosenzweig's response is that such purposes are made clear only in the flow of life itself. To discover this, in Rosenzweig's words, "to avail himself of today, man must, for better or worse, put his trust in God" (93). Buber agrees with Levinas that the meaning of life, and of one's particular life, must be put "to the proof in action" (1970, 159). Yet, he also insists that this meaning, revealed through revelation, is ineffable, since "you do not know how to point to or define the meaning, you lack any formula or image for it" (159).[12]

For Rosenzweig and Buber, the issue of the meaning of a life must ultimately allude to one's community and to the wider human world. This understanding is manifest in the *Star*, whose third "book" concerns the two religious communities of Judaism and Christianity, and ultimately the community of all persons (2005). It also is expressed in terms of the love of neighbor: "Love is really oriented toward the embodiment of all those—men and things—that could at any moment take this place of its neighbor, in the last resort it applies to everything, it applies to the world" (234). Buber alludes to the context of one's community, politics, and history in discussing that meaning which entails responding to the call of the divine:

> The human person belongs, whether he wants to acknowledge it and take it seriously or not, to the community in which he is born or which he has happened to get into... The Single One, the man living in responsibility, can carry out his political actions as well... only from that ground of his being to which the claim of the fearful and kind God, the Lord of history and our Lord, wishes to penetrate.
>
> (1965, 66)

Overlaps and Unique Features

As stated earlier, no consistent correlation can be documented between the crucial place of the concept of meaning in contemporary psychoanalysis and an openness and appreciation for religion. Still, the emergence of the topic of meaning paves the way for a re-evaluation of religion, and certainly adds a fertile area to the dialogue between the post-Freudian psychoanalysts and the Jewish philosophers featured in this study. There are both overlaps and unique features in the understandings of the term "meaning" in psychoanalysis and in Jewish philosophy. The most important area of agreement concerns the insight that meaning is an intersubjective creation. A meaningful life cannot be seen as merely the product of a single individual; it is grounded in significant relationships. Aron concisely expresses this from the psychoanalytic perspective: "Meaning is generated relationally and dialogically, which is to say that meaning is negotiated and co-constructed" (1996, xii). Noteworthy is Benjamin's equation of recognition and meaning in her statement, "Recognition is that response from the other which makes meaningful the feelings, intentions, and actions of the self" (1988, 12). This intersubjective feature is echoed in Levinas' insistence on the "meaningfulness of the face" of the other (1998, 162), and Buber's discussion of revelation, that divine–human meeting, in terms of "the inexpressible confirmation of meaning" (1970, 158).

In all, there are three arenas in which the term "meaning" is used—or alternately, three dimensions of the concept of meaning—within the discourse of psychoanalysis: the intersubjective, the combination of intrapsychic and intersubjective, and life as a whole. First, as just mentioned, there is that understanding that "the meanings generated by the self are all interactive products" (Mitchell 1993, 125). Most remarkable is Benjamin's view that meaning is created in the very act of contacting another's mind, through such experiences as sharing feelings (1988, 30). The sense of being valued as a person by another is a further important feature that accrues to this domain. Second, psychoanalytic discourse attributes meaning to a distinctive, dialectical psychic process and to a wide-ranging psychic organization characterized by integration, wholeness, comprehensiveness, and articulation. In this sphere that combines the intrapsychic and the intersubjective, the integration of unconscious and conscious, fantasy and reality, the somatic and mental is central. Third, there is also an important concern with the life of vitality and creativity. In this context, a person's *uniqueness* is expressed through the *individuality* of her or his life of fantasy, creativity, and productivity.

Jewish philosophical discourse identifies two arenas for the use of the term "meaning": the sphere of divine–human interaction, and the domain of ethics.[13] First, the Jewish philosophers believe that there must be a transcendent, transforming call in order for a life to be fulfilled. The transcendent also provides the individual with an elemental trust in life and introduces the whole vocabulary about having a unique destiny. For example, Levinas alludes to this notion of destiny through the multi-layered term "election" (1998, 169). Second, they also insist that meaning can only accrue to a life that is driven by the fundamental responsibility for others. For the philosophers, *individuality* is expressed through the *uniqueness* of the tasks one is given, and the web of responsibilities woven throughout everyday life. Actually, the two uses—divine–human and ethical—of the term "meaning" in the Jewish philosophers' lexicon often overlap in this context, since God is seen as the source of ethics (revelation) and the origin (creation) and ultimate guide of the world (redemption). The individual's tasks and responsibilities mark out one's place in the community and even one's divine–human role or mission in world-history. The inclusion of the language of the divine in the discussion of meaning allows Buber to speak of this participation in, or responsibility for, "the being of the world":

> Each man stands in an objective relationship to others; the totality of this relationship constitutes his life as one that factually participates in the being of the world.... It is his share in the human order of being, the share for which he bears responsibility.
>
> (1999b, 121–122)

Thus, we have two fecund perspectives on meaning, both surveying important dimensions of human life. Levinas' statement about psychoanalysis, that it is limited to addressing "what is" or the immanent nature of the human, is meant as a critique, but it can also be seen as an acknowledgment of the authenticity of two different purviews.[14] His view of meaning, that the fully human life is not simply a given, that persons have a divine calling and ethical task, is powerful, but it is obviously dependent on a particular living faith in the transcendent. However, it is difficult to disagree with the portrait of a full human life, particularly in terms of the role of fantasy and creativity, proposed by the psychoanalysts. Does the appreciation for fantasy, creativity, and "the analytic third"—the insight that deep interactions between persons can open us up to unanticipated and unforeseen meaning—not attend to a transcendence within immanence? And, on the other hand, does not the language of the Jewish philosophers about the divine dimension of the interhuman offer a different viewpoint and vocabulary to speak of the origin of this miraculous *novum*?

Notes

1 See, for example, Mitchell (1993, 175).
2 In *An Outline of Psychoanalysis*, Freud speaks of putting "psychology upon foundations similar to those of any other science, such as physics" (1949, 105). Of course, there were many reasons for Freud's effort to utilize the current model of science. Loewald, for instance, sees Freud drawing upon science's "unprejudiced, objective attitude" (1978, 8), as well as his view of the "closeness of instinctual life to biological life" (10).
3 Freud's views are always more complex, intriguing, and suggestive than any account can present. At times he expresses a more hermeneutical as well as limited sense of the grasp of science (1949, 105–106).
4 While Freud also uses this expression, Loewald's style of referring to and transforming Freud's vocabulary is legendary. This aspect of his style is well described by James Jones in "Hans Loewald: The Psychoanalyst as Mystic," (2001, 794).
5 It is significant that Loewald, as well as Rosenzweig and Levinas, dispute the general view that thinking is essentially a monologue of the self with itself. Loewald's notion of "con-scire," Rosenzweig's conception of "speech-thinking" (1999, 86–87), and Levinas' view that the origin of thinking or "reason" can be traced to the response to the other (1969, 208), all portray thinking as dialogical. For Loewald and Levinas this—having the other in mind—is true for all thinking, and for Rosenzweig it is characteristic of authentic thinking.
6 See Chapter 2 of the present work.
7 Hoffman cites Ogden in providing a fine definition of "dialectic": "A dialectic is a process in which each of two opposing concepts creates, informs, preserves, and negates the other, each standing in a dynamic (ever changing) relationship with the other" (1998, 200).
8 There are other developments in psychoanalysis that further the possibility of such a re-evaluation of religion. These have been discussed in the course of this chapter and book, and are also recognized by psychoanalytic commentators. One of these is the widespread critique of science as being able to provide the ultimate, objective portrait of reality. Aron and Henik have directly linked this critique to the possibilities of dialogues similar to ours. They write:

> In accord with this shift in our view of science and rationality, our contemporary epistemology gives greater recognition to the subjectivity of the scientist and of the psychoanalyst… This shift creates the environment for interdisciplinary dialogue between religious studies, Jewish thought and modern psychoanalysis.
>
> (2010, 20)

Another change in psychoanalytic theory concerns the appreciation of fantasy and illusion, which Celia Brickman indicates "took the sting out of Freud's critique of religion as illusion" (Aron and Henik 2010, 33). She notes Winnicott's view of transitional space and the transitional object having deeply influenced the recognition of the positive role of illusion in human life:

> Winnicott names the product of this transitional activity *illusion*, understood not as a wishful defense against reality, but as part and parcel of how we navigate the relationship between external reality and our inner worlds. Transitional experience is seen as the source of creativity, and of cultural and religious expression throughout life. Many analysts who have contributed to the literature that has made room in psychoanalysis for a positive evaluation of religion have been greatly indebted to Winnicott's work. (32–33)

9 A more detailed presentation and critique of this topic is presented in the first section of the Conclusion of the present work.

10 Levinas' attitude comes through in the words, "the search for which still excites the talk, become quotidian, men and women claiming to be preoccupied with the 'meaning of life'?" (1998, 152).

11 Buber (1965, 163–181) and Levinas (2000, and innumerable other places) directly contest Heidegger's position that the confrontation with one's own death is the ultimate source of meaning. Levinas' position is explored in Chapter 6 of the present work.

12 Also see Buber's discussion in "The Question to the Single One" (1965, 68–69).

13 Many commentators identify the prominence of ethics in Jewish philosophy as one of its distinguishing features. In this vein Steven S. Schwarzschild writes, "The view held here… is that philosophy is Jewish by virtue of a transhistorical primacy of ethics" (Cohen and Mendes-Flohr 1988, 629).

14 Overall, these three Jewish philosophers do not condemn as illegitimate the perspectives of the natural or social scientific disciplines, such as biblical criticism or psychoanalysis. This certainly is the case with Buber's discussion with the psychologist Carl Rogers (Buber 1999b, 246–270). However, they do see these disciplines as unable to seriously attend to the fullness of the religious life. Rosenzweig writes:

> Just as the student of William James knows how to put every "religious experience" into the correct cubbyhole of the psychology of religion, and a Freudian student can analyze the experience into its elements of the old yet ever new story… We know it differently, not always and not in all things, but again and again. We know it only when—we do [that is, within individual and communal religious life]. (1961, 244)

In response to the Freudian conclusion that religion is just a self-delusion, Rosenzweig so characteristically quips, "It is your own fault if you run within striking distance of the psychologist's knife! Why did you blab?" (1961, 243).

References

Aron, Lewis. 1996. *A Meeting of Minds: Mutuality in Psychoanalysis.* Hillsdale, NJ: Analytic Press.

—. 2004. "God's Influence on my Psychoanalytic Vision and Values." *Psychoanalytic Psychology* 21 (3): 442–451.

Aron, Lewis and Adrienne Harris, eds. 2005. *Relational Psychoanalysis Volume 2: Innovation and Expansion.* Hillsdale, NJ: Analytic Press.

Aron, Lewis, and Libby Henik, eds. 2010. *Answering a Question with a Question: Contemporary Psychoanalysis and Jewish Thought.* Boston, MA: Academic Studies Press.

Aron, Lewis, and Karen Starr. 2013. *A Psychotherapy for the People: Toward a Progressive Psychoanalysis.* New York: Routledge.

Benjamin, Jessica. 1988. *The Bonds of Love: Psychoanalysis, Feminism, and the Problem of Domination.* New York: Pantheon Books.

—. 1995. *Like Subjects, Love Objects: Essays on Recognition and Sexual Difference.* New Haven, CT: Yale University Press.

—. 1998. *Shadow of the Other: Intersubjectivity and Gender in Psychoanalysis.* New York: Routledge.

—. 2007. "Intersubjectivity, Thirdness, and Mutual Recognition: A Talk Given at the Institute for Contemporary Psychoanalysis, Los Angeles CA." Institute for Contemporary Psychoanalysis. Accessed November 6, 2015. http://icpla.edu/wp-content/uploads/2013/03/Benjamin-J.-2007-ICP-Presentation-Thirdness-present-send.pdf.

—. 2012. "Beyond Doer and Done To: An Intersubjective View of Thirdness." In *Relational Psychoanalysis Vol. 4: Expansion of Theory*, edited by Lewis Aron and Adrienne Harris, 91–130. New York: Routledge.

Berger, Peter L. 1967. *The Sacred Canopy: Elements of a Sociological Theory of Religion.* Garden City, NY: Doubleday and Company.

Buber, Martin. 1965. *Between Man and Man.* Translated by Ronald Gregor Smith. New York: Collier Books.

—. 1970. *I and Thou.* Translated by Walter Kaufmann. New York: Charles Scribner's Sons.

—. 1999. *Martin Buber on Psychology and Psychotherapy: Essays, Letters, and Dialogue.* Edited by Judith Buber Agassi. Syracuse, NY: Syracuse University Press.

Campbell, Colin. 2001. "A New Age Theodicy for a New Age." In *Peter Berger and the Study of Religion*, edited by Linda Woodhead, Paul Heelas, and David Martin, 73–85. London: Routledge.

Cohen, Arthur A., and Paul Mendes-Flohr, eds. 1988. *Contemporary Jewish Religious Thought: Original Essays on Critical Concepts, Movements, and Beliefs.* New York: Free Press.

Cooper, Steven H. 2000. *Objects of Hope: Exploring Possibility and Limit in Psychoanalysis.* Hillsdale, NJ: Analytic Press.

Elliott, Anthony, ed. 1999. *Freud 2000*. New York: Routledge.
Freud, Sigmund. 1949. *An Outline of Psychoanalysis*. Translated by James Strachey. New York: W. W. Norton and Company.
—. 1961. *Civilization and Its Discontents*. Translated and edited by James Strachey. New York: W. W. Norton and Company.
—. 1964. *The Future of an Illusion*. Translated by W. D. Robson-Scott. Garden City, NY: Anchor Books.
Geertz, Clifford. 1973. *The Interpretation of Cultures*. New York: Basic Books.
Hoffman, Irwin Z. 1998. *Ritual and Spontaneity in the Psychoanalytic Process. A Dialectical–Constructivist View*. Hillsdale, NJ: Analytic Press.
Jones, James W. 2001. "Hans Loewald: The Psychoanalyst as Mystic." *Psychoanalytic Review* 88 (6): 793–809.
—. 2002. "The Experience of the Holy: A Relational Psychoanalytic Analysis." *Pastoral Psychology* 50 (3): 153–164.
Levinas, Emmanuel. 1969. *Totality and Infinity: An Essay on Exteriority*. Translated by Alphonso Lingis. Pittsburgh, PA: Duquesne University Press.
—. 1981. *Otherwise Than Being or Beyond Essence*. Translated by Alphonso Lingis. The Hague: Martin Nijoff Publishers.
—. 1998. *Of God Who Comes to Mind*. Translated by Bettina Bergo. Stanford, CA: Stanford University Press.
Loewald, Hans W. 1978. *Psychoanalysis and the History of the Individual: The Freud Lectures at Yale*. New Haven, CT: Yale University Press.
—. 2000. *The Essential Loewald: Collected Papers and Monographs*. Hagerstown, MD: University Publishing Group.
Mitchell, Stephen A. 1988. *Relational Concepts in Psychoanalysis: An Integration*. Cambridge, MA: Harvard University Press.
—. 1993. *Hope and Dread in Psychoanalysis*. New York: Basic Books.
—. 1997. *Influence and Autonomy in Psychoanalysis*. Hillsdale, NJ.: Analytic Press.
—. 2000. *Relationality: From Attachment to Intersubjectivity*. Hillsdale, NJ: Analytic Press.
—. 2003. *Can Love Last?: The Fate of Romance Over Time*. New York: W. W. Norton and Company.
Ogden, Thomas H. 2004. *Reverie and Interpretation: Sensing Something Human*. Lanham, MD: Jason Aronson.
Rosenzweig, Franz. 1961. *Franz Rosenzweig: His Life and Thought*. Edited by Nahum N. Glatzer. New York: Schocken Books.
—. 1999a. *Franz Rosenzweig's "The New Thinking."* Edited and translated by Alan Udoff and Barbara E. Galli. Syracuse, NY: Syracuse University Press.
—. 1999b. *Understanding the Sick and the Healthy: A View of World, Man, and God*. Translated by Nahum Glatzer. Cambridge, MA: Harvard University Press.
—. 2005. *The Star of Redemption*. Translated by Barbara E. Galli. Madison, WI: University of Wisconsin Press.

Saler, Benson. 1993. *Conceptualizing Religion: Immanent Anthropologists, Transcendent Natives, and Unbounded Categories*. New York: Berghahn Books.

Smith, Jonathan Z. 1978. *Map is Not Territory: Studies in the History of Religion*. Leiden: Brill.

Tracy, David. 1987. *Plurality and Ambiguity: Hermeneutics, Religion, Hope*. San Francisco, CA: Harper & Row.

Chapter 6

Beyond "Betrayal"

On Responsibility

Hans Loewald and Emmanuel Levinas were two of Martin Heidegger's many students of Jewish heritage[1] who felt betrayed by him when he both spoke and acted in strong support of the Nazi regime. Their anguish was vividly expressed: "I am deeply grateful for what I learned from him [Heidegger], despite his most hurtful betrayal in the Nazi era, which alienated me from him permanently" (Loewald 2000, xlii–xliii), and "One can forgive many Germans, but there are some Germans it is difficult to forgive. It is difficult to forgive Heidegger" (Levinas 1990a, 25). While haunted by their teacher's treachery, they could not completely divorce themselves from his influence, or refuse to admit his important intellectual legacy. This complex, ambivalent stance is similar to what Richard Wolin finds in his study of some of Heidegger's other Jewish students (2001). As he writes in *Heidegger's Children*, "his 'children' sought to philosophize *with Heidegger against Heidegger*, thereby hoping to save what could be saved, all the while trying to cast off their mentor's long and powerful shadow" (7–8).

This study will begin with a concise account of Heidegger's relation to Nazism, followed by a précis of his 1927 classic *Being and Time*, focusing on the view of responsibility and the wider purview of human relations. It will then turn to discussions of the complex responses to Heidegger seen through Loewald's psychoanalytic understanding of intersubjectivity and responsibility, and through Levinas' philosophic rendering of these themes. The concluding section will widen the presentation to examine the importance given to responsibility in some post-Freudian psychoanalytic deliberations, and in the work of the two modern Jewish philosophers Franz Rosenzweig and Martin Buber.

Heidegger argued that a person's life is irrelevant to her or his philosophic legacy, and his supporters add that, despite his activities in the early 1930s, his philosophy itself was unrelated and uncontaminated. His relationship to National Socialism is well documented. The most overt acts of support occurred during the first year of the regime, 1933. Heidegger took over as Rector of the University of Freiburg and was vigilant in enforcing one of the earlier Nuremberg laws, the "law for the Preservation of a Permanent Civil Service," which banned Jews from government service, including at Germany's universities. In his inaugural address he lauded the new "spiritual" movement of the time and affirmed its ties to his own work as well as to the fate of the people, history, and Being. Jacques Derrida wrote of this, "[The *Rectorship Address*] capitalizes on the worst... the sanctioning of Nazism and the gesture that is still metaphysical" (1989, 40). Heidegger infamously declared in one speech of the time, "Let not ideas and doctrines be your guide. The *Führer* is the only German reality and its law" (cited in Wolin 2001, 10). Those Jewish students still working with him, including his intimate Hannah Arendt, were sent away. He prevented his famous mentor of Jewish descent, Edmund Husserl, from using the university library in his old age, and also withdrew the dedication to Husserl in the second edition of *Being and Time*. Although Heidegger remained as Rector for only one year, he had enough time to fully implement the regime's will. These were not isolated incidents. Heidegger gave earlier speeches that were blatantly anti-Semitic, and he never repudiated or apologized for what he had said and done. At the end of the war a university commission found him guilty of actively supporting the National Socialists and permanently took away his right to teach (Wolin 2001).

As Wolin indicates, Hannah Arendt, Karl Löwith, Hans Jonas, and Herbert Marcuse, who were also some of Heidegger's Jewish students, responded to their teacher's treachery with, minimally, a critique of his work. They saw his flirtation with evil as an extension of themes in *Being and Time*, and were particularly interested in exploring deeper notions of human relationships and responsibility. In particular, in a study that compared Heidegger and the Jewish philosopher Franz Rosenzweig, Löwith insisted that Heidegger's fall was not accidental, but fully corresponded to his philosophy. As he states it, "This political commitment... was not—as naïve people thought—a deviation from the main path of his philosophy" (1942, 75).

Heidegger's *Being and Time*

It was around the time of the publication of *Being and Time* that Loewald and Levinas studied with Heidegger, and it was in relation to that text that their later responses should be understood. On the first page, Heidegger affirms that the aim of the book is "to work out the question of the meaning of *Being*" (1962, 19), which is the problematic of "fundamental ontology" (227). For him, Being cannot properly be comprehended by ferreting out some essence, as philosophy had insistently attempted throughout its history. Rather, Being should be understood as it shows itself, that is, in its acts or in time. In this context, he focuses on the one entity for whom "Being is an *issue* for it" (32), that is *Dasein* or the existing individual. The issue of the meaning of its existence is not only distinctive to humans, but essential or constitutional. To understand this, one must explore Dasein "in its temporality and historicality" (42).

The central issue for Dasein has to do with the authenticity of its own existence, whether it decisively chooses itself or just loses itself in the everyday world. Living in the world, humans are initially concerned with attending to things, doing things, making things. Humans do not just stand and observe things in an uninvolved manner, but turn to them with purposes. The first kinds of entities that Dasein finds, at hand as it were, are equipment or tools. This points to persons coming to be in a world of human-fashioned objects already there.

In understanding how humans exist in the world, it is to their principal emotions or moods that one must turn. Moods are in this way prior to and more definitive than ideas in disclosing the nature of human existence. The three most revealing moods are fear, evasion, and anxiety. These show Dasein as thrown into a world, not first choosing itself or the universe around it, and concerned with how it is to live in this given situation. One primary feature of Dasein is its ability to project itself into the future by assessing its possibilities within a world already there.

In the midst of the everyday, Dasein is cast into public life, lost in the "they" with its idle talk, superficial curiosity, and amorphous ambiguity. This is a fallen life of inauthenticity and alienation from itself. The sole escape from this is achieved by turning away from others ("all its relations to any other Dasein have been undone" (Heidegger 1962, 294)) and facing the reality of one's own death. In facing death, a person comes to discover who he or she really is to be. As Heidegger writes, "Death is Dasein's *ownmost* possibility. Being towards this possibility discloses to Dasein its *ownmost* potentiality-for-Being, in which its very Being is the issue" (307).

It is conscience that calls Dasein out of its fallenness into the they, to the possibility of choosing itself. This is also expressed in terms of guilt: "The call of conscience has the character of an *appeal* to Dasein by calling it to its ownmost potentiality-for-Being-its-Self; and this is done by way of *summoning* it to its ownmost Being-guilty" (Heidegger 1962, 314). Guilt refers to the state in which Dasein first finds itself, the default position of "irresoluteness," "of one's lostness in the 'they'" (345). Still, Dasein has the ability to take over guilt with resoluteness.

Yet, authenticity requires more than resoluteness in the present about one's future living in the face of death. It also entails standing up to one's historicity or anchorage in the past. One must take up, even choose, who one already is and where one already stands—fate—while being aware at the same time that this fate with which one finds oneself is actually unchosen. Heidegger closes the penultimate section with an appropriate concluding statement for the whole work: "Resoluteness constitutes the *loyalty* of existence to its own Self" (1962, 443).

What is the place of other persons in this scenario? Other persons do exist and they are significant features of living in the world. However, as we saw, before looking at others, *Being and Time* considers cultural things, tools, that are ready-at-hand. When others are encountered, it is always from a perspective of one's own interests. As Heidegger states it, "In characterizing the encountering of *Others*, one is again still oriented by that Dasein which is in each case one's *own*" (1962, 154). Still, other persons are not treated as things or tools, but are objects of a special kind of concern called "solicitude" (*Fürsorge*). Solicitude may be something superficial or significant. Superficial solicitude, which has many forms, helps the other evade responsibility to himself or herself, and the need for resoluteness. True solicitude aids or frees the other in recognizing the need to decisively make oneself in the face of death. Heidegger writes, "It helps the Other to become transparent to himself *in* his care and to become *free for* it." However, he does not describe this type of positive solicitude further, and even notes that such an effort would be "beyond the limits of this investigation" (1962, 159). Thus, while the author of *Being and Time* does present this dimension of "being with" others, it is dwarfed by the importance of the topic of being lost in the crowd. Further, this relationship is only an existential possibility, neither a responsibility, nor a requirement for one's own authenticity.

Overall, in *Being and Time*, conscience, guilt, authenticity, and responsibility are not achieved in human relationships, but are clearly self-referential, although there is also a continuing refrain that the referent is not just the self, but the call of Being or one's own being. The preponderance of human relationships are alienating, and, most importantly, deceptively so. Only by breaking off relationships is authenticity achieved. The sole test of life is facing death, and this individualizes in the most extreme form. In Heidegger's words, "The non-relational character of death, as understood in anticipation, individualizes Dasein down to itself" (1962, 308). In essence, Dasein is constituted by a deep-seated concern for itself and its responsibility is solely to itself.

Finally, to say that *Being and Time* is a complex and ambiguous book is an understatement. There is no one "true" reading, but there are good and bad readings and I submit that this brief discussion is a balanced one. It follows a number of critics, in particular, Löwith (1942), Martin Buber (1965), and some feminist theorists, including Tina Chanter (2001). Despite the many attempts to uncover, extend, or augment hints in *Being and Time* concerning the responsibility to others,[2] there is, at the least, no rejoinder to John Caputo's challenge that entirely missing is "the body in need, the body of the suffering, the bodies of those who lay claim to those who are well-off" (1993, 68).

Hans Loewald: A "Heideggerian Reworking of Freud"

While I do not want to suggest that the complicated relationship of Hans Loewald toward his teacher provides the single key to understanding his tremendously vital and original oeuvre, that relationship does highlight some of its essential features.[3] Loewald studied with Heidegger for three years until 1926. Stephen Mitchell writes of the influence of Heidegger that "in many respects, Loewald's life's work might be regarded as a kind of Heideggerian reworking of Freud's basic concepts" (2000, 11–12). Despite this, there are few direct references to Heidegger in Loewald's corpus. Two of the most extensive are written around the same period, in 1978–1979, after many decades of virtual silence.

Loewald's deeply reflective essays *Psychoanalysis and the History of the Individual* (1978), which were delivered as the *Freud Lectures* at Yale University, include a long reference to Heidegger. This comes, fittingly, in his first lecture "Man as Moral Agent," in the context of the discussion of the developmental step of integrating the unconscious material of the id into the higher organization of ego. He calls this process "owning up," that is, owning or personally taking up desires, fantasies, and memories that are embedded in the mind, but not originally chosen by or with the consent of the subject. Loewald writes:

> This appropriation, this owning up, integrating the id into one's life context as an individual self, is then a developmental task or, in a different framework, an existential task. I believe that Heidegger's concepts of *Geworfenheit*—man is thrown into the world, unplanned and unintended by himself—and *Entwerfen*—the taking over and actively developing the potentialities of this fact—have grown in the same soil.

A footnote follows these lines, which refers to *Being and Time* and notes that Heidegger's "philosophical elucidation of human existence" is different from Freud's psychoanalytic discourse, which includes "the differentiation of unconscious and conscious mentation [mental activity]." Still, both authors hold to the notion: "Become what you are" (19).

Heidegger's name also appears in the "Preface" to *Papers on Psychoanalysis*, articles published between 1951 and 1979. A part of this passionate and revealing paragraph was already included at the beginning of this chapter:

> Philosophy has been my first love. I gladly affirm its influence on my way of thinking while being wary of the peculiar excesses a philosophical bent tends to entail. My teacher in this field was Martin Heidegger, and I am deeply grateful for what I learned from him, despite his most hurtful betrayal in the Nazi era, which alienated me from him permanently.
>
> (Loewald 2000, xlii–xliii)

This statement is followed by a reference to Freud as someone "who has remained for me, through his writings, that living presence" (xliii).

It is clear from the above citations that Loewald does not completely leave either philosophy or Heidegger behind when he takes up his vocation as a psychoanalyst. The former, his "first love," is not totally spurned. This is explicit in his acceptance and interpretation of the challenge that the *Freud Lectures* entailed. In the "Preface" he says that he sees himself as being asked "to attend to and articulate some of the wider humanistic and philosophical implications of psychoanalysis and its influence on modern life and contemporary sensibility" (1978, ix–x). At the end of the *Lectures* he returns to this note, offering that they "turned out to be… tentative philosophical reflections on psychoanalysis." However, he also admits that this is not accidental, since "some of the things I have discussed I have wanted to say for a long time" (77). Anticipating what we will soon explore, it appears that he actually had been saying many of these things for a long time.

Two essential features of philosophy, which have important positions in *Being and Time*, were perennial concerns for Loewald. The first is that "love of truth or wisdom" which is built into the constitution of the Greek word itself, *philo-sophia*. For Heidegger, the goal of his book is to understand the truth of Being as revealed through the truth of human existence, Dasein. In the essay "Psychoanalytic Theory and the Psychoanalytic Process" Loewald discusses that "love of truth" which he saw animating all scientific endeavors, especially as practiced in psychoanalysis (2000). He writes that "in our field the love of truth cannot be isolated from the passion for truth to ourselves and *truth in human relationships*" (297; my emphasis). It is this latter, relational aspect that is of overriding importance to him, while clearly peripheral to his teacher.

This departure from Heidegger is also evident in that goal of self-knowledge which has defined philosophy from its beginning, encapsulated in the famous Socratic maxim to "Know thyself." In *Being and Time* Dasein has as its distinguishing feature the solitary task of uncovering the meaning of its existence. Loewald's understanding of this quest highlights intersubjectivity or "interrelatedness," the view that the self cannot be known independently of its multifaceted relationships with others (2000). He writes:

> Our object, being what it is, is the other in ourselves and our self in the other. To discover truth about the patient is always discovering it with him and for him as well as for ourselves and about ourselves. And it is discovering truth between each other, as the truth of human beings is revealed in their interrelatedness. (297–298)

There is a haunting reference in Loewald's earlier cited comments about philosophy that cannot be left unaddressed: his statement about "being wary of the peculiar excesses a philosophical bent tends to entail" (2000, xlii). It is not entirely evident what Loewald has in mind here, but there are hints in some of his reflections that we have just read. It might be a reference to the tendency of philosophic thought to become an end in itself, ignoring life concerns. More pointedly, in keeping with Loewald's dedication to the "truth of human beings… in their interrelatedness" (298), it undoubtedly includes the idea that truth cannot be separated from care for or treatment of the other in her or his concrete life; in other words, truth must be therapeutic.

Fundamental to Loewald's work are those twin concepts of Heidegger, *Geworfenheit* and *Entwerfen*, to which he refers earlier. The first points to Heidegger's insistence that philosophy cannot start with an examination of the human abstracted from the tangible situation in which life is lived ("facticity"). Heidegger's account of Dasein, the being there of human existence, includes such features as language, the cultural heritage, and particularly, the inevitability of death. Loewald also grounds his reflection and therapy in concrete life. The "thrown into the world, unplanned and unintended by himself" for Loewald significantly adds the Freudian legacy, which includes the unconscious, repression, transference, and defense (1978, 19). He sees these processes as driven by one's "ghosts" from the past (2000, 248–249), those repudiated dreams, wishes, fantasies, and memories, as well as the earliest relations with parents. Freud's "living presence" is also felt in Loewald's insistence that the body in all of its material and sensible dimensions not be ignored (xliii). This aspect, which is one of the features that Loewald appreciates in Freud in contrast to his appraisal of Jung (413–416), is also a detail that his first teacher does not take up in *Being and Time*. While Heidegger certainly gives voice to the importance of the passionate nature of life, Loewald, following Freud, recognizes that passions cannot be detached from the body and gender (125).

While there are significant differences between Heidegger and Freud/Loewald in portraying the situation into which one is thrown, we remember that *Entwerfen*, "the taking over and actively developing the potentialities of this fact" of being thrown, is seen by Loewald as joining together his two teachers under the precept, "Become what you are" (Loewald 1978, 19). Although no person has chosen the contents of her or his unconscious, Loewald holds that a pivotal task of becoming a full person is to, as far as possible, take these up and integrate them into one's consciousness or reflection. This is his transformation of Freud's dictum—he calls it an "appeal" (2000, 95)—that "*Wo Es war, soll Ich werden*; where id was, there ego shall come into being" (1978, 18). Loewald writes, "To own up to our own history, to be responsible for our unconscious, in an important sense means, to bring unconscious forms of experiencing into the context and onto the level of the more mature, more lucid life of the adult mind" (21). The technical term he uses for this process is "sublimation," and he views it as a task both "evolutionary" and "moral" (75–76). Loewald clarifies this requirement by adding that it does not mean that unconscious contents are to be repudiated or repressed, for repression only galvanizes their disturbing power to haunt or overwhelm mature life. Such early wishes, fantasies, and memories are *us*, and one must draw upon them to live a fully personal, meaningful life.

The moral feature of this task is deepened through Loewald's translation of Freud's central notion of the superego. Classically the superego develops as the child, in the midst of a crisis, torn by incest and aggressive passions in relation to his or her parents, repudiates these passions and appropriates parental codes as his or her own. Loewald sees this process, which Freud holds is the key transformation of mental life, as unending, which brings one face to face with both guilt and, possibly, atonement. While the child's experience with parricide and incest are usually only in fantasy or dreams, there is real existential guilt. They symbolically tell of the child breaking off intense early identifications with the parents, to move toward more mature and reciprocal relations. Thus, there is an ending of something, a killing-off of something, but only through this process are more adult interactions (object relations) possible. If guilt is accepted for these symbolic crimes, then a reorganization of mental life ensues, and with it a richer life is opened up. In his dramatic words, "Without the guilty deed of parricide there is no individual self worthy of that name" (Loewald 2000, 394).

Despite the psychological nature of the material being addressed here, two additional philosophical elements, which Loewald may well have taken from Heidegger, add to this complex story. The first is the temporal dimension of existence as revealed in the temporality of moods. In this sense, Heidegger finds that most moods are correlated with the past of Dasein. For his part, Loewald connects the three basic psychic structures or processes with time frames. The id is the projection of the past warded-off features into the present. The superego is the promised development or "voice of conscience"—in terms of standards, demands, ideals, hopes, reproaches, and punishments—for the future (1978, 23).

The ego is the accessible present psychic performance of the person. In terms of owning-up, the task is to make past features accessible, and to integrate the moral future into the present. As Loewald presents this, "That man can own up to his past and thus gain some measure of mastery of his present life and the shape of his future, is part of his experience of time and implicit in the whole undertaking of psychoanalysis" (2000, 139).

Heidegger's impact can also be seen in the way that approach and object are connected. The nature of the objects Dasein encounters always corresponds to the basic attitudes that are taken. For Loewald, the development of the person and the engagement with objects, actually the very texture of the objects, are correlated. For example, in the first engagement with the world, since the infant is merged with the mother, no distinct object or objects are encountered. As the ego begins to differentiate from the mother, she begins to exist for the infant as distinct. Ego and object develop together. In terms of the process of owning up, integrating the moral dimensions of the parents transforms the ego so that it can relate to the parents as mature objects, rather than treating them in childish ways as just loving or, alternately, threatening extensions of the self.

How, then, does Loewald's treatment of responsibility differ from Heidegger's? For Heidegger, one is responsible to oneself and to Being for the nature of the life one chooses to live. That guilt has virtually the same referents is telling. This essentially closed circle of responsibility, the "to whom" and "for what" only notes other persons as those whom one is with; at most in solicitude there is the hint that the individual can help to free the other to choose her or his own life decisively.

Loewald also sees responsibility, at least partially, in terms of choosing, featuring the psychological dimension of owning up to the contents of the unconscious. The process of owning up is virtually synonymous with responsibility. As we saw earlier, for Loewald, "to own up to our own history, to be responsible for our unconscious," delineates what it means to be "mature" or an "adult" (1978, 21). Thus, to become a full person is to accept responsibility *for* the way one lives out what one has originally been given. However, others are not absent from this scenario. Choosing for oneself has significant implications for relationships with others, because the human is essentially intersubjective. Mental development is a moral task, where guilt for the inevitable and necessary breaking of immature infantile bonds—shattering intimate ties with the other—must be atoned for. Thus, one is responsible *to* both the self and *to* others. Here other persons extend beyond the primary caregivers, since the earliest patterns of relationship continue to be salient for later interactions. In other words, if infantile approaches to the first significant persons are not transformed, then later relationships with other persons will be circumscribed by such alternating patterns as idealization or denigration.

This portrait of "man as moral agent" must be augmented by Loewald's personal decision to become a psychoanalyst (1978, 1). This choice goes well beyond that possible "solicitude" in Heidegger's text, that helps the other to come to an authentic resolution about itself. For Loewald, the analyst's work with the patient is modeled on some features of the mother's crucial and loving care for her infant. He writes, for example:

> We note that the analyst's interpretation is a form of active mirroring, reflecting back to the patient his behavior in a different light, in terms of higher, more comprehensive and more articulate mental organization—analogous to the parental mirroring function in infancy and childhood. (21)

Additionally, the goal of that psychoanalytic "truth of human beings… in their interrelatedness" (2000, 298), which Loewald so passionately seeks, is a fundamentally therapeutic one. Thus, both in terms of theory and vocation, Loewald's approach to responsibility decisively departs from that of his teacher.

Emmanuel Levinas: Hellenic *Sophia* Infused with Hebrew *Ahavah*

Levinas' work in its entirety stands as a deep protest against the Holocaust. In his essay "Signature," he writes that his intellectual development "is dominated by the presentiment and the memory of the Nazi horror" (1990a, 291). The dedication to his second defining book, *Otherwise Than Being or Beyond Essence* (1981), reinscribes this reflection:

> To the memory of those who were closest among the six million assassinated by the National Socialists, and of the millions on millions of

> all confessions and all nations, victims of the same hatred of the other man, the same anti-Semitism. (x)

During the Holocaust Levinas was in a labor camp as a French prisoner of war from 1940 to 1945, and feared that this confinement was a mere way-station to the killing camps (Malka 2006, 262). At the same time, in Lithuania his father and brothers were murdered. His response to the Holocaust is to offer a scorching critique of the longstanding intellectual and political forces that led to that destructive caesura, and to fashion a counter-narrative about the binding power of human relationships that could withstand those powers.

Levinas' compound, almost tortuous relationship to Heidegger reflects this theme. In 1928 he went to Freiburg to study with the creator of phenomenology, Edmund Husserl. However, once there he was captivated by Husserl's brilliant student, Martin Heidegger. Levinas was deeply influenced by this emerging star and continued to insist that no one could understand modern philosophy unless they went through the Heideggerian portal. Yet, Levinas was equally insistent that his teacher's reprehensible actions could not be ignored ("it is difficult to forgive Heidegger" (1990a, 25)). What Paul Ricoeur terms Levinas' "permanently polemical rapport" sums up those halting statements about Heidegger interjected throughout Levinas' writings (cited in Malka 2006, 162), which are in the vein of: "When I pay homage to Heidegger, it is always costly to me, not because of his incontestable brilliance" (1998b, 92); and "This is the case, whatever the debt of every contemporary thinker might be to Heidegger, a debt that he often owes to his regret" (2000, 8).

Levinas believes that the basis for Heidegger's allegiance to National Socialism is cast early in his philosophy itself. He especially criticizes such basic features of *Being and Time* as the elevation of Being over human existence, the pervasive denigration of everyday social life of the crowd or "*das Mann*," the discussion of encountering things before the meeting with other persons, the veneration of the legacy of "*das Volk*," and, finally, the complete lack of an ethics, despite a few peripheral asides to the contrary. Levinas' overall judgment is aptly captured in the statement, "The absence of concern for the other in Heidegger and his personal political adventure are bound together" (2001, 186).

Levinas' attitude toward philosophy is equally ambivalent. Personally, he sees himself as a philosopher, even though he worked most of his adult life as a school principal at the *Ecole Normale Israelite Oriental* in Paris. His philosophic writings span sixty years, while it was only in his fifties that an academic position at University of Poitiers was offered, which eventually led to another at the Sorbonne. More significant is his complex stance toward the discipline itself. He lauds philosophy's rigor, clarity, and universality, that presupposition of the equality of humans, which accompanies the elevation of a common reason and a justice for all. Yet, there is a reverse side to this all-encompassing "wisdom." Permitting nothing outside of its grasp, philosophy is also synonymous with totality. Denying otherness and rejecting transcendence, it perpetuates a closed system where what is left mirrors itself, "the same." However, this does not mean that philosophy cannot be redeemed. Levinas highly values its ability to be self-reflective, that is, "to question itself, and ultimately to unsay itself" (1986, 22). More importantly, "Greek" or Hellenic *sophia* can be infused with "Hebrew" *ahavah*, that love for the neighbor, the poor, orphan, widow, and stranger proclaimed by the biblical prophets. In this connection Levinas writes, "My concern everywhere is precisely to translate this non-Hellenism of the Bible into Hellenic terms" (1998b, 85). This infusion without synthesis issues in a new definition of philosophy, substituting that traditional "love of wisdom" with "the wisdom of love in the service of love" (1981, 162). Thus, with Levinas as with Loewald, the questioning of Heidegger's philosophy leads to a rethinking of the philosophic discipline itself.

Actually, the whole course of Levinas' writings can be seen as a dialectical confrontation with Heidegger. It might begin with his first essay "On Escape" of 1935, which was later published as a book, and culminates in his *Otherwise Than Being* (1981). In terms of the first, the rejection of Heidegger's view of the self that comes to rest ultimately with itself is seen in the note that "escape is the need to get out of oneself" (2003, 55). There is also found in the last lines a sense of direction while the goal is yet unclear, of "getting out of being by a new path" (73). By the time of *Totality and Infinity* of 1961, which marks Levinas' first signature philosophic book and his emergence as an important philosopher in France, the goal is fully clarified. It is the other, viewed through the optics of ethics, that breaks both the violence of philosophy's identification of thought with being and the emptiness of the self given over to itself. Through the relation to the other, which stands outside of thought as an Infinite, the decentered self finds its meaning. *Otherwise than Being* (1981) radicalizes this movement, quoting from Pascal's *Pensées*: "'That is my place in the sun.' That is how the usurpation of the whole world began" (1981, vii)—and finding authenticity for the individual in its "substitution" for the other.

Over the course of this confrontation—or what Ricoeur terms this "polemical rapport"—the central features of Heidegger's philosophy are either contorted or totally refused. *Difficult Freedom* highlights one major contrast: "In the place of ontology—of the Heideggerian comprehension of the Being of being… a relation with the Other" (1990a, 293). In place of the primacy of Dasein's self-concern, Levinas features the self obsessed with and hostage to the other. Levinas accepts the truth of Heidegger's thrownness, but this original situation—unchosen yet inescapable—is described in terms of the overriding obligation to the other. The treatment of death is especially telling. Rejecting the view that authenticity arises through facing one's own death, Levinas insists that the concern for the death of the other is the very definition of the human. Finally, in contrast to a text without an ethics, Levinas announces that "Ethics is First Philosophy" (1989, 75–87).

The theme of responsibility is at the core of Levinas' sweeping break with Heidegger and with the whole tradition of the philosophy of being. For Levinas, human existence is bifurcated. There is first that aspect that ties the human to the rest of animal life. From this direction, each I or self is the center of the universe. The ruling principle is self-interest, that *conatus essendi* (self-preservation) of Spinoza, which most philosophers continue to regard as a natural given. The self seeks comfort, finds pleasure in life, and encounters others out of this approach. Regardless of how this attitude may be "tempered," or how solicitous one is for the other, in Levinas' view, where such natural egoism reigns, responsibility is banished. Put another way, he writes that "for ethical thought… *the self*, as this primacy of what is mine, is *hateful*" (1986, 26).

This entrenched egoism cannot be escaped through the self's efforts, despite the hollowness and disgust that inevitably accompany it. The self must be wrenched out of itself by another power for meaning and authenticity to ensue. This power comes from the encounter with the other, a meeting not initiated by the self, but unwillingly undergone. This other is neither my object nor my equal. Rather, the one beside me is totally outside of my designs, and ethically accosts me. This situation reveals the second dimension of human existence. According to Levinas, prior to or more original than human egoism is the concern for the other. It is the very basis of *human* life. Thus, there is an aspect of the life of persons, a second register, that transcends natural life and Being. Not sought out of need and incapable of being fulfilled, there is a metaphysical "desire" for the Infinite. The situation out of which this desire is evoked is the face-to-face relation.

The face of the other opens the way to my responsibility. By the term "face" Levinas does not intend to point to or signify a specific part of the human body, but the full human presence of the one encountered. He writes, "A face is a trace of itself, given over to my responsibility" (1981, 91). The face addresses me in two ways, as Levinas writes: "The transcendence of the Other, which is his eminence, his height, his lordship, in its concrete meaning includes his destitution, his exile, and his rights as a stranger" (1969, 76–77). By "height" Levinas is referring to the other's priority over the self's own interests, as well as the unavoidable obligation that the other confers. The term "destitution" relates to the vulnerability of the other that comes through the face. I am haunted by the lack of defense seen in the face of the other, in the presence of my "natural" instinct to be. For Levinas this is similar to the lack of legal protection for the stranger, abandoned in my land or country. The obligation or commandment not to kill expresses these two aspects of the encounter with the other. "Thou Shalt Not Kill" is an imperative. It cannot be avoided and nullifies every other interest or concern. It is also a reminder that the other's life is fragile. As obligation in the presence of fragility, "'Thou shalt not kill' signifies… 'thou shalt do everything in order that the other may live'" (2001, 272).

Especially in his later work, Levinas uses hyperbole to accentuate the radical nature of, the surplus in, responsibility. He writes of being a hostage to the other, or alternately being persecuted. Responsibility for the neighbor is likened to an obsession, and the self finds itself substituted for the other. These expressions are reminders or reinforcements of a number of lessons, which directly clash with the way ethics is traditionally presented.[4] Responsibility is not taken up from out of one's freedom, and actually precedes any question of decision. Levinas also insists that responsibility has no limits, and incessantly quotes Dostoyevsky: "We are all responsible for everyone else—but I am more responsible than all the others" (1986, 31). Thus, no single action or group of actions fulfills one's responsibility. Additionally, one is responsible not just for one's actions, but even for those of the other person. In this regard, substitution "means, in the ultimate shelter of myself, not to feel myself innocent, even for the harm that another does" (1998b, 91). While this last idea may appear unrealistic, it concretely means that if one person harms another, this is of real concern to me. Finally, reciprocity cannot be a consideration in this asymmetrical relation to the other.

Of course, the command "Thou shalt not kill!" is not itself without a reference. While Levinas insists that his ethics stands on its own, he acknowledges that it is inspired by the Jewish tradition. He also believes that the term "God" has a legitimate place in philosophy (1989, 166–189), while vigilant in his effort not to allow it to be a theme appropriated into, that is, subordinated to, a system. Levinas thus often just speaks of the "trace." At times he connects this to the face. In his words, "The trace is not just one more word: it is the proximity of God in the countenance of my fellow man" (1998a, 57). At other times he finds that the term arises, that is, "God… comes to mind" (1998b, v), in the ethical response or open hands that one offers to the neighbor.

One of the most outstanding features of Levinas' discussion of responsibility, and again particularly pointed toward Heidegger, is its linkage with the topic of death.[5] For Levinas that subject is driven by a concern *not* about the self, but for the other. He writes, "The fear for the other man does not turn back into anguish for *my* death. It overflows the ontology of the Heideggerian *Dasein*" (1998b, 176). The facticity of death is revealed in the face of the other, which "in this nakedness is an exposure unto death: nakedness, destitution, passivity, and pure vulnerability" (1998a, 167). While the neighbor's death is inevitable, the requirement to not let her or him die alone still stands. Levinas writes that the other "is alone and can undergo the supreme isolation we call death—and there is, consequently, in the Face of the Other always the death of the Other" (104).

Finally, while anxiety over the face of the other is so expressive of what responsibility means for Levinas, he is not reticent to speak of responsibility and love, especially in his later essays and interviews. For Levinas, these two terms are not opposites or incompatible. The response to the face that stands for responsibility is also the true meaning of love. With a reference to Pascal, Levinas writes that "responsibility is the love without concupiscence" (2001, 108). What could be more a testament to love than to be with the other when she or he is facing the ultimate challenge of death? In this case, Levinas' phrase "*me voici*"—French for the biblical "*hineni*" (2000, 188), refers to a *being there* that is a witness to responsibility, to a love that lingers beyond death.

Toward a Recovery of the Suppressed?

Responsibility as either for the self—in Loewald's words, "owning up"—or to the Other—the defining characteristic of Levinas' philosophy—is suppressed, as it were, within the history of psychoanalysis. It is missing in the explicit writings of the discipline's founder, although Freud does address issues concerning the therapist's relationship to the patient (1990). He also has an allusive statement that one is responsible for one's dreams, which Loewald characteristically uses as an imprimatur for his position (Loewald 1978, 7).[6] Some of the factors behind Freud's attitude are well known. He sees himself battling some social conventions such as the moralistic stigmatizing of the mentally ill and the hypocrisy of late Victorian Europe in its attitudes toward sex. He also determines that the obsessive, crushing demands of what he calls the superego have to be addressed, and not reinforced in therapy. Finally, Freud's accounts of the underlying processes of the psyche in terms of hydraulic, electric, and other mechanical-like forces leave little room for personal responsibility. As Roy Schafer writes, "The mechanistic and organismic language of metapsychology… by its nature… excludes concepts like responsibility from explanation" (1976, 233).[7] Still, the original spirit behind Freud's new "science" is deeply ethical. It promises relief to patients experiencing years of overwhelming and inescapable suffering. He provides a method that eschews both surgery and hypnotism, a "talking cure" that builds up the conscious agency of his patients.

The topic of responsibility in relationships does appear in some of the first generation of post-Freudians. For example, there is an ethical feature in Melanie Klein's developmental narrative, in terms of the second, "Depressive Position." For her, the infant is at first overwhelmed by aggressive and destructive drives, fear, anxiety, and paranoia. It projects the drives onto the mother, and responds with destructive fantasies toward her (1986, 40). Following this "Paranoid–Schizoid" foundation, the infant experiences remorse. In its feelings of guilt, loss, and reparation, there is something analogous to accepting responsibility for "the disaster created through its sadism" (48). Erik Erikson's unique examination of the later stages of the individual's "psychosocial" development brings him to highlight personal virtues important for a mature and fulfilling life, including responsibility (1963). He describes the sixth of eight developmental stages, "Intimacy vs. Isolation," in terms of the individual struggling with "the capacity to commit himself to concrete affiliations and partnerships and to develop the ethical strength to abide by such commitments, even though they may call for significant sacrifices and compromises" (263). Of the seventh stage, "Generativity," he writes about "the concern in establishing and guiding the next generation" and of bequeathing something valuable that comes from the self (267).

In light of the attention that the relational psychoanalysts give to issues of meaning and authenticity in their writings and therapy, coupled with the intersubjective basis for their approach, it is surprising that the topic of responsibility is virtually ignored in their literature. A perusal of the book indices of the major figures in the movement confirms the dearth of both "ethics" and "responsibility" as topics. This lacuna is evidenced in Stephen Mitchell's summary discussion of contemporary relational trends concerning what he labels "Mode 4: Intersubjectivity," which focuses on recognizing and being recognized by another as a person (2000). He writes, "Being fully human (in Western culture) entails being recognized *as a subject* by another human subject." Here at the conscious, intentional level is the notion that authenticity and fulfillment require mutual recognition of persons as subjects in their "own right" (64). Still, the discussion does not explicitly acknowledge that one might owe the other this recognition, or that the patient's ultimate healing includes the realization of this responsibility to the other.

The reticence to speak of responsibility extends to the influential work of Jessica Benjamin, who Mitchell cites as an important theorist of intersubjectivity. Benjamin gives recognition of the other's independence and inviolability a central place in her work. She asserts that "we have a need for recognition and we have a capacity to recognize others in return, thus making mutual recognition possible" (1995, 30). Until recently she shunned using the term "responsibility" in conjunction with recognizing the other, because she believed that prescriptive language about normative ideals does not have a place in psychoanalytic discourse (20–21). However, in a very significant late reflection about what she terms the moral third, Benjamin affirms the need to "bring the ethical into our practice." She writes of one's responsibility for the other in terms of "the broader vision of becoming an active bystander that makes humans socially responsible, empowered to witness if not to change and thus to recognize the pain and affirm the dignity of those who suffer" (2012, 129).

Where contemporary psychoanalytic voices do feature substantial treatments of the patient's responsibility to others, these often reveal the influence of the main subjects of our treatment, Loewald or Levinas.[8] One of these theorists is Roy Schafer, who was a student of Loewald. Schafer's first book, *A New Language for Psychoanalysis* (1976), features a number of dimensions of responsibility as part of its central argument. He speaks of taking responsibility for one's life, even for events not chosen. He writes, "More and more, the analysand indicates a readiness to accept the responsibility of life as action… [However] it does not imply a belief on one's part that one has caused one's whole life or can cause it from now on" (146). This statement is reminiscent of Loewald's treatment of "owning up." Schafer also discusses one's responsibility for others as an important ingredient of the mature life. In *Tradition and Change in Psychoanalysis*, he writes of "that well-developed sense of responsibility that takes into account the feelings of others and so recognizes that others do matter" (1997, 102).

David Goodman's recent publication, *The Demanded Self: Levinasian Ethics and Identity in Psychology* (2012), is a fine example of the effort to highlight the topic of responsibility within the discourse of psychoanalysis. As the subtitle indicates, his work, and that of other theorists whom he notes (112, 186), reflects the impact of Levinas' philosophy on the discipline. Goodman extends Levinas' notion of "*hineni*" to speak of "The self lived as *hineni*" as "a self, first and foremost, forever responsive to the other" (125). He sees this rendering of the meaning of a self as deepening and transforming the attenuated portrait of what constitutes the patient's health or an authentic human life that is currently the norm in psychology and psychoanalysis.

Following Goodman, I would suggest that Levinas' message is especially relevant to the portrayal of what constitutes the ultimate *telos* of the analytic interaction, the patient's movement toward a full human life. While such a goal might be unreachable in the deepest sense, and especially difficult in the face of the complex details of any particular patient's life, it still can have significant impact on how therapy is understood and conducted. The contemporary discourse of psychoanalysis often leaves such a goal underdeveloped, or presents it in too narrow a vein. Levinas' understanding of responsibility is significant for discussing what might constitute that full life, or flourishing, in the patient. Would we ever call a person healed or healthy in any deeper sense, who could not at times be responsible for the other? Responding to the other does not just fulfill an ethical obligation, it also provides the patient with a sense of competence, relevance, and meaning. Of course, there is a question of how the need for responsibility might be communicated by the therapist. Certainly not as a lesson, didactic or prescriptive—as Freud warned—but indirectly, and of course only incompletely, through the questions asked, the responses made, and the concern shown in the therapeutic dialogue. Put in another way, Levinas is a significant resource for addressing the issue that Mitchell believes brings patients to seek psychoanalytic treatment today, the quest for "a revitalization and expansion" of the "capacity to generate experience that feels real, meaningful, and valuable" (1993, 24). Levinas holds that both authenticity and meaning cannot be reached directly, but arise when the self is forgotten, out of a life of responsibility for the other.

In concert with Levinas' position, the topic of responsibility is omnipresent in the writings of the two Jewish philosophers Franz Rosenzweig and Martin Buber. This is not surprising to those who have any familiarity with the history of Jewish philosophy. What Steven Schwarzschild termed "the transhistorical primacy of ethics" is the single distinctive feature of the discipline in the context of the wider history of Western philosophy (1987, 629). This is true of Jewish philosophy whether it has taken its point of departure from Aristotelianism in the medieval period or Idealism and Existentialism in the modern.

Franz Rosenzweig's *The Star of Redemption*, which is frequently acclaimed as the most significant work in the field of modern Jewish philosophy, features the theme of responsibility (2005). The book narrates how the elements of God, world, and humans are structured through the relationships of Creation, Revelation, and Redemption. The latter two relationships are based on the commandments to love God and the neighbor. In particular, Redemption, which is understood by Rosenzweig in terms of bringing permanence and substance to the everyday world of flux, is achieved entirely through human actions. Humans are responsible for redemption of the world, and this process proceeds step by step through the fulfillment of the responsibility for the neighbor or "next one." Put in another way, Rosenzweig affirms that each person has a unique mission in the world, defined as the response/responsibility for the other. Rosenzweig poetically writes, "Precisely here, in this commandment of love of the neighbor, his Self is finally definitively confirmed in its place… Out of the infinite chaos of the world, a neighbor, his neighbor, is placed before his soul" (257).

As the author of *I and Thou*, it may not be the topic of responsibility that is usually associated with Martin Buber. However, this would be a misconception. While Buber most often characterizes the I–Thou relationship in terms of mutuality and reciprocity, he also finds responsibility to be a necessary component. He holds, for example, that "Love is responsibility of an I for a Thou" (1970, 66). His famous text has a treatment of God's calling and the unique mission of the individual in terms of turning to the other that is analogous to what Rosenzweig presented. Thus we find: "When a man steps before the countenance, the world becomes wholly present to him… He is not rid of responsibility… [but takes up] the power of loving responsibility for the unexplorable course of the world" (157).

An even more explicit discussion of responsibility is found in Buber's essay "A Question to the Single One." It is ostensibly a response to a major theme found in some of Søren Kierkegaard's works, which concerns the tension or conflict between the relationship to God and those with both one's intimate other and "the crowd." Buber powerfully contests this opposition, writing: "[The ethical] means an *essential* action and suffering in relation to men, which are co-ordinated with the essential relation to God" (1965, 56). He also equates responsibility with answerability to the other:

> Responsibility presupposes one who addresses me primarily, that is, from a realm independent of myself, and to whom I am answerable. He addresses me about something that he has entrusted to me and that I am bound to take care of loyally. (45)

How does one move beyond betrayal? For Loewald and Levinas this includes an honest expression of their feelings of hurt and abandonment brought about by the actions of their teacher, as well as an acknowledgment of the debt for what had earlier been received. However, they go further than this. Through their work in psychoanalysis and philosophy, they endeavor to fulfill some of the promise of their teacher's work and their respective disciplines' calling, while rejecting and correcting for those philosophical elements that they see as having contributed to their teacher's pernicious political position. A major feature of this correction is to speak of the role of responsibility to others in a life of meaning and authenticity. As we have seen, their legacy has already had an impact on psychoanalytic theory and practice, and hopefully this influence will continue to grow.

Notes

1 Loewald's father was Jewish. Levinas was an Orthodox Jew, whose Judaism always occupied a central place in his life and thought. For the latter see Solomon Malka's *Emmanuel Levinas: His Life and Legacy* (2006).
2 Critics who find an ethical concern in *Being and Time*, in terms of the relationship to the other, focus on Heidegger's discussions of being with others, the call of conscience, and solicitude. For example, Jean Greisch writes, "One must keep in sight the breadth of the Heideggerian 'with,' which is capable of containing the moment of abandonment and of being delivered over to the other" (Raffoul and Pettigrew 2002, 102). Frank Schlow sees in conscience the experience of "the attunement that echoes the claim of the other" (38), and in solicitude "a way of responding to the welfare of the other" (36).
3 Jonathan Lear's excellent introduction to Loewald's collected papers and monographs offers another approach to the question of responsibility, and his relationship to Heidegger (2000).
4 As noted in Chapter 4, Hilary Putnam speaks of Levinas' philosophy, as well as those of Franz Rosenzweig and Martin Buber, in terms of "moral perfectionism." This type of moral theory recognizes that "it is only by keeping an 'impossible' demand in view" that the individual can realize her or his highest potentiality for living (2008, 72).
5 Much of Levinas' last efforts focused on the twin subjects of Heidegger and death (2000).
6 There is also Freud's "fundamental rule," of the responsibility of the patient in analysis to say whatever comes into his or her mind.
7 Levinas' well-known hostility to psychoanalysis is a reflection of his view that the discourse about the unconscious did not break with the self, self-consciousness, and presence (1989, 93).
8 A little afield, the subjects of responsibility and ethics are fully manifest in the extensive writings of the French feminist philosopher and psychoanalyst Luce Irigaray. In addition, she has authored two critical pieces on Levinas, which question his stereotyped view of the feminine, and insist that even intimate love relations include an ethics of *Eros* (see Oppenheim 2006, 175–219).

References

Buber, Martin. 1965. *Between Man and Man*. Translated by Ronald Gregor Smith. New York: Collier Books.

—. 1970. *I and Thou*. Translated by Walter Kaufmann. New York: Charles Scribner's Sons.

Benjamin, Jessica. 1995. *Like Subjects, Love Objects: Essays on Recognition and Sexual Difference*. New Haven, CT: Yale University Press.

—. 1998. *Shadow of the Other: Intersubjectivity and Gender in Psychoanalysis*. New York: Routledge.

—. 2012. "Beyond Doer and Done To: An Intersubjective View of Thirdness" and "Afterword." In *Relational Psychoanalysis Vol. 4: Expansion of Theory*, edited by Lewis Aron and Adrienne Harris, 91–130. New York: Routledge.

Caputo, John D. 1993. *Demythologizing Heidegger*. Bloomington, IN: Indiana University Press.

Chanter, Tina. 2001. "The Problematic Normative Assumptions of Heidegger's Ontology." In *Feminist Interpretations of Heidegger*, edited by Nancy J. Holland and Patricia Huntington, 73–108. University Park, PA: Pennsylvania State University Press.

Derrida, Jacques. 1989. *Of Spirit: Heidegger and the Question*. Translated by Geoffrey Bennington and Rachel Bowlby. Chicago, IL: University of Chicago Press.

Erikson, Erik H. 1963. *Childhood and Society*. New York: W. W. Norton and Company.

Freud, Sigmund. 1990. "Observations on Transference-Love: Further Recommendations on the Technique of Psycho-Analysis III." In *Essential Papers on Transference*, edited by Aaron Esman, 36–48. New York: New York University Press.

Goodman, David M. 2012. *The Demanded Self: Levinasian Ethics and Identity in Psychology*. Pittsburgh, PA: Duquesne University Press.

Heidegger, Martin. 1962. *Being and Time*. Translated by John Macquarrie and Edward Robinson. New York: Harper and Row Publishers.

Klein, Melanie. 1986. "A Contribution to the Psychogenesis of Manic-Depressive States." In *Essential Papers on Object Relations*, edited by Peter Buckley, 40–70. New York: New York University Press.

Lear, Jonathan. 2000. "Introduction." In *The Essential Loewald: Collected Papers and Monographs*, edited by Norman Quist, ix–xl. Hagerstown, MD: University Publishing Group.

Levinas, Emmanuel. 1969. *Totality and Infinity: An Essay on Exteriority*. Translated by Alphonso Lingis. Pittsburgh, PA: Duquesne University Press.

—. 1981. *Otherwise Than Being or Beyond Essence*. Translated by Alphonso Lingis. The Hague: Martin Nijoff Publishers.

—. 1986. *Face to Face with Levinas*. Edited by Richard A. Cohen. Albany, NY: State University of New York Press.

—. 1989. *The Levinas Reader*. Edited by Seán Hand. Oxford: Basil Blackwell.

—. 1990a. *Difficult Freedom: Essays on Judaism*. Translated by Seán Hand. Baltimore, MD: Johns Hopkins University Press.

—. 1990b. *Nine Talmudic Readings*. Translated by Annette Aronowicz. Bloomington, IN: Indiana University Press.

—. 1998a. *Entre Nous: On Thinking-of-the-Other*. Translated by Michael B. Smith and Barbara Harshav. New York: Columbia University Press.

—. 1998b. *Of God Who Comes to Mind*. Translated by Bettina Bergo. Stanford, CA: Stanford University Press.

—. 2000. *God, Death, and Time*. Translated by Bettina Bergo. Stanford, CA: Stanford University Press

—. 2001. *Is It Righteous To Be?: Interviews with Emmanuel Levinas*. Edited by Jill Robbins. Stanford, CA: Stanford University Press.

—. 2003. *On Escape: De l'évasion*. Translated by Bettina Bergo. Stanford, CA: Stanford University Press.

Loewald, Hans W. 1978. *Psychoanalysis and the History of the Individual: The Freud Lectures at Yale*. New Haven, CT: Yale University Press.

—. 2000. *The Essential Loewald: Collected Papers and Monographs*. Hagerstown, MD: University Publishing Group.

Löwith, Karl. 1942. "M. Heidegger and F. Rosenzweig or Temporality and Eternity." In *Philosophy and Phenomenological Research*, 3: 53–77.

Malka, Salomon. 2006. *Emmanuel Levinas: His life and Legacy*. Translated by Michael Kigel and Sonja M. Embree. Pittsburg, PA: Duquesne University Press.

Mitchell, Stephen A. 1993. *Hope and Dread in Psychoanalysis*. New York: Basic Books.

—. 2000. *Relationality: From Attachment to Intersubjectivity*. Hillsdale, NJ: Analytic Press.

Oppenheim, Michael. 2006. *Jewish Philosophy and Psychoanalysis: Narrating the Interhuman*. Lanham, MD: Lexington Books.

Putnam, Hilary. 2008. *Jewish Philosophy as a Guide to Life: Rosenzweig, Buber, Levinas, Wittgenstein*. Bloomington, IN: Indiana University Press.

Raffoul, François and David Pettigrew, eds. 2002. *Heidegger and Practical Philosophy*. Albany, NY: State University of New York Press.

Rosenzweig, Franz. 2005. *The Star of Redemption*. Translated by Barbara E. Galli. Madison, WI: University of Wisconsin Press.

Schafer, Roy. 1976. *A New Language for Psychoanalysis*. New Haven, CT: Yale University Press.

—. 1997. *Tradition and Change in Psychoanalysis*. Madison, CT: International Universities Press.

Schwarzschild, Steven S. 1987. "Modern Jewish Philosophy." In *Contemporary Jewish Religious Thought: Original Essays on Critical Concepts, Movements, and Beliefs*, edited by Arthur A. Cohen and Paul Mendes-Flohr, 629–634. New York: The Free Press.

Wolin, Richard. 2001. *Heidegger's Children: Hannah Arendt, Karl Löwith, Hans Jonas, and Herbert Marcuse*. Princeton, NJ: Princeton University Press.

Conclusion

Strong as Death

We have been pursuing a dialogue between some relational psychoanalysts and three Jewish philosophers featuring their discourses on love, which view the presence of the other as the singular venue for meaning and authenticity. There are remaining questions which, while incontrovertibly significant, have been held in abeyance until now. How does the fact of human mortality impact these two languages of love? Does the inevitability of death subvert, intensify, or point to another register in the portrayal of intersubjectivity?

Hoffman's Dialectical Constructivism

Irwin Hoffman is widely recognized as providing the most sustained and illuminating discussion of the challenge of death within the relational stream.[1] The first two chapters of his principal work *Ritual and Spontaneity in the Psychoanalytic Process* are titled "The Dialectic of Meaning and Mortality in the Psychoanalytic Process" and "Death Anxiety and Adaptation to Mortality in Psychoanalytic Theory" (1998). The fact of human mortality and the psychic anxiety that this creates are fundamental features of Hoffman's book and play central roles in his overall position. He designates his approach as "dialectical constructivism," which always has, in his words, "the dialectic of meaning and mortality… in the background" (xvii). He writes, "The dialectical constructivism that I am espousing is intimately tied to death anxiety and the adaptation to mortality since all constructed reality goes on… in the face of the prospect of nonbeing and meaninglessness" (xx). The constructivist element points to the social and individual contribution to all human experiences and to the interpretation of these.

For Hoffman death is not just a negative, threatening factor—its impact as the ultimate symbol of the inescapable meaninglessness and loss that haunts life. He writes, "The very annihilation that jeopardizes our sense that anything we care about matters, paradoxically, is what infuses caring with the meaning that it has" (1998, 18). The consciousness of the limited time we have provides a unique intensity and importance to our living. It reinforces the significance of every moment, provides a sense of urgency, since we know that these are limited. He often cites Martin Heidegger as the theorist best known for examining the way that the confrontation with death predicates the very value of life. Consonant with this understanding, Hoffman sees pretensions to human immortality as undermining human meaning. As he writes, "Ironically, therefore, a human being's sense of self, threatened as it may be by awareness of mortality, is also profoundly jeopardized by a 'promise' of immortality" (xvii).

However, unlike Heidegger's heroic individualistic portrayal of authentically facing death—that death is essentially mine and all human relations are consequently undone—Hoffman's relational perspective is illustrated through discussions of the early role of parents and the possibility of later analytic contributions. In terms of the former, he notes, "Parents, the 'gods' of infancy and childhood, have the power to give children a sense of being 'chosen,' that is, of being valued as creative centers of experience and choice in their own right" (1998, 11). The early and foundational sense of being loved and valued, as well as in turn loving and being attached to these seemingly omnipotent beings, sustains persons when they subsequently experience those inevitable events of meaninglessness, loss, and mortality, or what Hoffman enchantingly designates as the "insults of the human condition" (xxviii). He further adds that those who have come to feel "chosen" are empowered in turn to affirm the meaningfulness of their children's actions and lives.

Hoffman claims that many psychoanalysts, starting with Freud, maintained perspectives that were "generally characterized by avoidance and denial" of the anxiety before death (1998, xix). Of course the biological fact of death was not ignored, and in his later years Freud proposed the dual instinct theory of the pervasive conflicting drives within the mind of *Eros* and *Thanatos*. Still, Hoffman finds that there has been little effort devoted to the psychoanalytic examination of death's paradoxical relation to meaning, as the supreme challenge as well as the defining structure for the value of human life. In this regard, Hoffman believes that the psychoanalyst actually has an important role in reinforcing early parental support as well as addressing its inevitable deficiencies. He writes, "Psychoanalysis as an institution... has just that underlying purpose: finding that means within consciousness for confronting and 'going beyond' mortality, that is, the means for investing the particulars of living in the context of—even through—awareness of their negation" (47).[2]

Allusions to religion punctuate Hoffman's treatment of this feature of the psychoanalyst's role. This is already foreshadowed by the quotation above, which characterized parents, with their power and authority, as "the 'gods' of infancy and childhood" (1998, 11). The analyst is a later significant other whose focused concern has super-ordinary meaning for the patient, and the patient's transference love both responds to and reinforces the early parental position. Hoffman's statement follows upon this: "Sometimes the analysis is a background support for living, functioning in a way that is analogous to the way religion functions in many people's lives" (255). However, he is also very determined to limit this association between psychoanalysis and religion, emphasizing the unique deferral of authority and self-critical climate that the therapist elicits.

A deeply ambivalent attitude pervades Hoffman's treatment of religion, in conjunction with his discussion of meaning and mortality. On the positive side, in addition to some references to religion's comparable therapeutic functions, he sees the possibility of what might be called a mature religious consciousness providing insight into the reality of the human condition. He envisions the Genesis story of creation as "the story of humankind, forging, against a background of chaos, a sense of significance and order." There is also a quotation from the influential twentieth-century theologian Paul Tillich, that "God... is the power of being itself, prevailing over against non-being, overcoming estrangement, providing us the courage to take the anxiety of finitude, guilt, and doubt upon ourselves" (1998, 16).

Yet, the prevailing attitude toward religion in Hoffman's work is anything but positive. There is a persistent linking of religion with ideas and promises of immortality, so that religion becomes synonymous with the "'promise' of immortality" (1998, xvii). For example, he speaks of "religious belief in an afterlife" as providing consolation (60), and refers to the psychoanalyst George Pollock concerning "the religious notion of immortality" (41). The precise meaning and problematic of this "promise" is revealed in Hoffman's reference to a statement by Franz Kafka that "the idea of immortality refers to the wish for the infinite extension into time of the self" (35), and to Pollock's assertion:

> Thus the [religious] notion of immortality is a way of arresting or reversing the irreversible flow of time toward death… This optimistic hope of a world to come, where time has stopped and there is reunion and everlasting continuity, is a defense against the total helplessness associated with the "nothingness" of nonlife, be it death or the earliest states of infancy. (41)

Since it is precisely the reality of mortality and the finite time allotted to human existence which provide the context and overall meaning for human life, the indissoluble connection with the idea of immortality is unequivocally ruinous for religion in Hoffman's eyes.

Hoffman offers other, related characterizations of religion. One appears in his effort to distinguish the approach of psychoanalysis from religion. Psychoanalysis as "critically challenging and interpretative" is opposed to "a religious belief system," and "many expressions of organized religion," which play upon the "innate appetite for belief in an absolute authority" (1998, 256–257). Here, in agreement with Freud, religion is seen as grounded in the infant's limitless trust and love for her or his first caregivers (11–12). Like many other critics, Hoffman remarks—one would think approvingly—that religion has lost its power as a "secure mooring" in Western society (xviii). In all, religion stands for those unquestioned and illusory beliefs in the promise of eternal life and in the necessity for submission to an omnipotent, omniscient Caregiver.[3]

As presented earlier in Chapter 2, Jessica Benjamin offers a similar evaluation of religion, although the direct association with immortality is not emphasized as it is with Hoffman. For her, religion tenders the promise of redemption in exchange for the believer's complete submission to its absolute authority. It is therefore in direct conflict with the naked reality of the human condition, with its inevitable elements of injustice, loss, and incompleteness.

These views about the unvarnished, inescapable "indignities" of the human condition are mirrored in brief statements by other relational authors. Thomas Ogden speaks of the development of a mature sense of calm in the face of our finitude, and of how "there can be no triumphs when it comes to time" (2004, 264). Stephen Mitchell similarly relates that "understanding does not provide much solace for, among other things, real loss, grief over lost opportunities, irreconcilable conflicts, and, ultimately, death" (1993, 213). His book *Can Love Last?* is punctuated with the term "tragic" and, following one of its appearances, he quotes Harold Bloom: "Love dies or else lovers die, those are the pragmatic possibilities" (2003, 55).

Jewish Philosophers' Other Register

Despite some differences, the Jewish philosophers of encounter share a basic approach to the topic of love and death. It comes through in many different places in their texts, and this presentation will necessarily be both selective and abbreviated.[4] In the course of this discussion we will examine not dualities, but dialectical combinations that have essential roles in their overall position, or in their alternative narrative: love and death, faith and trust, meaning and responsibility, life and eternity.

The key to the Jewish philosophers' position on love and death concerns, of course, the relationship to God. The relationship is usually understood in terms of faith, but the term the Jewish philosophers prefer is *trust*. Trust in God is the foundation for trust in the meaning of one's life and necessarily in life itself. As we have seen in Chapter 2, the Jewish philosophers regard trust as the basis for the possibility of love, that is, for authentic human relationships. Still, how does their position confront the challenge or challenges of death? The threat of death is two-fold: to the physical survival of the individual person, and then to that life of the individual, of those relationships to or love with others. Is there any meaning to either of these, if death has the final word?

The Jewish philosophers do not ignore the topic of death. They acknowledge that while it is inescapable, death is not stronger than love. The individual buoyed by trust is assured that meaning survives, that most importantly, nothing significant in life—which is love—is lost. This trust in God, lived out in the world, points to a different discourse or story about life than that of the psychoanalysts. The centerpiece, actually the entrée to the story, concerns authentic human relationships, which are characterized by love and responsibility. The specifics of the story, especially in terms of death, are not given or fixed, which is to say that among other things the Jewish philosophers are not literalists. The story is both allusive and fully real-truth. It is not about the self, one's perseverance in being. What is clear is that the trust or assurance, while at times difficult to maintain, can ultimately withstand the test.

Death and the fear of death are persistent themes in Franz Rosenzweig's writings. Among other factors, biographical "*absurda*" probably weighed heavily on his thought:[5] the draft for his major work, *The Star of Redemption*, was written while serving in the army during World War I; his father also died during this period; and soon after the book was published Franz was diagnosed with Lou Gehrig's disease. He continued to write during the last years of his young life, while progressively losing control over his body. Three of Rosenzweig's works are especially germane to his stance in regard to the topic of death: the aforementioned *Star*, its adaptation in the "Büchlein"—*Understanding the Sick and the Healthy*, and one of his later lectures on the *Star*.

The skeleton of the *Star* consists of three parts: the philosopher's panicked effort to escape death through the contrived division separating the immortal soul from the perishable body, the dialogue of love between God and his beloved, and the individual's trusting journey back into the world. Rosenzweig begins by suggesting that it is often the fullness of life that suffers when a solution to death is proffered. However, for him the only authentic remedy, not to death but to the fear of death, is trust. This trust emerges from the call to love, initiated by God and answered by the individual. In Rosenzweig's words, "Revelation teaches us to trust in the Creator, to await the Redeemer" (2005, 404). Trust in oneself and the meaning of one's life issues from the trust in the divine other. It extends to all of one's life, because the individual knows that "nothing can happen to it" (181). With this assurance, the person can enter back into life. Here the individual's assigned "share in the whole truth" (439) is verified through acts of loving the next one—the neighbor—punctuating the journey.

Two related tropes in the *Star* concern the terms "eternity" and "the Kingdom." These belong to that parallel and sometimes intersecting narrative that addresses that which is outside of time and history. The experience of being loved by God and the ensuing acts of fulfilling the commandment of loving the neighbor are not transient. They are events that have become ensouled, that is, transformed into moments of eternity. They usher in the redemptive Kingdom. Thus, it is not the soul that is eternal, as it were, but the moments of love, of authentically being together, which are never lost. This is how Rosenzweig expresses it:

> Eternity is a today that would be conscious of being more than today. And to say that the Kingdom is eternally coming means that its growth

> is no doubt necessary, but that the rhythm of this growth is not definite, or, more exactly: that the growth does not have any relationship to time. An existence that has once entered into the Kingdom cannot fall back outside again; it has entered under the sign of the once-and-for-all, it has become eternal. (2005, 241)

Understanding the Sick and the Healthy follows the basic storyline and reaffirms themes that earlier appear in the *Star*. The "attempt to elude death" results in a premature dying, that is, the paralytic inability to live fully in the world (Rosenzweig 1999, 102). However, persons can learn to live and act responsibly in the world, through an awareness that there is One who "summons man by name." Rosenzweig summarizes this insight with the statement: "To avail himself of today, man must, for better or worse, put his trust in God" (93). Still, this trust does not extinguish the reality of death. In Rosenzweig's words, "There is no remedy for death; not even health. A healthy man, however, has the strength to continue towards the grave" (103).

A captivating section on marriage in Rosenzweig's lecture "Faith and Knowledge" provides a different forum for his lesson about love and death. It begins with the statement that marriage understands "'the and' between love and death," because it is not just built upon some ephemeral exchange of effervescent feelings. Marriage is that concrete "love… 'at work'" (1998, 109). It recognizes that it lives in the midst of death, "death media in vita," but at the same time "overcomes" it. Rosenzweig continues, "A marriage is not after all destroyed through the loss of one partner… For if it was good, then it saved every day because it—lived every day, from the first, with the knowledge of death" (110). Rosenzweig does not underestimate the challenge of sustaining the belief that moments are "saved," while being cognizant of the inevitability of death. A glimpse into this demanding/defining struggle is seen in Rosenzweig's acknowledgment: "But to learn this is a difficult art and costs much strength and pains. No one learns it otherwise. We can only pray that the strength for these pains be given to us and does not run out. Amen." (111).

Elements of Martin Buber's global narrative concerning love and death are woven throughout his long authorship. It is helpful to begin with his late book of 1951 *Two Types of Faith*. Its main point is that the Hebrew term *emunah* should be translated as "trust," rather than "faith" (2003, 28).

In the work, Buber describes *emunah* as a fundamental trust in God that permeates all of one's life. He writes:

> But the realization of one's faith... [takes place] in the man's whole life, that is in the actual totality of his relationships, not only towards God, but also to his appointed sphere in the world and to himself... By its very nature trust is substantiation of trust in the fullness of life in spite of the course of the world which is experienced. (40)[6]

Many interconnected features of trust are elaborated here: in God, in one's place and mission in the world, and in the "fullness" or meaningfulness of life itself. In terms of intersubjectivity, this trust is carried by the believing/trusting individual throughout all of one's relationships with others.[7]

The topic of death is scarcely mentioned in Buber's defining work, *I and Thou*. Still, essential ingredients of his overall position are presented there: the expansive understanding of the term "love," reference to another dimension of existence, and the link between divine revelation and meaning. For Buber, love is synonymous with the responsibility one has to the other, to the Thou. Since everyone is potentially a Thou or neighbor for the I, this also implies the fundamental equality of all persons. In his words, "Love is responsibility of an I for a Thou: in this consists what cannot consist in any feeling—the equality of all lovers" (1970, 66). Another of the distinguishing features of the approach of I and Thou is that it is beyond, or not limited by, our conceptions of space, time, and history. From this it follows that the I–Thou relation constitutes the only access to presence: "The present—not that which is like a point... but the actual and fulfilled present—exists only insofar as presentness, encounter, and relation exist. Only as the Thou becomes present does presence come into being" (63).

In the section in *I and Thou* which focuses on the nature of revelation, Buber takes up the issue of meaning:

> The inexpressible confirmation of meaning... is guaranteed. Nothing, nothing can henceforth be meaningless. The question about the meaning of life has vanished. But if it were still there, it would not require an answer. You do not know how to point to or define the meaning, you lack any formula or image for it, and yet it is more certain for you

> than the sensations of your senses... It wants to be demonstrated by us in this life and this world.
>
> (1970, 158–159)

Thus, the dialogue with the divine provides a confirmation of meaning, perhaps of that meaning already revealed in the life between persons. Of course, such a meaning—of life—escapes all formulations, but can be an abiding impression more strongly felt than the reports of the senses. The meaning is about this life and is verified through one's responsive/responsible actions in the world.

The essay "The Dialogue Between Heaven and Earth" elaborates Buber's understanding of human life as a response to the divine. He relates that "heaven" speaks to persons in the "language of events and situations" by which they feel addressed: ethically addressed. The language of one's answer is through "our actions and attitudes, our reactions and our abstentions" (1972, 216). In other words, at different times—Buber might say at all times—persons live with ethical challenges or summons. They can allow themselves to be aware of these, or refuse to be attentive. Further, answers are expressed through actions, whether in responsibility or in abstention. For Buber, this is the language of "the dialogue between heaven and earth" (214).

Two final references from Buber's corpus are oriented directly toward the topic of death. The first, which is appropriately part of his response to Heidegger's thanatic-centered philosophical anthropology, mirrors those famous lines from the biblical Song of Songs. Buber writes:

> A *great* relation exists only between real persons. It can be strong as death, because it is stronger than solitude, because it breaches the barriers of a lofty solitude, subdues its strict law, and throws a bridge from self-being to self-being across the abyss of dread of the universe.
>
> (1965, 175)

Buber designated the single-paragraph piece "After Death," composed in 1927, as the final entry in his last book, *A Believing Humanism: My Testament, 1902–1965*. In it, that elemental faith or trust in God is called before the challenge of death.[8] Buber insists that this faith does not refer to or rely on some doctrine of immortality, but a trust in that "absolute person" whom we designate by the term God (1970, 181). It opens the way to that other discourse that features the term "eternity":

> The genuine faith speaks: I know nothing of death, but I know that God is eternity, and I know this, too, that he is my God. Whether what we call time remains to us beyond our death becomes quite unimportant to us next to this knowing, that we are God's—who is not immortal, but eternal. Instead of imagining ourselves living instead of dead, we shall prepare ourselves for a real death which is perhaps the final limit of time but which, if that is the case, is surely the threshold of eternity. (1999, 231)

The topics of death, ethics, and meaning are woven throughout Levinas' works, especially from the time of his first major text, *Totality and Infinity* (1969). Among other reasons for this is his complex personal and philosophical relationship to Heidegger and the latter's extremely influential ensemble of these themes. As Jacques Derrida wrote, "And yet all of Levinas's thought, from the beginning to the end, was a meditation on death, a meditation that diverted, disconcerted, and set beside itself everything in philosophy, from Plato to Hegel and Heidegger" (1999, 120). While Levinas fully acknowledges the reality and challenge of death, he believes that the face-to-face relation, that is, one's ethical calling by another, evokes and belongs to another narrative.

In *Otherwise Than Being or Beyond Essence* Levinas juxtaposes two ways of looking at human life, or much better, two ways of living and their accompanying realities. On one side is the truth of *conatus essendi*. If the individual's life is defined in terms of self-preservation and being for himself or herself, then death clearly puts an end to that singular drama and whatever meaning it contained. However, a second "approach" confronts humans in the face of the other. The authentic response to the ethical call of the other signals another possible meaning to one's life. In this case the death of the individual does not herald the death of that meaning. Levinas writes:

> The self inasmuch as, in an approach, it abrogates the egoism of perseverance in being, which is the imperialism of the ego, introduces meaning into being… Mortality renders senseless any concern that the ego would have for its existence and its destiny… The approach,

> inasmuch as it is a sacrifice, confers a sense on death. In it the absolute singularity of the responsible one encompasses the generality or generalization of death. In it life is no longer measured by being, and death can no longer introduce the absurd into it.
>
> (1981, 128–129)

Levinas utilizes a unique vocabulary to demarcate the realm of ethics. He often speaks of diachrony (1998, 159–177), affirming that the relationship to the other which responds to the height and vulnerability of the face belongs to a different time. This relationship is not within the purview of being, of time and space, of the self's desires, decisions, accomplishments, and "place in the sun."[9] Another term is "holiness." Taken from religious discourse, it points to this otherwise dimension, and the actions that constitute it:

> In all these reflections, what emerges is the valorization of holiness as the most profound upheaval of being and thought, through the advent of man… The human (love of the other, responsibility for one's fellowman, an eventual dying-for-the other, sacrifice even as far as the mad thought in which dying for the other can concern me well before, and more than, my own death)—the human signifies the beginning of a new rationality beyond being. (228)

Levinas' later work includes that expansive use of the term love. The ethical responsibility to the other is for him synonymous with love. He maintains the traditional association of love as that unique bond to the "one and only." Of course, fully unconventionally, everyone who is met is precisely this "one." He also characterizes this love as distanced from any return to the self—in particular the erotic encounter—for it is "outside all concupiscence." As part of the "order" of holiness, love must also be that excess beyond both being and death (1998, 199).

Neither the terms faith nor trust make much of an appearance in Levinas' writings, particularly within the philosophic division of these. His "Jewish" authorship, that is, his Talmudic expositions and such essays as "A Religion for Adults," "Israel and Universalism," and "Loving the Torah More Than God," do describe a trust and faithfulness to both God and to the Torah (1990a). For example, in an allusion to the enigmatic Sinai experience when the Jewish community agreed to do God's word before even hearing what had to be done, he refers to Israel's fundamental trust: "Through trust in him who speaks, we promise to obey and now will listen to what he tells us" (1990b, 42).[10]

Levinas' general reluctance to use the terms faith or even trust is the result of his insistence that God is not experienced or known directly, but through the response to the neighbor. This is well expressed as: "The knowledge of God comes to us like a commandment, like a *Mitzvah*. To know God is to know what must be done" (1990a, 17). Still, this reticence does not prevent Levinas from speaking of a closeness, an intimacy with God, which accompanies the life dedicated to the other: "The Justice rendered to the Other, my neighbour, gives me an unsurpassable proximity to God. It is as intimate as the prayer and the liturgy which, without justice, are nothing" (18); and: "The intimacy… [with] the strong God is won through a terrible ordeal" (144).

Finally, Levinas does not equivocate concerning the difficulty of that "ordeal." It requires taking a stance against the law of *conatus essendi* that dominates both society and life, by giving to the other with open hands, without reference to anything in return. In a statement where he does use the term "faith," Levinas expresses the etiquette proper to offering his severe teaching. It cannot be asked of another, and it is a most demanding ideal to present even to oneself.[11]

> The beginning of faith is not at all the promise, and faith is not at all something that one can preach, because it is difficult to preach—that is to say, to propose to the other—something without promise. But one can preach it to oneself, one can ask it of oneself: I am not saying that I always manage to consent to it.
>
> (2001, 78)

Without Conclusion

While there are contemporary psychoanalysts who have a more positive view of religion than Hoffman, including Michael Eigen, Lewis Aron, Marie Hoffman, and as we have seen in Chapter 2, the later Benjamin, the most interesting for our purposes are somewhat earlier thinkers. Erik Erikson, through his treatment of trust, and Hans Loewald, in his discussion of eternity, represent at this point significant dialogue partners for the Jewish philosophers.

Although Erikson, who died in 1994, is often depicted as an ego psychologist, his work anticipates some features of the group of psychoanalysts who have been the focus of this presentation. This is particularly true concerning his famous "Eight Ages of Man" (1963, 247–274) and its starting point with the first psychosocial stage, "Trust vs. Mistrust." Similarly to many contemporary psychoanalysts, Erikson grounds the development of the psyche in that first interaction, between mother and infant. Through the mother's overall attentive and consistent response to the infant, the latter is given a "basic trust." Erikson writes that "the nuclear conflict of basic trust versus basic mistrust in mere existence is the first task of the ego, and thus first of all a task for maternal care" (249). More specifically, this is a trust in both the self and the world, or as Erikson states it, in "the goodness of one's strivings and… the kindness of the powers of the universe" (251).

Emphasizing the relational quality of trust, Erikson refers to the *Webster's Dictionary* definition that trust is "the assured reliance on another's integrity" (Erikson 1963, 269). He directly connects this trust to two topics that have recently been discussed, meaning and death. In terms of the former he finds that parents "must also be able to represent to the child a deep, an almost somatic conviction that there is a meaning to what they are doing" (249). The tie between adult integrity, infantile trust, and the challenge of death is expressed as: "Healthy children will not fear life if their elders have integrity enough not to fear death" (269).

Finally, some of Erikson's direct references to religion resonate with important themes delineated by the Jewish philosophers. He writes, "The parental faith which supports the trust emerging in the newborn, has throughout history sought its institutional safeguard… in organized religion. Trust born of care is, in fact, the touchstone of the *actuality* of a given religion." Erikson draws a non-reductive parallel between this basic trust achieved in childhood and religious experiences central to at least theistic varieties: "All religions have in common the periodical childlike surrender to a Provider" (1963, 250).[12]

A fuller account of Loewald's stunning exploration of the topic of "eternity" has been described in Chapter 5. In condensed form, Loewald suggests that "the experience of eternity" (1978, 62), which he situates in primary process mentation, is found in "mystical and other timeless experiences" (76). This is a "prototypical" experience of timelessness, and thus outside the grids of space and time that dominate conscious—secondary process register—life. These experiences come together to represent "the sum total of our life, in archetypal form" (66). The theme of meaning—the meaning of one's life—is featured in his statement, "As experience augments and grows in an individual's life course, these instants… contain more and more meaning which is poured into the *nunc stans*" (65). Further, Loewald sees the mature task of religion as expressing the "dialectic of eternity and temporality" (77), which thus provides some conscious, symbolic access to that meaning.

Neither Erikson's nor Loewald's treatments are psychologically reductive, proposing that religion is just some projection stemming from the child's early experience. They also do not equate religion to a literalism or what philosophers of religion describe as "realism."[13] Rather, their treatments of trust and eternity point the way to an appreciation from a psychological perspective of the basic human challenges and issues that mature religion attempts to address. Erikson's discussion of trust beginning with the mother–infant relation corresponds both to the earlier suggestion that it is trust that beats at the heart of Benjamin's discussion of recognition and intersubjectivity, and to that conception of trust forwarded by the Jewish philosophers, a trust in the meaningfulness of one's life and in life itself. These discourses envision a conception of trust that meets the challenge of death. They also feature a view of eternity, which is the placeholder not of the resurrected body, but of that meaning created in significant relationships. It is this meaning which withstands the ravages of both time and mortality. These are the keys to recognizing the scope and strength of love, which, in this, the fullest sense, is "strong as death."

The words, our words—trust, love, divine sanctuary (eternity, Kingdom), no man can remain alive (death), life—reverberate together in the last lines of that symphonic narrative, which is Rosenzweig's *The Star of Redemption*:

> To walk humbly with your God—nothing more is asked for here than a wholly present trust. But trust is a great word. It is the seed from which faith, hope and love grow, and the fruit that ripens from it. It is the easiest of all and just for that reason the hardest. It dares at every moment to say Truly to Truth. To walk humbly with your God—the words are above the gate, the gate that leads out from the mysterious, wonderful illumination of the divine sanctuary where no man can remain alive. But whither do the winds of the gate open? You do not know?
>
> INTO LIFE.
>
> (2005, 447)

Notes

1 See, for example, Steven Cooper's *Objects of Hope* (2000, 116, 226).
2 A critique of Hoffman's exposition that sees death as a stark, unvarnished fact that unequivocally destroys meaning can be assembled from the very perspective of his own guiding principles, constructivism and relationality. For the constructivist no human event is understood and even experienced outside of the context of a cultural platform and the stories that this makes available. In addition, should it be taken for granted that the individuality of one's death completely sabotages that relational creation which is human meaning? These points will be examined later in the Conclusion.
3 All of this is reminiscent of the view of religion offered by Jane Flax, whom he often quotes. Flax sees religion as an illusory and dangerous transcendental promise of some kind of redemption for all at the end of history (1993, xiii, 31, 114). Also, see the discussion of Flax in my *Jewish Philosophy and Psychoanalysis* (Oppenheim, 243).
4 Also see my *Jewish Philosophy and Psychoanalysis*, on "Death" (Oppenheim 2006, 235–245).
5 Rosenzweig's statement concerning Kierkegaard might well apply equally to himself, when he wrote to Buber that "behind each paradox of Kierkegaard one senses biographical *absurda*, and for this reason one must *credere*" (Rosenzweig 1999, 33).
6 The last lines in Buber's quotation mirror an important sentiment in William James' *The Varieties of Religious Experience*. In the midst of a very circumscribed discussion of the nature of religion, James makes the somewhat audacious but profound statement: "If any one phrase could gather its [religion's] universal message, that phrase would be, 'All is *not* vanity in this Universe, whatever the appearances may suggest'" (2004, 29).
7 In the essay "Genuine Dialogue and the Possibilities of Peace" of 1953, Buber elaborates on the idea that authentic speech or dialogue between persons has become increasingly scarce because a basic trust is lacking. This is a trust in "Being," or God (1999, 201).
8 In a footnote in his autobiography, Emil Fackenheim provides the dramatic biographical context for this selection: "This book was Buber's very last; the cited passage is the last in the book itself, but it was written before 1933, in 1927. Buber was still able to proofread before his death. He died on June 15, 1965" (2007, 290).
9 This is a phrase from Blaise Pascal's *Pensées* that Levinas frequently quotes, and appears with a few other citations at the beginning of *Otherwise Than Being or Beyond Essence* (1981, vii).
10 For Levinas, the term "Israel" stands for both the historic Jewish people and that ethical dimension open to everyone, which defines the very nature of the human (1990b, 98).
11 Hilary Putnam's discussion of Levinas as a "moral perfectionist" adds another perspective to this (2008, 72–73).

12 Erikson's use of the word "childlike," rather than childish, clearly distinguishes his presentation from Freud's view of religion as infantile.
13 A much cited text on philosophy of religion discusses religious realism in terms of holding certain beliefs concerning the "transempirical": "These beliefs are conveyed in language that contains assertions that religious believers take as making truth-claims and defended by arguments meant to show that there is good reason to think that these beliefs are true" (Peterson *et al.* 2013, 26).

References

Buber, Martin. 1965. *Between Man and Man*. Translated by Ronald Gregor Smith. New York: Collier Books.
—. 1970. *I and Thou*. Translated by Walter Kaufmann. New York: Charles Scribner's Sons.
—. 1972. *On Judaism*. Edited by Nahum N. Glatzer. New York: Schocken Books.
—. 1999. *A Believing Humanism: My Testament 1902–1965*. Translated by Maurice Friedman. Amherst, NY: Humanity Books.
—. 2003. *Two Types of Faith*. Translated by Norman P. Goldhawk. Syracuse, NY: Syracuse University Press.
Cooper, Steven H. 2000. *Objects of Hope: Exploring Possibility and Limit in Psychoanalysis*. Hillsdale, NJ: Analytic Press.
Derrida, Jacques. 1999. *Adieu: To Emmanuel Levinas*. Translated by Pascale-Anne Brault and Michael Naas. Stanford, CA: Stanford University Press.
Erikson, Erik H. 1963. *Childhood and Society*. New York: W. W. Norton and Company.
Fackenheim, Emil. 2007. *An Epitaph for German Judaism: From Halle to Jerusalem*. Madison, WI: University of Wisconsin Press.
Flax, Jane. 1993. *Disputed Subjects: Essays on Psychoanalysis, Politics and Philosophy*. New York: Routledge.
Hoffman, Irwin Z. 1998. *Ritual and Spontaneity in the Psychoanalytic Process. A Dialectical–Constructivist View*. Hillsdale, NJ: Analytic Press.
James, William. 2004. *The Varieties of Religious Experience: A Study in Human Nature*. New York: Touchstone.
Levinas, Emmanuel. 1969. *Totality and Infinity: An Essay on Exteriority*. Translated by Alphonso Lingis. Pittsburgh, PA: Duquesne University Press.
—. 1981. *Otherwise Than Being or Beyond Essence*. Translated by Alphonso Lingis. The Hague: Martin Nijoff Publishers.
—. 1990a. *Difficult Freedom: Essays on Judaism*. Translated by Seán Hand. Baltimore, MD: Johns Hopkins University Press.
—. 1990b. *Nine Talmudic Readings*. Translated by Annette Aronowicz. Bloomington, IN: Indiana University Press.
—. 1998. *Entre Nous: On Thinking-of-the-Other*. Translated by Michael B. Smith and Barbara Harshav. New York: Columbia University Press.

—. 2001. *Is It Righteous To Be?: Interviews with Emmanuel Levinas*. Edited by Jill Robbins. Stanford, CA: Stanford University Press.

Loewald, Hans W. 1978. *Psychoanalysis and the History of the Individual: The Freud Lectures at Yale*. New Haven, CT: Yale University Press.

Mitchell, Stephen A. 1993. *Hope and Dread in Psychoanalysis*. New York: Basic Books.

—. 2003. *Can Love Last?: The Fate of Romance Over Time*. New York: W. W. Norton and Company.

Ogden, Thomas H. 2004. *Reverie and Interpretation: Sensing Something Human*. Lanham, MD: Jason Aronson.

Oppenheim, Michael. 2006. *Jewish Philosophy and Psychoanalysis: Narrating the Interhuman*. Lanham, MD: Lexington Books.

Peterson, Michael, William Hasker, Bruce Reichenbach, and David Basinger. 2013. *Reason and Religious Belief: An Introduction to the Philosophy of Religion*. Oxford: Oxford University Press.

Putnam, Hilary. 2008. *Jewish Philosophy as a Guide to Life: Rosenzweig, Buber, Levinas, Wittgenstein*. Bloomington, IN: Indiana University Press.

Rosenzweig, Franz. 1998. *God, Man, and the World: Lectures and Essays*. Edited and translated by Barbara E. Galli. Syracuse, NY: Syracuse University Press.

—. 1999. *Understanding the Sick and the Healthy: A View of World, Man, and God*. Translated by Nahum Glatzer. Cambridge, MA: Harvard University Press.

—. 2005. *The Star of Redemption*. Translated by Barbara E. Galli. Madison, WI: University of Wisconsin Press.

Index